Hazing (Ragging) at Universities: A Legal Perspective

Aashish Srivastava · Neerav Srivastava ·
D. K. Srivastava

Hazing (Ragging) at Universities: A Legal Perspective

Springer

Aashish Srivastava
Department of Business Law and Taxation
Monash University
Clayton, VIC, Australia

Neerav Srivastava
Law School
Monash University
Clayton, VIC, Australia

D. K. Srivastava
Toorak, VIC, Australia

ISBN 978-981-99-5217-5 ISBN 978-981-99-5215-1 (eBook)
https://doi.org/10.1007/978-981-99-5215-1

This Springer imprint is published by the registered company Springer Nature Singapore Pte Ltd.
The registered company address is: 152 Beach Road, #21-01/04 Gateway East, Singapore 189721, Singapore

To Shastra and Naren, Who have always fought for minorities, the disadvantaged, and those who are bullied or discriminated against. Naren passed away peacefully on 10 November 2023. Naren made friends for life. He was loyal, down to earth, and self-effacing. He had a great sense of humour. His adventures and misadventures—told with a distinctive chuckle—are part of local folklore. He never sought to live anything other than an ordinary life. Still, if life is measured by how giving a person is and whether we have left the world a better place, then Naren's place is in the stars. The affection in which he is held means that his star shines bright.

Contents

Chapter 1
Introduction

"You don't expect to send your child off to college…and they come back in a coffin"[1] said a bereaved mother. This statement sums up what hazing is doing to young students who join colleges and universities in the hope of a brighter future.

Hazing is described as "a rite of passage [to groups] wherein youths, neophytes, or rookies are taken through traditional practices by more senior members in order to initiate them into the next stage of their cultural, religious, academic, or athletic lives".[2] Hazing should not be confused with bullying although both involve humiliation, degradation, and physical and mental abuse.[3] Hazing is the price of admission. Bullying does not purport to be inclusive, and the victim cannot be seen as a willing participant. With hazing, victims ostensibly submit to it.

---

[1] This is how a bereaved mother described her pain in a BBC documentary on hazing deaths in the U.S. See 'Frat Boys: Inside American Fraternities', *BBC* (online, 23 June 2016) https://www.bbc.co.uk/programmes/b07hns97; Sam Wollaston, 'Frat Boys: Inside America's Fraternities Review—What Happens When the Party Turns Sour', *The Guardian* (online, 24 June 2016) https://www.theguardian.com/tv-and-radio/2016/jun/24/frat-boys-inside-america-fraternities-review.

[2] Brian Trota and Jay Johnson, 'A Brief History of Hazing' in Jay Johnson & Margery Holman (eds.), *Making the Team: The Inside World of Sport Initiations and Hazing* (Canadian Scholar's Press, 2004) p. X.

[3] The purpose of hazing is to initiate a new member to a group; the member is targeted because they want to be accepted by the group. Once accepted (i.e., the initiation phase passes), hazing ends. On the other hand, in bullying, the bully targets the victim, often with an evil motive to exclude or alienate him. Furthermore, unlike hazing, the victim does not know if and when the harassment will end. See Hank Nuwer, *Wrongs of passage: Fraternities, sororities, hazing, and binge drinking* (Indiana University Press, 1999); Aaron Jeckell, Elizabeth Copenhaver & Alex Diamond (2018) 'The Spectrum of Hazing and Peer Sexual abuse in Sports: A Current Perspective', 10(6) *Sports Health* 558, https://doi.org/10.1177/1941738118797322; Jennifer Lamb, Debra J Pepler, Wendy Craig (2009) 'Approach to Bullying and Victimization', 55(4) *Canadian Family Physician* 356.

A. Srivastava et al., *Hazing (Ragging) at Universities: A Legal Perspective*,
https://doi.org/10.1007/978-981-99-5215-1_1

The practice of hazing often descends into barbarism.[4] There can be murder, suicide, grievous hurt and sexual assault, forced alcohol consumption, and lewd and cruel games. Hoover classifies hazing into four categories: (i) acceptable behaviour, (ii) questionable behaviour, (iii) alcohol-related behaviour, and (iv) unacceptable behaviour.[5] The University of Colorado Boulder divides hazing into three categories: "subtle, harassment and violent".[6]

In this book, we define hazing as:

> initiation of new students (freshers) by senior students into a university,[7] including its clubs (e.g., fraternities and sororities) or residential colleges, that involves embarrassment, humiliation, physical or psychological abuse, forced or coerced alcohol or drug consumption, sexually demeaning practices, [assault and other offences against the person], and sexual assault regardless of the freshers' consent.

1.1 History of Hazing

The practice of hazing has existed since the time of Plato.[8] In Greece, in the eighth century A.D., new entrants to sporting events (including Olympics) were humiliated and teased with the object of inculcating team spirit.[9] In the middle-ages, hazing (known as pennalism) prevailed in European universities.[10] New students were forced to act as servants and had to be subservient to the upperclassmen. Hazing (known as fagging) also existed at Oxford and Cambridge universities.[11] Senior students at those universities had a right "to make the younger ones do what [they] like and what the younger one[s] generally dislikes".[12]

---

[4] Neerav Srivastava, Aashish Srivastava, and DK Srivastava (2019) 'A million winslows: Private liability of universities for ragging in India', 19(2) *Oxford University Commonwealth Law Journal* 227.

[5] Nadine Hoover (1999) 'National Survey: Initiation Rites and athletics for NCAA Sports Teams', https://www.alfred.edu/about/news/studies/_docs/hazing.pdf. However, the problem with the hazing behaviour continuum is that it implies that some hazing activities are acceptable, 'which ignores the possibility that the same hazing activity could be perceived as acceptable by some but as physically, psychologically, and/or emotionally harmful by others'. See Curtis Fogel and Andrea Quinlan (2021) 'Sexual assault in the locker room: Sexually violent hazing in Canadian sport', 27(3) *Journal of Sexual Aggression* 353.

[6] University of Colorado Boulder, 'Examples of Hazing', *Office of Victim Assistance* https://www.colorado.edu/ova/examples-hazing.

[7] The word university or universities in this book has been used in a wide sense to include any higher education or tertiary institution.

[8] Nuwer (n 3).

[9] Dhananjay Mahapatra, 'Ragging Needs Social Ban, More than Laws', *The Times of India* (online, 22 March 2009) https://timesofindia.indiatimes.com/home/sunday-times/deep-focus/ragging-needs-social-ban-more-than-laws/articleshow/4298362.cms?pcode=461.

[10] Ruth Sterner (2008) 'The History of Hazing in American Higher Education', https://ruthsterner.files.wordpress.com/2008/05/histpdf.pdf, p. 2.

[11] Ibid.

[12] Hank Nuwer, *Broken Pledges.* (Longstreet Press Inc., 1990) p. 117.

There is evidence of hazing at Harvard University of freshmen by upperclassmen as early as 1657.[13] The Phi Beta Kappa Society, founded on 5 December 1776 at the College of William and Mary in Williamsburg, Virginia, was the first fraternal organisation in the U.S.[14] The founders of this society intended to promote good fellowship, with "friendship as its basis and benevolence and literature as its pillars".[15] Evidence of hazing existed at the fraternity as early as 1781. Between 1828–1845 several fraternities emerged in the U.S.[16] In 1867, a society called I. C. Sorosis founded the nation's first women's fraternity (called sorority)[17] at Monmouth College in Illinois: Pi Beta Phi.[18] The African-American community saw fraternity discipline as a means of defining manhood.[19] Hazing has a long history in the British and other colonial armies.[20]

The justification for hazing has been that students "must experience some interpersonal tension and risk because growth into full maturity requires this".[21] A student joining a fraternity or sorority creates a strong bond with other members of such an organisation. It also enhances their self-esteem, helps shake their inhibitions and inferiority complex and makes them tough and resilient.[22] A similar belief exists in other countries, such as India and Sri Lanka, that hazing helps freshers develop their personality, breaks the ice between them and seniors, and facilitates long-lasting friendships with other students.[23] The psyche of some hazers is that they have the

---

[13] Nuwer (n 3); Alexandra Lehman (2014) 'A Brief History of Fraternity/Sorority Paddles and Recommendations', *Fraternal Law Newsletter,* https://fraternallaw.com/newsletter2/a-brief-history-of-fraternity-sorority-paddles-and-recommendations.

[14] William T. Hastings, *Phi Beta Kappa as a Secret Society* (United Chapters of Phi Beta Kappa, 1965) p. 84.

[15] Ibid. See also Janice Fivehouse (1968) 'The History of the Alpha Chapter of Phi Beta Kappa', *Masters Thesis*, https://scholarworks.wm.edu/etd/1539624652.

[16] Albert Clark Stevens, *The Cyclopaedia of Fraternities* (Book on Demand Ltd., 2013) p. 346 [first published by Hamilton Printing and Publishing Company (1899)].

[17] The term "sorority" was invented by a professor of Latin who felt the word "fraternity" was inappropriate for a group of ladies. See William Raimond Baird, Jack L Anson and Robert F Marchesani, *Baird's Manual of American College Fraternities* (Baird's Manual Foundation, 20th ed, 1991).

[18] Fivehouse (n 15).

[19] Sara Delamont (2005) 'Black Haze: Violence, Sacrifice, and Manhood in Black Greek-Letter Fraternities', 30(5) *Studies in Higher Education* 629.

[20] Simon Walker (2023) 'Toughening up: Bullying in the British Army during the First World War', 31(1) *Journal of Military and Veterans Health* 19.

[21] Robert D Bickel and Peter F Lake (1997) 'The Emergence of New Paradigms in Student-University Relations: From In Loco Parentis to Bystander to Facilitator', 23(4) *Journal of College and University Law* 755, p. 787.

[22] Liesbeth Mann, Allard R. Feddes, Bertjan Doosje & Agneta H. Fischer (2016) 'Withdraw or Affiliate? The Role of Humiliation during Initiation Rituals', 30(1) *Cognition and Emotion* 80.

[23] Harsh Agarwal, *Psychology Behind Ragging*, Paper presented at the seminar "Legal Awareness Programme on Anti-Ragging" in the session "Understanding Psychology Behind Ragging" chaired by the acting Chief Justice of Delhi High Court, organised by the Delhi Legal Services Authority (DLSA), in the Vallabhbhai Patel Chest Institute (VPCI) Auditorium (New Delhi, India, March 20, 2010) http://www.humiliationstudies.org/documents/AgarwalPsychologyBehindRagging.pdf.

right and the duty to pass on hazing traditions to new students: do-unto-others what others did to you.

In Australia, it is believed initiation rituals instil respect and submission in freshers towards senior students and the college as an institution. Those freshers who comply with initiation rituals are rewarded with social acceptance and go on to occupy the position of power held by senior students.[24]

These justifications are, in part, reflected in the theory of why hazing occurs. A common[25] theory is 'dominance': hazers seek to establish or reaffirm a dominant position concerning hazees. The commitment theory is that severe gang initiations act to 'weed out the weak and uncommitted', such as those seeking to join a fraternity, because newcomers are an unknown quantity.[26] Finally, 'automatic accrual theory' holds that hazing prevents the near-term exploitation of group-controlled benefits by new members.[27]

1.2 Prevalence of Hazing Worldwide

Despite attempts to control hazing it continues unabated. Hazing is common at university campuses; its clubs, societies and residential colleges. In some countries it is endemic. The focus of this book is on examining hazing problems in educational institutions. It is also prevalent in the defence forces.[28] In the U.S., hazing is woven into the fabric of student life and campus culture.[29] More than half (55%) of

[24] EROC Australia (2018) 'The Red Zone Report - An Investigation into Sexual Violence and Hazing in Australian University Residential Colleges', https://apo.org.au/sites/default/files/resource-files/2018-02/apo-nid134766.pdf, p. 82.

[25] On it being common Aldo Cimino (2011) 'The Evolution of Hazing: Motivational Mechanisms and the Abuse of Newcomers' 11 *Journal of Cognition and Culture* 241 traces this 'Durkheim (1912) notes that group members haze newcomers to "make them understand how superior [they feel]" (p. 318). Bryshun (1997) writes that athletic hazing allows veterans to have their dominant position "consolidated" (p. 100). Whiting (1958) argues that hazing in male adolescent initiations is used to suppress "open and violent revolt" (p. 361). Honeycutt (2005) describes veterans of a discussion group hazing to "maintain their power" (Analysis section, final paragraph). Robidoux (2001) describes athletic hazers "celebrating their power over rookies" (p. 104). Keating et al. (2005) suggest that vertically-organized groups use severe initiations to "establish social control" (p. 107). Waldron and Kowalski (2009) write that athletic hazing rituals "help maintain…the power structure of the team" (p. 292). Nuwer (2000) actually defines hazing as an imposition of dominance, stating that hazing involves "any activity that requires new members to show subservience to old members" (p. 20), and so on (e.g., Webster, 1908; Stone, 1946; Johnson, 2001; Allan and DeAngelis, 2004; Tooby et al., 2006)'.

[26] JD Vigil (1996) 'Street baptism: Chicano gang initiation', 55 *Human Organization* 149, p. 151.

[27] Cimino (n 25).

[28] Richard Evans (2013) 'Hazing in the ADF: A Culture of Denial?,' 10(3) *Australian Army Journal* 113.

[29] Elizabeth J Allan & Mary Madden (2008) 'Hazing in View: College Students at Risk: Initial Findings from the National Study of Student Hazing', *Stop Hazing*, https://stophazing.org/wp-content/uploads/2020/12/hazing_in_view_study.pdf.

the students involved in campus activities have been victims of hazing. In Canada, sexually violent hazing, has been reported in sporting clubs.[30]

Initiation ceremonies are also common in Europe and the U.K. The British Universities Sports Association (BUSA) states that nudity is forced upon new participants in sports and games.[31] Experts believe extreme and dangerous hazing rituals and initiation ceremonies in the U.K. have come over from the U.S. U.K. universities have so far struggled to stop hazing.[32] The *Universities U.K.* organisation has warned university leaders to take hazing seriously and said that students involved in dangerous and degrading rituals can be charged with perpetrating torture and jailed.[33] In Belgium, in January 2023, a correctional court found five students guilty of involuntary manslaughter for the hazing-related death of a fresher.[34] In another incident in 2021, a 20-year-old student at the University of Leuven (K.U. Leuven) died from hypothermia and organ failure after participating in an initiation ritual.[35] In France, universities are grappling with hazing incidents, despite a law banning initiation ceremonies (known as *la rentrée*) during the welcome week for first-year university students.[36]

In the Asia–Pacific, hazing is prevalent in universities and their residential colleges. Australian universities' residential colleges are known for hazing activities. According to the Australian Human Rights Commission report, *Change the Course: National Report on Sexual Assault and Sexual Harassment at Australian Universities* worrying levels of sexual harassment and assault exist; a situation that may not be improving.[37] The Red Zone Report by End Rape on Campus Australia (EROC) vividly portrays hazing as a culture of humiliation forced upon freshers joining a

---

30 Fogel and Quinlan (n 5).

31 Mark Groves, Gerald Griggs and Kathryn Leflay (2012) 'Hazing and Initiation Ceremonies in University Sport: Setting the Scene for Further Research in the United Kingdom', 15(1) *Sport in Society* 117.

32 Eleanor Busby, 'Universities Struggling to Stop Dangerous Initiations and Hazing Rituals on British Campuses', *The Independent* (online, 26 December 2019) https://www.independent.co.uk/news/education/education-news/hazing-initiation-ceremonies-universities-students-alcohol-binge-drinking-ed-farmer-a9255776.html.

33 Marc Horne, 'Organisers of Student Hazing Rituals Face Jail for Torture, Universities Told', *The Times* (online, 6 February 2023) https://www.thetimes.co.uk/article/organisers-of-student-hazing-rituals-face-jail-for-torture-universities-told-ctqc8fsmw.

34 Lukas Taylor, 'Five People Found Guilty Following Student Death in Hazing Ritual', *The Brussel Times* (online, 21 January 2023) https://www.brusselstimes.com/356171/five-people-found-guilty-following-student-death-in-hazing-ritual.

35 Lauren Walker, 'Antwerp Looks to Ban Hazing "Ritual of Humiliation"', *The Brussel Times* (online, 15 September 2021) https://www.brusselstimes.com/belgium-education/185103/antwerp-looks-to-ban-hazing-ritual-of-humiliation.

36 Catherine Benett, 'French Universities Brace for New Wave of Hazing with "La Rentrée"', *France* 24 (online, 3 September 2018) https://www.france24.com/en/20180831-french-universities-brace-new-wave-crackdown-hazing-rituals-la-rentree.

37 Australian Human Rights Commission (2017) 'Change The Course: National Report on Sexual Assault and Sexual Harassment at Australian Universities', https://humanrights.gov.au/our-work/sex-discrimination/publications/change-course-national-report-sexual-assault-and-sexual, p. 187.

university.[38] The report states that 'there is a clear link between the coercion of hazing rituals and the high rates of sexual assault and harassment at colleges'.[39] It highlights gruesome hazing incidents, for example: forcing a fresher (girl) to drink beer poured on a boy's genital; exposing sexual activities of freshers through graphic and embarrassing photos; and locking freshers in a bathroom and throwing vats of dead fish on them.[40]

In Indian universities, hazing (called ragging) has reached endemic proportions. While there is no recognised initiation ritual, the various indignities to which the freshers are subjected have a remarkable similarity to that in the U.S. In July 2022, a student hanged herself to death. Her suicide note said that three senior students mentally harassed her.[41] In the same month, senior medical college students coerced freshers to imitate sex acts using pillows, slap each other, and make derogatory remarks against female students in their class.[42] According to a report, 40% of Indian university students face hazing, but only 8.6% report it.[43]

In Sri Lanka, hazing (also called ragging) is a significant problem in state universities. According to a study, more than half (51%) of those surveyed suffered physical abuse, one-third (34%) faced psychological abuse, a quarter (24%) were physically abused, and 17% suffered sexual harassment. In one incident, a group of freshmen in Sri Lanka were taken to a remote location by their seniors and sexually abused and

---

[38] EROC Australia (n 24). See also, Madeline Ward, Lara Sonnenschein and Nina Dillon Britton, 'Racism, Sexism, Hazing: New Allegations Surface over Behaviour at St Andrew's College', *Honi Soit* (online, 17 May 2020) http://honisoit.com/2020/05/racism-sexism-hazing-new-allegations-surface-over-behaviour-at-st-andrews-college/.

[39] Ibid, p. 84.

[40] Ibid, p. 6.

[41] 'Odisha Girl Dies by Suicide; Blames Ragging by College Seniors in Last Note', *India Today* (online, 3 July 2022) https://www.indiatoday.in/cities/bhubaneswar/story/odisha-girl-suicide-ragging-by-seniors-bjb-autonomous-college-1969648-2022-07-03.

[42] Bobbins Abraham, 'Ragging Horror In Indore Medical College, Students Forced To Do Unnatural Sex, Slap Each Other', *IndiaTimes* (online, 27 July 2022) https://www.indiatimes.com/news/india/ragging-in-indore-mgm-medical-college-575799.html.

[43] Mohan Rao et al. (2015) 'Psychosocial Study of Ragging in Selected Educational Institutions in India' https://www.ugc.ac.in/pdfnews/7661310_Psychosocial-Study-of-Ragging.pdf, pp. 45 & 142.

tortured.[44] Hazing also exists in other Asia–Pacific countries such as Malaysia,[45] the Philippines,[46] Thailand[47] and Pakistan.[48]

1.3 Disastrous Consequences of Hazing

Hazing has been justified as a benign team-building exercise to help freshers into a new environment. However, its consequences can be disastrous. It can result in death, physical injuries, and psychological harm. Physical injuries have included alcoholic coma, hematemesis, multi-organ system failure, hypoxic brain damage, HIV, Hepatitis C, unwanted pregnancy and sexually transmitted infections.[49] The Daily Mail of the U.K. reported in June 2022 that since 1838 fraternity initiation rituals have killed nearly 500 college students in the U.S.[50] In the U.K. and E.U., between 1950 and 2007, 250 hazing deaths occurred.[51] In India, from 2011 to 2019, 54 students committed suicide due to hazing.[52] In Sri Lanka, 20 students have committed suicide due to hazing.[53]

---

[44] 'Ragging at Universities: Grave Human Rights Violation - News Features', *Daily Mirror* (online, 3 March 2017) https://www.dailymirror.lk/news-features/Ragging-at-Universities-Grave-Human-Rights-Violation/131-124790

[45] R S N Murli, 'Student Ragging Turns Extreme', *The Star* (online, 4 June 2014) https://www.thestar.com.my/news/nation/2014/06/04/student-ragging-turns-extreme-seniors-force-freshmen-to-strip-and-perform-lewd-acts-on-each-other.

[46] Ofelia M Bawan, Marilou P Pascual and Arneil G Gabriel (2017) 'Hazing and Organizational Tradition in a Higher Education Institution in the Philippines: What Has the Law Got to Do with It?', 5(12) *Open Journal of Social Sciences* 110; *Dandy L Dungo & Gregorio A Sibal, Jr v. People of Philippines* (Supreme Court of Philippines, 1 July 2015).

[47] 'Mother of Thai Hazing Victim Decries Slow Police Probe', *ucanews.com* (online, 8 June 2021) https://www.ucanews.com/news/mother-of-thai-hazing-victim-decries-slow-police-probe/96574.

[48] Shafaq Taseen et al. (2021) 'Ragging: A Harmless Tradition or Menace? Perspective of Newly Admitted Medical Students of Karachi, Pakistan', 17(8) *European Scientific Journal* 123.

[49] Michelle A Finkel (2002) 'Traumatic Injuries Caused by Hazing Practices", 20(3) *The American Journal of Emergency Medicine* 228, p. 229.

[50] Jennifer Smith, 'America's Dark Hazing History: Initiation Rituals Have Killed Dozens', *Mail Online* (online, 9 June 2022) https://www.dailymail.co.uk/news/article-10900563/Americas-dark-hazing-history-sick-initiation-rituals-killing-young-men-1905.html.

[51] Jorge Srabstei (2008), 'Deaths Linked to Bullying and Hazing", 20(2) *International Journal of Adolescent Medicine and Health* 235.

[52] Priyesh Mishra, 'The Disease of Ragging is not Stopping in the Country, 4696 Cases Registered in Seven Years', *Amar Ujala* (online,13 Jun 2019) https://www.amarujala.com/india-news/ragging-in-educational-institute-4696-cases-registered-in-last-7-years-in-ugc.

[53] Himaya Perera and Asiri Ekanayake, 'Tradition vs Trauma: Hazing in Universities Worsen', *The Sunday Times* (online, 3 May 2020) https://www.pressreader.com/sri-lanka/sunday-times-sri-lanka/20200503/282664689550934.

A BBC documentary describes the plight of students in U.S. fraternities[54]: a student was forced to binge drink and eat raw onions and sticks of butter until he vomited. He was then blindfolded with his hands behind his head and repeatedly beaten with boat paddles until his skin split open. In October 2021, a 19-year-old freshman at the University of Missouri joined the fraternity Phi Gamma Delta. During hazing he suffered alcohol poisoning and became blind and crippled. He is unable to walk and has to use a wheelchair.[55]

As for the emotional and psychological consequences of hazing, in a U.S. study, nearly three-quarters of all hazing victims reported sleep deprivation, deterioration in academic grades, post-traumatic stress, and mental instability.[56] Similar adverse effects of hazing have been found in India and Sri Lanka.[57] In India, two-thirds of the hazed victims reported having lasting emotional problems, adversely impacting their self-esteem and confidence.[58] Research has shown that sexual assault and harassment victims are prone to have post-traumatic stress and anxiety disorders, depression and heightened feelings of fear, grief, and shock.[59] They also struggle with academic work and find maintaining a healthy social life and relationships challenging.[60]

1.4 Hazing and the Law

Hazing laws fall into three categories: disciplinary proceedings by the university; criminal sanctions; and civil proceedings brought by the hazee against the hazer and/or the university.

Most universities, sporting clubs, fraternities, and sororities have anti-hazing policies. A perpetrator of hazing can face disciplinary action under such policies. Criminal sanctions can also be imposed by the courts. Forty-four U.S. states have specific

---

[54] Lucy Waterlow and Erica Tempesta, 'College Student Recalls How He Was Beaten during Hazing in BBC's Frat Boys Documentary', *The Daily Mail* (online, 23 June 2016) https://www.dailymail.co.uk/femail/article-3654776/College-student-recalls-brutally-beaten-boat-paddles-urinated-branded-horrific-hazing-ritual-new-documentary-exposing-dark-fraternities.html.

[55] Smith (n 50).

[56] Nadine C Hoover & Norman J Pollard (2000) 'Initiation Rites in American High Schools: A National Survey Final Report', https://eric.ed.gov/?id=ED445809.

[57] Hemamalie Gunatilaka, Dushan Jayawickrama & Ananda Rathnayake (2022) 'Prevalence of Ragging and Sexual and Gender Based Violence in Srilankan State Universities', *UNICEF*, https://www.unicef.org/srilanka/media/2431/file/Prevalence%20of%20Ragging%20and%20Sexual%20and%20Gender%20Based%20Violence.pdf, p. 13.

[58] RK Raghavan et al. (2007) 'The Menace of Ragging in Educational Institutions and Measuress to Curb It', https://nitc.ac.in/app/webroot/img/upload/MENACE.pdf.

[59] Chiara Sabina and Lavina Y Ho (2014) 'Campus and College Victim Responses to Sexual Assault and Dating Violence: Disclosure, Service Utilization, and Service Provision', 15(3) *Trauma, Violence & Abuse* 201.

[60] Australian Human Rights Commission (n 37); Anne Wagner and Jamie Lynn Magnusson (2005) 'Neglected Realities: Exploring the Impact of Women's Experiences of Violence on Learning in Sites of Higher Education', 17(4) *Gender and Education* 449.

anti-hazing statutes, making hazing a criminal offence. Arizona is the latest state to criminalise hazing. The Arizona statute came into force on 24 September 2022. Under the new law, if a person dies during hazing, those involved could be convicted of manslaughter. If the victim suffers a bodily injury, the perpetrators can be charged with assault. In addition, those who were not directly involved in hazing but assisted in the planning of hazing would also be held accountable.

Both, India and Sri Lanka, have a federal body, called the University Grants Commission (UGC).[61] The UGC grants accreditation and funding to universities and higher education institutions (HEIs). It has formulated regulations and guidelines to address hazing. In India, the *Regulations on Curbing the Menace of Ragging in Higher Educational Institutions* 2009 ('UGC Regulations')[62] set out measures that universities must adopt to eliminate hazing and provides various sanctions against universities and HEIs, which fail to adopt such measures. Fourteen out of 28 states in India also have enacted an anti-hazing statute.[63] The statutes provide strict punishment for hazing, abetment to hazing, and conspiracy to haze. In addition, where hazing involves a criminal act, hazers can be charged both under the state anti-hazing statute and the general criminal law of the county, i.e., the *Indian Penal Code, 1860* (IPC). In those states that do not have an anti-hazing statute, an action against the perpetrator is only possible under the IPC. In July 2022, the police in the State of Madhya Pradesh, which does not have a specific anti-hazing statute, registered cases against the hazers under various sections of the IPC.[64] Like India, Sri Lanka[65] and the Philippines[66] have anti-hazing legislation, albeit at a federal level, and a penal code that also punishes hazing. Recalcitrant university officials, who refuse to deal with hazing situations, may also face criminal sanctions.

Canada, the U.K., Australia, and Malaysia do not have a specific law on hazing. In such countries hazing may be punished under the general criminal law of the land.[67]

---

[61] University Grants Commission (UGC) was formed in 1945 to oversee the work of the three Central Universities of Aligarh, Banaras and Delhi. After Indian Independence, it was entrusted with the responsibility of reporting current and future needs of education and suggest as well as implement provisions to improve the educational system of all the universities in India. For details, see www.ugc.ac.in.

[62] The All India Council for Technical Education (AICTE) and the Medical Council of India have made regulations similar to those of the UGC. *See* AICTE (Prevention and prohibition of ragging in technical institutions including deemed to be universities imparting technical education) Regulations 2009; Medical Council of India (Prevention of Prohibition of ragging in Medical Colleges/ Institutions) Regulations 2009.

[63] The States are: Andhra Pradesh, Assam, Chandigarh, Goa, Himachal Pradesh, Jammu and Kashmir (was downgraded from state to a union territory on 5 August 2019), Karnataka, Kerala, Maharashtra, Tamil Nadu, Telangana, Tripura, Uttar Pradesh and West Bengal.

[64] Sections 342 (wrongful confinement), 294 (obscene act), 323 (voluntarily causing hurt), and 506 (criminal intimidation) of the Indian Penal Code 1860.

[65] Prohibition of Ragging and other Form of Violence in Educational Institutions Act, No. 22 of 1998.

[66] Bawan, Pascual and Gabriel (n 46).

[67] It all depends on the nature of the hazing act. For example, if hazing involves beating and paddling the victim, criminal law pertaining to assault applies.

A civil claim by a hazee against the hazer or a university can only be made under the general law. The hazer can be sued in tort for intentional torts or negligence. A university can potentially be sued for negligence, breach of contract, or under consumer laws.

1.5 Outline of the Book

The aim of this book is to look into the hazing laws of the U.S., India, Sri Lanka and Australia. The reason for choosing these countries is that hazing incidents are much higher in these countries than in many other countries. The book discusses the state of hazing and respective laws in these jurisdictions. By looking at a number of jurisdictions, it is hoped that hazing-prevention measures in one jurisdiction informs other jurisdictions. Likewise, one jurisdiction can learn from another.

Chapter 2 examines the hazing laws of the U.S. It begins with an overview of the atrocities committed against a pledge[68] during hazing rituals. The next section of the chapter analyses the criminalisation of hazing by state anti-hazing statutes. A problem with the state hazing statutes is a lack of consistency, including the definition of 'hazing'. Some statutes define hazing to include both physical and emotional harm, while some other refer to only physical harm. A few states impose a duty on universities to implement hazing prevention measures. Where any administrator or employee is aware of hazing but fails to make a reasonable attempt to prevent it, they may be criminally liable. The discussion then moves on to private law liability in torts and contracts. This part discusses intentional tort claims against the hazer and the potential liability in negligence of universities and their fraternities and sororities.

Chapter 3 is on India. This chapter begins by highlighting the problem of hazing on university campuses. This part focuses on the critical role of the Supreme Court of India in addressing the issue of hazing. The Supreme Court has not only defined hazing but directed the UGC to draft regulations that set out measures for universities to adopt to eliminate hazing. In the next part of the chapter, the UGC Regulations are examined. Thereafter, the chapter compares and contrasts the hazing laws of 14 states. Like the U.S., hazing laws of India differ from state to state. This section also discusses the IPC provisions that can be applied to a hazing scenario. Furthermore, it analyses the judicial decisions where hazers have appealed against the disciplinary action taken by the university. Next, the discussion moves to tortious liability of universities towards students.

Like India, hazing in Sri Lanka has reached endemic proportions. Chapter 4 begins with discussing atrocities committed by senior university students against freshers. Thereafter, Sri Lanka's UGC Regulations, hazing statute, penal code and private law liability of universities are discussed.

Chapter 5 begins by highlighting the problem of hazing at Australian university residential colleges. New students suffer from hazing in the 'orientation week' (O

[68] A pledge is one who joins a fraternity or sorority.

week). Alcohol fuels hazing practices. In extreme cases, there has been sexual assault and rape. Australia has no specific anti-hazing statute like the U.S., India and Sri Lanka. Hazing-related proceedings are brought under the general law. The chapter discusses the potential liability of a hazer and then universities. Thereafter, the chapter examines the psychological and cultural factors that lead to hazing. Finally, the chapter proposes a comprehensive legal strategy to tackle hazing in Australia.

Chapter 6 is the conclusion.

Chapter 2
Hazing in the U.S.

> *I lost so much that night; my only child, a best friend. I sent him off to ... get a higher education. And they sent him back in a body bag.*
> *—Parents of a fresher who died in a hazing incident*
> ('REACH-Info_updatedAug2022.Pdf' https://stophazing.org/wp-content/uploads/2022/08/REACH-Info_updatedAug2022.pdf)

Hazing in the U.S. universities[1] is often used as a formal introduction to organisations, such as fraternities and sororities. Senior students, as part of what is called initiation ceremonies, require freshers (also called initiates or pledges) to perform certain embarrassing, humiliating, dangerous and potentially illegal activities. It endangers their physical and mental well-being.

As part of hazing, students have been assaulted, kidnapped, beaten up, forced to drink excessive alcohol, perform sexual acts and consume disgusting food.[2] Some recent examples of hazing testify how hazing is affecting the well-being of students and destroying university culture.[3] In February 2021, a 19-year-old Virginia Commonwealth University fresher[4]—Adam Oakes—died from alcohol poisoning at a fraternity event. Six former fraternity members were found guilty of the fresher's death and charged with misdemeanour. Ironically, they have been exempted from serving any term of imprisonment and ordered to visit university campuses across the country to share how the incident leading to Adam's death has affected them

---

[1] The term "university" in this chapter refers generally to all institutions of higher education defined in the U.S. Code Title 20. Education § 1001.

[2] Elizabeth J Allan and Mary Madden (2008) '*Hazing in View: College Students at Risk: Initial Findings from the National Study of Student Hazing*', *Stop Hazing*, https://stophazing.org/wp-content/uploads/2020/12/hazing_in_view_study.pdf; Joshua A Sussberg (2003) 'Shattered Dreams: Hazing in College Athletics', 24(3) *Cardozo Law Review* 1421; R Brian Crow & Scott R Rosner (2002) 'Institutional and Organizational Liability for Hazing in Intercollegiate and Professional Team Sports', 76(1) *St. John's Law Review* 87.

[3] See 'Hazing The Deadly Ritual at Fraternities and Sororities', *Independent Lens* (Directed by Byron Hurt and Natalie Brown, 12 September 2022) https://www.pbs.org/independentlens/documentaries/hazingfilm/.

[4] Also known as freshman in the U.S.

A. Srivastava et al., *Hazing (Ragging) at Universities: A Legal Perspective*,
https://doi.org/10.1007/978-981-99-5215-1_2

and others. The university paid about one million dollars to the deceased's family to settle the matter and promised to reform its approach to oversee fraternities and sororities.[5]

There is ample evidence and literature on hazing in the U.S. universities, fraternities, sororities, athletic teams and marching bands.[6] 44 out of 50 states in the U.S. have passed specific statutes to declare hazing an offence. Such statues also lay down various punishments for different hazing acts. Yet, hazing continues unabated. More and more students are being victimised. Since 2000 more than 100 students have died because of hazing. Six deaths occurred in 2021.[7] According to a national study conducted in 2008, more than half (55%) of the participants associated with fraternities and sororities[8] and athletic teams experienced hazing.[9] "25% of coaches or Greek organisations [(fraternities and sororities)] advisors were aware of the group's hazing behaviours [and] 25% of the behaviours occurred on-campus in a public space".[10] Half of which was recorded and posted on public websites.[11]

A significant issue with controlling hazing is that most of the victims (9 out of 10) do not consider themselves hazed and believe hazing has positive outcomes and creates group affiliation and solidarity.[12] Freshers hardly understand how hazing is

[5] Eduardo Medina, 'A Virginia University Will Pay Hazing Victim's Family Nearly $1 Million', *The New York Times* (online, 20 September 2022) https://www.nytimes.com/2022/09/20/us/vcu-adam-oakes-hazing-settlement.html; Eric Kolenich, 'VCU Settles with Family of Adam Oakes, Who Died in Hazing Incident, for $995,000', *Richmond Times-Dispatch* (online, 16 September 2022) https://richmond.com/news/local/education/vcu-settles-with-family-of-adam-oakes-who-died-in-hazing-incident-for-995-000/article_0a249cd9-2c52-5e29-abb5-48a45b672e3a.html.

[6] In recent years hazing related death has also been reported from military organisations, college/university marching bands and high schools. See Benjamin D Ganellen (2016) 'When Marching to the Beat of the Drum Means Beating the Drummer: An Analysis of Hazing in University Marching Bands', 2016(5) *University of Illinois Law Review* 2309; Barbara B Hollmann (2002) 'Hazing: Hidden Campus Crime', 2002(99) *New directions for Student Services* 11; Shelly Campo, Gretchen Poulos and John W Sipple (2005) 'Prevalence and Profiling: Hazing among College Students and Points of Intervention', 29(2) *American Journal of Health Behavior* 137; Gregory Scott Parks et al. (2013) 'White Boys Drink, Black Girls Yell...: A Racialized and Gendered Analysis of Violent Hazing and the Law', *SSRN Electronic Journal* https://www.ssrn.com/abstract=3004714; Sussberg (n 2).

[7] Hank Nuwer, 'Tracking Hazing Deaths', *Unofficial Hazing Clearinghouse*, https://www.hanknuwer.com/.

[8] In most states the anti-hazing statutes use the term organisation for fraternities and sororities.

[9] Allan and Madden (n 2).

[10] Ibid.

[11] Ibid. In one hazing incident, a website showed photographs of students posing in sexually suggestive positions, and one woman passed out drunk while a teammate wrote on her face. See Brad Wolverton, 'Hazing Photos Spur Debates on Complicity of Coaches', *The Chronicle of Higher Education* (online, 2 June 2006) https://www.chronicle.com/article/hazing-photos-spur-debates-on-complicity-of-coaches/.

[12] Allan and Madden (n 2).

ruining their lives and future prospects. Research shows[13] it creates a harmful campus climate and hinders a positive learning environment.[14]

This chapter begins with looking into the sociological background of hazing in detail. The next section analyses relevant statutory provisions of anti-hazing statutes. However, they lack uniformity. The third section thoroughly discusses intentional torts and liability in negligence of universities, fraternities and sororities. Finally, the chapter ends with concluding remarks and suggestions for reform.

2.1 Four Hundred Years of Hazing

An Oxford university student brought hazing to Harvard College as early as 1641. The first student was punished for hazing 43 years later.[15] There were two hazing-related deaths in the nineteenth century. Hazing reached endemic proportions in the late twentieth century. Between 1970 and 1999, 56 students died due to hazing.[16]

Fraternities and sororities are known for hazing-related deaths and injuries. The first Fraternity, Phi Beta Kappa, was formed in 1776 at the College of William and Mary in Williamsburg on 5th December 1776. Over the next couple of centuries, several fraternities and sororities were established.[17] However, the Greek organisations of the past differed from those of today. Their purpose was to encourage members to discuss and debate wide-ranging and controversial (social and political) topics and thereby assist their institutions.[18] There was a sea change in the characteristics of fraternities after the end of World War II. They became famous for "beer, sex and rock and roll".[19]

In early days, fraternities and sororities were mainly white organisations. As a reaction to such organisations, the first African-American Greek organisation was founded in 1906 at Cornell University (followed by many others). The idea was to help integrate African-American students into universities, which were predominantly

---

[13] Aldo Cimino and Benjamin J Thomas (2022) 'Does Hazing Actually Increase Group Solidarity? Re-Examining a Classic Theory with a Modern Fraternity', 43(5) *Evolution and Human Behavior* 408.

[14] Jorge Srabstein (2008) 'Deaths Linked to Bullying and Hazing', 20(2) *International Journal of Adolescent Medicine and Health* 235.

[15] Hank Nuwer, *Wrongs of Passage: Fraternities, Sororities, Hazing, and Binge Drinking* (Indiana University Press, 1999).

[16] Ibid.

[17] The fraternities were: Kappa Alpha-1825, Phi Gamma Delta-1848, Sigma Chi-1852, Sigma Alpha Epsilon-1856, Alpha Tau Omega-1865, and Sigma Nu-1869. The sororities were Beta Phi-1867, Kappa Alpha Theta-1870, Kappa Kappa Gamma-1870, Delta Gamma-1872, Alpha Delta Pi-1904, and Phi Mu-1904.

[18] Alan D DeSantis, *Inside Greek U. Fraternities, Sororities, and the Pursuit of Pleasure, Power, and Prestige* (University Press of Kentucky, 2007).

[19] Ibid, p. 5.

white institutions. Compared to predominantly white Greek organisations, violence is higher in African-American fraternities.[20] They "push pledges to the limits of their endurance and strength, as if the pledges were prisoners performing for ancient emperors".[21]

Hazing has spread from its origins in Greek-letter organisations to universities' sports and marching bands.[22] The first recorded incident occurred in 1923 at Hobart College: a fresher was beaten and thrown into a lake by senior team members.[23]

A survey of 325,000 college athletes indicates: (a) 79% experience hazing,[24] (b) 20% of hazing activities involve crimes such as destroying property, kidnapping others and making prank phone calls; (c) 52% are forced to participate in alcohol-related hazing, including drinking games; and (d) 66% suffer humiliating hazing (such as being yelled at, forced to wear embarrassing clothes, subjected to sleep deprivation).[25] Despite all these atrocities, 60% of hazees said they would not report hazing to university administrators.[26]

Hazing is also much prevalent in universities' marching bands.[27] In 2011 a student at Florida A&M University died after suffering internal bleeding during the practice of a hazing tradition (known as Crossing Bus C).[28] Fifty-six per cent of marching bands and other performing arts organisation members experience hazing.[29]

---

[20] Parks et al. (n 6); Nuwer (n 15).

[21] Nuwer (n 15) p. 187.

[22] SK Fields, CL Collins and RD Comstock (2010) 'Violence in Youth Sports: Hazing, Brawling and Foul Play', 44(1) *British Journal of Sports Medicine* 32; Sussberg (n 2); Hollmann (n 6).

[23] Sussberg (n 2).

[24] Nadine Hoover (1999) 'National Survey: Initiation Rites and Athletics for NCAA Sports Teams', https://www.alfred.edu/about/news/studies/_docs/hazing.pdf.

[25] Ibid.

[26] Ibid.

[27] Ganellen (n 6). In another incident of 2014 Ohio State University fired its Marching Band's Director for permitting and encouraging hazing abuse, including acts of sexual harassment, of its students.

[28] The 'Crossing Bus C' tradition involves a student forcing his way from the front of a bus to the back, ploughing through band members who tackle, block, kick and punch him with drum mallets.

[29] Allan and Madden (n 2). A study involving interviews of 1215 college marching band members found that almost one-third (30%) of members experienced hazing (mostly yelling); surprisingly, 12% encouraged hazing. See Jason M Silveira & Michael W Hudson (2015) 'Hazing in the College Marching Band', 63(1) *Journal of Research in Music Education* 5; Ganellen (n 6).

Forced alcohol drinking is widespread in fraternities and sororities. Students who join fraternities consume a lot more alcohol than others.[30] Alcohol plays a significant role in 35–40% of all hazing incidents.[31] Students face both direct and indirect peer pressure to consume alcohol. Direct pressure involves drinking alcohol at the instruction of other fraternity or sorority members or face punishment. Indirect pressure includes the easy availability of alcohol and drinking at fraternity and sorority events because others are doing the same thing.[32] In October 2021, a University of Missouri student and freshman pledge of the Phi Gamma Delta fraternity suffered brain damage from alcohol poisoning after drinking three-fourth bottle of vodka.[33] The student involved cannot now walk or converse.

Assaults, including sexual assault, and battery, are common during hazing. In March 2017, nine Texas athletes, as part of hazing rituals, sexually assaulted and sodomised junior team members. They put various items, including soda water bottles, steel pipes, baseball bats and a carbon dioxide tank, into the rectum of the victims.[34] The hazers were arrested and charged with sexual assault and sodomy of junior team members. In another case, the prosecutor charged fifteen suburban Chicago teenagers with misdemeanour battery for their alleged part in a videotaped hazing in which high school girls were beaten and showered with filth.[35] In *Helton v. State of Indiana*,[36] Helton, a youth group member, hit two pledges forty times in the head and six times in the chest as part of the initiation ceremony.

Despite anti-hazing policies that warn students of the dangers of hazing, incidents of deaths and severe injuries continue to hit the mainstream media.

---

[30] Henry Wechsler, George Kuh and Andrea E Davenport (2009) 'Fraternities, Sororities and Binge Drinking: Results from a National Study of American Colleges', 46(3) *NASPA Journal* 395; H Wechsler et al. (2000) 'College Binge Drinking in the 1990s: A Continuing Problem. Results of the Harvard School of Public Health 1999 College Alcohol Study', 48(5) *Journal of American College Health* 199; JR Cashin, CA Presley and PW Meilman (1998) 'Alcohol Use in the Greek System: Follow the Leader?', 59(1) *Journal of Studies on Alcohol* 63; Byron L LeFlore (1998) 'Alcohol and Hazing Risks in College Fraternities', 7(2) *The Review of Litigation* 191.

[31] Damon C Richardson (2014) 'University Officials' Perceptions about Felony Hazing Laws', *Doctoral Thesis*, p. 32.

[32] Brian Borsari, John TP Hustad and Christy Capone (2009) 'Alcohol Use in the Greek System, 1999–2009: A Decade of Progress', 2(3) *Current Drug Abuse Reviews* 216.

[33] The video footage of the pledge night shows the freshman passing out after consuming a bottle of vodka, and while doing so, another fraternity member poured beer down his throat using a tube and funnel. See 'Danny Santulli's Family on "Good Morning America": Prosecute the Fiji Brothers Responsible', *Columbia Daily Tribune* (online, 11 June 2022) https://www.columbiatribune.com/story/news/education/campus/2022/06/11/danny-santulli-family-missouri-hazing-fiji-surveillance-video-phi-gamma-delta/7580183001/.

[34] Katie Mettler, 'Alleged "Sadistic Hazing Rituals" Lead to 13 Arrests of Male Student Athletes in Small Texas Town', *Washington Post* (online, 25 October 2021) https://www.washingtonpost.com/news/morning-mix/wp/2017/04/14/alleged-sadistic-hazing-rituals-lead-to-13-arrests-of-male-student-athletes-in-small-texas-town/.

[35] Amy E. Nevala & Susan Kuczka '15 Students Face Battery Charges in Hazing Brawl', *Chicago Tribune* (online, 17 May 2023).

[36] 1993, 624 N.E.2d 499.

Most U.S. states have drafted specific statutes to prevent and punish hazing. These statutes are discussed in the next section.

2.2 Anti-hazing Legislation

As noted before forty-four out of 50 U.S. states have enacted anti-hazing laws.[37] However, the penalties provided under these laws do not limit or affect the right of an educational institution to enforce its own penalty against hazing. Anti-hazing laws of a state are either part of the criminal/penal code or the education code and vary from state to state. It is beyond the scope of this chapter to analyse statutory provisions of hazing in all the states. We have therefore selected some states to illustrate how state laws seek to protect pledges.

States differ in their definition of what constitutes hazing. The differences in the definition of hazing at the state level have led to a situation where certain activities are illegal in one state but permissible in another state.[38] Some states, such as New York[39] and Illinois, limit the definition of hazing to only physical harm. The anti-hazing law of Illinois defines hazing as:

> A person commits hazing who knowingly requires the performance of any act by a student or other person in a school, college, university, or other educational institution of this State, for the purpose of induction or admission into any group, organization, or society associated or connected with that institution if:
>
> (a) the act is not sanctioned or authorized by that educational institution; and
> (b) the act results in bodily harm to any person.[40]

Other states, such as Ohio,[41] Texas,[42] and Michigan,[43] include both physical and emotional harm in the definition of hazing. The Ohio Anti-hazing Act defines hazing as:

> doing any act or coercing another, including the victim, to do any act of initiation into any student or other organization or any act to continue or reinstate membership in or affiliation with any student or other organization that causes or creates a substantial risk of causing mental or physical harm to any person, including coercing another to consume alcohol or a drug of abuse.[44]

---

[37] The states that do not have an anti-hazing law are New Mexico, South Dakota, Wyoming, Montana, Alaska and Hawaii.

[38] See Sussberg (n 2).

[39] New York State Law on Hazing, Article 120 – NY Penal Law Part 3, Title H, §120.16 & §120.17.

[40] See, e.g., 2010 Illinois Code :: Chapter 720 Criminal Offences :: 720 ILCS 120/ Hazing Act.

[41] Ohio Revised Code § 2903.31.

[42] Texas Education Code §51.936, Chapter 37, subchapter F § 37.151(6).

[43] Michigan Penal Code 750.411t.

[44] Ohio Revised Code § 2903.31 (A)(1).

Most states either broadly define hazing or give examples of behaviour that constitute hazing, i.e., beating or paddling a pledge, depriving a pledge of sleep, food, or water, or forcing a pledge to perform calisthenics that affects their health and safety, or forcing a pledge to drink a large quantity of alcoholic beverage.

The majority of states classify hazing as a misdemeanour. Under Texas law, where hazing causes serious bodily injury, it is a Class A misdemeanour; where it does not cause serious bodily injury, it is a Class B misdemeanour. If hazing results in the victim's death, it is a felony.[45] Under the California Penal Code,[46] hazing is a crime as long as there is a likelihood of serious physical injury to the victim. The prosecution does not need to prove that the victim, in fact, suffered physical injury. In such cases, hazing is a misdemeanour. This offence is punishable with a fine ($100–$5000) and/or up to one year in county jail (or on misdemeanour probation). If hazing has resulted in serious bodily injury or death of the victim, it is up to the prosecutor's discretion to charge the hazer with misdemeanour or felony.[47]

Pennsylvania and Texas anti-hazing laws include a 'safe harbour' provision that provides student protection if they report hazing. Also in Pennsylvania, an 'individual' is immune from criminal prosecution if the student is the first to seek urgent medical attention to prevent death or serious bodily injury to another person from hazing activities.[48] In Texas, a student is granted immunity from civil or criminal liability if the student voluntarily reports a specific hazing incident involving another student to the appropriate university official.[49] In December 2022, a lawmaker in Missouri proposed a similar 'safe harbour' provision for persons who 'placed a 911 call' for reporting an act of hazing and staying and assisting the victim until emergency services arrive on the scene.[50]

Massachusetts impose punishment on eyewitnesses and accomplices for not reporting hazing (e.g., university employees) to relevant authorities. A bystander present at the hazing scene could face fines for not reporting the matter, but only if they could have done so without endangering themselves or others:

> Whoever knows that another person is the victim of hazing … and is at the scene of such crime shall, to the extent that such person can do so without danger or peril to himself or

---

[45] Failure to report hazing is also a Class B misdemeanour. Texas Education Code § 37.152.

[46] CA Penal Code § 245.6 (2020).

[47] A hazer may face up to three years in prison or felony probation if convicted of a felony.

[48] 18 Pa. Stat. and Cons. Stat. § 2810.

[49] Texas Education Code § 37.155 IMMUNITY FROM PROSECUTION AVAILABLE - In the prosecution of an offense under this subchapter, the court may grant immunity from prosecution for the offense to each person who is subpoenaed to testify for the prosecution and who does testify for the prosecution. Any person reporting a specific hazing incident involving a student in an educational institution to the dean of students or other appropriate official of the institution is immune from civil or criminal liability that might otherwise be incurred or imposed as a result of the report. Immunity extends to participation in any judicial proceeding resulting from the report. A person reporting in bad faith or with malice is not protected by this section.

[50] Ethan Heinz, 'Proposed House Bill Would Protect Those Calling for Help in College Hazing Incidents', *ABC17NEWS* (online, 29 December 2022) https://abc17news.com/politics/missouri-politics/2022/12/29/bill-proposed-would-protect-those-calling-for-help-in-college-hazing-incidents/.

> others, report such crime to an appropriate law enforcement official as soon as reasonably practicable. Whoever fails to report such crime shall be punished by a fine of not more than one thousand dollars.[51]

It is worth noting that it is not uncommon for prosecutors to charge hazers under other penal code provisions relating to assault, battery, and forcible acts of sexual penetration.[52] For example, if hazing involves using force or violence on someone, a prosecutor may decide to charge the hazer for assault and battery.[53]

2.2.1 *Institutional Duty*

A few state statutes require universities to draft an anti-hazing policy, provide a copy of such policy to every student group and organisation (e.g. fraternities and sororities), and upload it on their publicly accessible website.[54] These statutes also require universities to educate students about hazing prevention and penalties for violating the institution's anti-hazing policy.[55] The university penalties may include (a) imposition of fines against those involved in hazing; (b) withholding of diplomas or transcripts of a hazer; (c) revocation of permission for an organisation (e.g. fraternity or sorority) to operate on campus or to otherwise operate under the recognition or sanction of the institution; and (d) imposition of probation, suspension, dismissal, or expulsion of a hazer.[56]

The Ohio Anti-hazing law requires the chancellor of higher education to develop a state-wide education plan for preventing hazing at universities. The plan requires at least a model anti-hazing policy and guidelines regarding anti-hazing education and training for students, staff and organisations (e.g. fraternities and sororities) affiliated with a university.

Furthermore, Ohio and Pennsylvania laws require universities to maintain a record (to be updated bi-annually) of all reported anti-hazing policy violations or anti-hazing laws for five years and upload them on a publicly accessible website.[57]

---

[51] Mass. Gen. Laws ch. 269, § 18.

[52] See *Helton v. State of Indiana* 624 N.E.2d 499 (1993); *Ex Parte Smith* (2006) 185 S.W.3d 887 (Texas); CA Penal Code § 289 - Forcible acts of sexual penetration.

[53] For example, under Californian Penal Code 240 and 242 PC Assault and Battery are a crime. CA Penal Code § 242 - Battery is defined as any willful and unlawful use of force or violence upon the person of another. CA Penal Code § 243 - A battery is punishable by a fine not exceeding two thousand dollars ($2000), and/or by imprisonment in a county jail not exceeding six months.

[54] *See, e.g.*, Mass. Gen. Laws ch. 269, §§ 17–19; Ohio Revised Code §§ 2903.311(B), 3345.19 (B)(C); 18 Pa. Stat. and Cons. Stat. § 2808(a)(2),(3).

[55] *See, e.g.*, Ohio Revised Code § 3345.19; 18 Pa. Stat. and Cons. Stat. § 2808.

[56] Ibid. - *See, e.g.*, Ohio Revised Code § 3345.19; 18 Pa. Stat. and Cons. Stat. § 2808.

[57] OHIO REV. CODE ANN. § 3345.19; 18 Pa. Stat. and Cons. Stat. § 2809.

2.2.2 *Condoning and Encouraging Hazing by Fraternities and Sororities*

Where a fraternity or sorority condones or encourages hazing, they commit an offence of misdemeanour punishable by a fine between $5000 and $10,000.[58] Pennsylvanian law provides that upon conviction of the fraternity or sorority, the court may order the forfeiture of property involved in hazing.[59]

Where a fraternity or sorority authorises hazing in disregard of anti-hazing policy and rules, it may not be allowed to operate on an institution's campus and may lose institutional recognition.[60] In some cases, fraternities and sororities have been permanently expelled[61] or suspended for a period for encouraging hazing in violation of the anti-hazing policy.[62]

Despite anti-hazing laws in the U.S., the criminal punishment prescribed does not seem to be a sufficient deterrent to hazers. Even in extreme cases of hazing causing death, the punishment given by the court is not severe. In Pennsylvania, a hazer who caused the hazee's death was just placed on five years probation, ordered to perform 100 hour of community service and pay a fine of $1000.[63]

---

[58] In Pennsylvania, the university may also be liable to the same amount if it intentionally, knowingly or recklessly promotes or facilitates hazing. See 18 PA. STAT. AND CONS. STAT. ANN. § 2805. In Texas, in case of personal injury, property damage, or other loss, it may impose a fine between $5000 and double the amount of that loss. TEX. EDUC. CODE ANN. § 37.153.

[59] 18 Pa. Stat. and Cons. Stat. § 2807.

[60] 18 Pa. Stat. and Cons. Stat. § 2808; Ohio Revised Code § 3345.19§.

[61] Maya King, 'Bowling Green Reaches $2.9 Million Settlement in Hazing Death', *The New York Times* (online, 23 January 2023) https://www.nytimes.com/2023/01/23/us/bowling-green-state-university-hazing-settlement.html.

[62] In January 2022, two Bowling Green State University (BGSU) fraternities (Delta Chi and Phi Delta Theta) were suspended for alleged hazing and alcohol incidents. In the same month, Phi Gamma Delta and Phi Delta Theta fraternities at the University of Kansas were suspended for five years after an investigation found forced alcohol consumption and physical abuse practices-See Jenson Strock, '2 BGSU Fraternities Suspended for Alleged Hazing, Alcohol Incidents', *wtol.com* (online, 25 January 2022) https://www.wtol.com/article/news/crime/bowling-green-state-university-fraternities-suspended-for-hazing-and-alcohol-violations/512-bb5bab48-247b-48c2-8a37-7ddbf5e6a7f6. In April 2022, Louisiana State University (LSU) suspended the Sigma Alpha Epsilon fraternity till 31 May 2023 for violating LSU's anti-hazing policy. After that, the fraternity will be on a two-year disciplinary probation period from 1 June 2023 through 31 May 2025 before being fully integrated as part of LSU's organisation - See ELYSE CARMOSINO, 'LSU Suspends Fraternity for Hazing after Alleged "Hell Week" Kidnapping, Assault', *The Advocate* (online, 9 April 2022) https://www.theadvocate.com/baton_rouge/news/lsu-suspends-fraternity-for-hazing-after-alleged-hell-week-kidnapping-assault/article_dc5dd2be-b793-11ec-bc7a-bf805b4ab8fd.html.

[63] David Keok, 'First of 37 Defendants in Baruch College Fatal Hazing Case Pleads Guilty', *Reuters* (online, 11 January 2017) https://www.reuters.com/article/us-new-york-hazing-death-idUSKBN14V0A2.

2.2.3 Consent to Criminal Hazing

Consent is a defence to a criminal action. But, consent must have been given freely without any pressure. When the consent is not influenced by threat or coercion, the defendant could argue that the victim's predicament or injury was caused due to his own act of consent and, therefore, there is no question of the defendant's liability. The test whether the victim's consent was freely given is an objective one.[64] 25 out of the 44 states specifically provide in their anti-hazing laws that the perpetrator of hazing cannot argue consent as a legal defence.[65] The Massachusetts Anti-Hazing Statute states that "consent shall not be available as a defence in any prosecution".[66]

In *Quinn v. Sigma Rho Chapter of Beta Theta Pi Fraternity*,[67] the plaintiff was a pledge of the defendant. To become a fraternity member, he was required to participate in the "Pledge Dad Night" initiation ceremony. During the ceremony, the fraternity members directed him to consume excessive alcohol. The plaintiff complied and, after considerable drinking, became unconscious. When he awoke, he could not properly use his hands or arms and suffered neurological damage. The Appellate Court of Illinois said:

> The social pressure that exists once a ...university student has pledged into a fraternal organisation is so great that compliance with initiation requirements places him or her in a position of acting in a coerced manner.[68]
>
> We cannot close our eyes to the fact that the abuse illustrated in the present case could have resulted in the termination of life and that plaintiff was coerced into being his own executioner. Therefore, we hold that a legal duty was created and the complaint states a cause of action in negligence.[69]

In *Oja v. Theta Chi Fraternity,*[70] the Supreme Court of New York had taken a similar view to that of the Appellate Court of Illinois. In *People v Lenti (Lenti II),* the Court clarified that "[c]onsent of the pledges certainly should not be a bar to prosecution" and "consent cannot be a defence when the public conscience and morals are shocked".[71]

---

64 See *Siesto v. Bethpage Union Free School.* Dist., N.Y. L.J., Dec. 30, 1999, p. 21 (N.Y. Sup. Ct.).

65 Qi Li (2002) 'Contract Liability in the Student-University Relationship: Case Law Implications for University Policies', *Ph.D. Thesis, Washington State University*, p. 106.

66 Mass. Gen. Laws ch. 269, § 17. See also Texas Education Code § 37.154. The California hazing law provides that "the implied or expressed consent of the person or persons against whom the hazing was directed shall not be defence to any action." - CA Penal Code § 245.6 (f).

67 507 N.E.2d 1193 (Ill. App.) 1193; Cf. *Ex Parte Barran* (1998) So.2d 203 (Ala.) and *Jones v. Kappa Alpha Order* (1997) 730 So.2d 197 (Ala.).

68 507 N.E.2d 1193,1198.

69 507 N.E.2d 1193,1197. See also *People v. Lenti*, 44 Misc. 2d 118, 253 N.Y.S.2d 9 (N.Y. Cnty. Ct. 1964).

70 (1997) 174 Misc. 2d 966; 667 N.Y.S.2d 650 (N.Y.). See also *Helton v. State of Indiana* (1993) 624 N.E.2d 499 (Indiana).

71 *People v. Lenti,* 46 Misc. 2d 682, 260 N.Y.S.2d 284 (N.Y. Cnty. Ct. 1965), p. 287–288.

On the other hand, in *Ex Parte Barran*[72] the Supreme Court of Alabama said that fraternities and sororities can use consent as a defence where the victim of hazing continued to be involved in the fraternity event after seeing other pledges leaving it because of abuse and violence. The court said:

> Plaintiff claims a coercive environment hampered his free will to the extent that he could not voluntarily choose to leave the fraternity. College students are not children. Save for very few legal exceptions, they are adult citizens, ready, able, and willing to be responsible for their own actions.[73]

This decision means fraternities in Alabama can use consent as a defence where the victim voluntarily participates in hazing activities.[74]

Specific anti-hazing laws of the 44 states provide criminal responsibility for those directly or indirectly involved in hazing. Members of fraternities and sororities can be held criminally responsible for the death or injury of the hazed victim. But, anti-hazing laws do not prevent the victim from filing a civil suit for damages. For example, Californian Anti-Hazing law states that "a victim of hazing may commence a civil action for injury or damages…against any participants in the hazing, or any organisation to which the student is seeking membership".[75] In fact, almost half (49.7%) of all court cases on hazing are about tort liability, including negligence.[76] The following section discusses university liability to a victim of hazing in torts.

2.3 Liability in Tort Law

While the purpose of criminal law is to punish the wrongdoer, that of tort law is to compensate the victim.[77] A criminal action may fail, but a tort action may succeed. One cannot be held criminally liable for an act done in the mistaken belief that it would not cause any injury or damage to the victim, but the wrongdoer could be held liable in the tort of negligence.[78]

---

72 (1998) 730 So. 2d 203 (Ala.).

73 (1998) 730 So. 2d 203 (Ala.) 206.

74 Qi Li (n 65), p. 79. It is worth noting the dissenting opinion of Shores, J. - I cannot condone a practice that exploits the desire to be admitted to "the fraternity" to the extent it is exploited here. As I understand it, a pledge must be willing to undergo the degrading, disgusting, and, no doubt, health-threatening practices to meet, again, "the fraternity's" high standards for admission. No one should be required to wallow in feces, vomit, urine, and God only knows what else, to gain admission to any "club". The sadness is that so many are willing to do so.

75 CA Penal Code § 245.6 (2020) (e).

76 Qi Li (n 65), p. 65.

77 Andrew Tettenborn, *Clerk & Lindsell on Torts. 23rd Edition, Mainwork & 1st Supplement* (Sweet & Maxwell UK, 2021).

78 Kit Barker (ed.), *The Law of Torts in Australia* (Oxford University Press, 5th ed, 2012). In a recent incident in the U.S., a Linfield college student who lost his one eye due to hazing filed an $8.3 million lawsuit against the college and Pi Kappa Alpha fraternity for impairment of his future earnings and career prospects - see 'Student's $8.3M Lawsuit Alleges Hazing Incident Cost Him His Eye', *Fox News* (online, 2 February 2017) https://www.foxnews.com/health/students-8-3m-law suit-alleges-hazing-incident-cost-him-his-eye.

2.3.1 Intentional Tort

2.3.1.1 Assault and Battery

Assault is any direct and intentional act of the defendant threatening the plaintiff that physical force will be used against him immediately.[79] Where a hazer threatens a pledge that if the pledge does not abide by his/her instructions, they will be coming to the pledge's place to beat the pledge up thoroughly, is an assault. Even a threat via email or a on any social media platform can constitute assault, provided a reasonable person in the position of the pledge would have taken the threat seriously.[80]

In contrast to an assault, where the plaintiff must prove that the use of physical force against him was about to occur, a battery requires the plaintiff to prove that physical force was, in fact, applied.[81] A fresher who is raped, sodomized, kicked, paddled, punched, banged against something, or physically or sexually assaulted may file a battery claim.[82] In *W v. Meah*, the victim of rape and severe attack received aggravated damages. Both, assault and battery protect a student's interest in maintaining their physical integrity, which hazers frequently violate.[83]

In *Helton v. State of Indiana* (1993),[84] discussed above,[85] the Court of Appeals of Indiana, referring to the Indiana Code, said that a person commits battery when he knowingly or intentionally touches another person in a rude, insolent, or angry manner.[86] The court further said that the general rule is that victim's consent is a defence to the charge of a battery, but there are exceptions.[87] Striking pledges "continuously in an area which is susceptible of injury as severe as permanent brain damage is an atrocious, aggravated battery for which consent is no defence".[88]

---

[79] *Read v. Coker* (1853) 13 CBR 850; 138 ER 1437.

[80] See e.g., *Police v. Greaves* [1964] NZLR 295.

[81] Nancy J Moore (2012) 'Intent and Consent in the Tort of Battery: Confusion and Controversy', 61(6) *American University Law Review* 1585.

[82] CA Penal Code § 289 - Forcible acts of sexual penetration are a serious felony; See also Nevala and Kuczka (n 35).

[83] (1986) 1 All ER 835.

[84] 624 N.E.2d 499. (Indiana).

[85] See above n 37.

[86] IND. CODE 35-42-2-1(a).

[87] The Supreme Court of Indiana in *Jaske v. State* (1989), Ind., 539 N.E. 2d 14, 18 laid down the exception to the general rule. Consent is not a defence in certain circumstances such as: (1) Where the defendant goes beyond acts consented to and beats to death the victim who consented only to the defendant's execution of the organization's initiation ritual of being struck in the stomach until he passed out; (2) Where it is against public policy to permit the conduct or resulting harm even though it is consented to, as where there are no sexual overtones and the battery is a severe one which involves a breach of the public peace, as well as, an invasion of the victim's physical security; (3) Where consent is ineffective as where it is obtained by fraud or from one lacking legal capacity to consent; (4) Where a deadly weapon is employed; (5) Where death results; or, (6) Where the battery is atrocious or aggravated.

[88] *Helton v. State of Indiana* (1993) 624 N.E.2d 499 (Indiana), p. 515.

Brueckner v. Norwich University[89] is a relevant case on assault and battery. Senior students employed by Norwich university in specific programs to educate incoming pupils hazed the plaintiff and endangered his bodily and emotional well-being. As the university was aware of ongoing hazing issues in the past but failed to take any action, the plaintiff's tort case against the institution for assault and battery, as well as negligent supervision, was successful. The lower court's decision to hold the university accountable and grant the victim compensatory and punitive damages[90] was upheld by the Supreme Court of Vermont.

2.3.1.2 False Imprisonment

False imprisonment is the total restraint on a person's liberty without any lawful justification. There is a complete physical restriction on a person's freedom of movement with no reasonable means to escape. For example, where the fresher does not leave a room fearing beating, he has an action in false imprisonment.[91] Likewise, when fraternity brothers, as part of the initiation ceremony, abduct a pledge and lock him in a room without any means to escape, the hazers will be liable for false imprisonment.[92]

In 2019, a pledge at Louisiana State University (LSU) Delta Kappa Epsilon fraternity was forced by fraternity brothers to strip down to his underwear and stand in an ice machine filled with half water and half ice for 30–45 min. The pledge did not attempt to escape from the ice machine, fearing he would be beaten up severely by the fraternity brothers. The police charged nine fraternity brothers with false imprisonment and hazing.[93] In another incident, a former pledge of a U.S. fraternity suffered burns, brandings, beatings and mental abuse during his time at the fraternity, causing him post-traumatic stress, including anxiety disorder.[94] He filed a complaint against the fraternity for battery, false imprisonment, and other wrongs, claiming compensatory and punitive damages.[95]

---

[89] [1999] No. &30 A.2d 1086. *Maines v. Cronomer Valley Fire Department* (1980) 50 N.Y.2d 535 (New York).

[90] The purpose of punitive damages is to "punish conduct which is morally culpable [and] to deter a wrongdoer from repetitions of the same or similar actions". See *Coty v. Ramsey Associates, Inc.*, 149 Vt. 451, 546 A.2d 196 (1988).

[91] *See Symes v. Mahon* [1922] SASR 447; *K v. Chan Wing* [1995] 1 HKC 470, CA.

[92] *See Knoll v. Board of Regents of University of Nebraska* [1999] 601 N.E. 2d 757 discussed below n 151 where the victim could have a good case in false imprisonment.

[93] Chris Woodyard, 'Police: DKE Frat Members Arrested for Hazing, Urinating upon LSU Pledges', *USA TODAY* (online, 14 February 2019) https://www.usatoday.com/story/news/nation/2019/02/14/9-lsu-fraternity-members-arrested-hazing-charges/2872824002/ ('*Police*').

[94] Megan Trimble, 'Penn State Fraternity Pledge Suffered Cigarette Burns, Alcohol Abuse during Hazing: Lawsuit', *pennlive (patriot news)* (online, 8 June 2015) https://www.pennlive.com/midstate/2015/06/kappa_delta_rho_penn_state_law.html.

[95] Ibid.

Where a successful action is brought in any of the above torts (assault, battery or false imprisonment), damages will be awarded for injury to feelings caused by indignity, humiliation and mental suffering, even if there was no physical injury. The court can also award separate damages for psychiatric injury.[96]

2.3.1.3 Defamation

Defamation consists in the publication of a false or derogatory statement about the plaintiff that affects the plaintiff's reputation in the community and tends to deter another from associating with the plaintiff. To succeed in a defamation case, the plaintiff must demonstrate that the defamatory statement was untrue and published. A defamation action cannot be based solely on a private email sent to the plaintiff. A defamatory statement must be published to a third party. Defamatory remarks on a blog post, a WhatsApp group message, or a YouTube video would suffice the criteria for publishing. In July 2022, male university students from a university in Bangkok were forced to strip naked while being evaluated by girls as part of hazing. The video of the incident was shared on Twitter. A similar incident in the U.S. will give the hazee a right to file a claim for damages under the tort of defamation.[97]

In August 2010, a Drake University student was charged with sexually assaulting another fraternity brother. He also took pictures and videos of the assaults and stored them on his computer.[98] The victim could have sued the hazer for the tort of defamation if the hazer would have uploaded the videos on social media.

Another incident involving defamation in 2011 is worth highlighting. The plaintiff and another student (both members of the Florida Marching Band) were severely beaten-up during hazing. The plaintiff survived while the other student lost consciousness and died from his wounds. In a story, Cox Media falsely claimed that the plaintiff caused or contributed to the death of the deceased and was therefore expelled from the institution. When the plaintiff complained, Cox Media updated the article stating that the plaintiff had not been suspended. Nevertheless, the plaintiff persisted in his defamation lawsuit since Cox Media failed to state that he had not contributed to the deceased's death. The parties resolved the matter through mediation.[99]

---

[96] *See Richardson v. Howie* [2004] EWCA Civ 1127; *Rowlands v. Chief Constable of Merseyside* [2007] WLR 1065.

[97] Joe Faretra, 'University Students Performed Naked Hazing Dance Ritual in Front of Women', *Dailystar.co.uk* (online, 19 July 2022) https://www.dailystar.co.uk/news/world-news/university-students-performed-naked-hazing-27516522.

[98] 'Drake University Senior Charged With Assaulting, Taping Fraternity Brother', *ABC News* (online, 7 August 2010) https://abcnews.go.com/US/drake-university-senior-accused-sexually-assaulting-fraternity-brother/story?id=11342144.

[99] Iulia Filip, 'Cox Accused of Defamation in Hazing Story', *Courthouse News* (online, 14 June 2012) https://www.courthousenews.com/cox-accused-of-defamation-in-hazing-story/.

Over the years, student victims of hazing have filed multi-million dollar claims in defamation.[100] Damages awarded in defamation cases are in line with those awarded for personal injuries.[101] Apart from compensatory damages, the court can also award aggravated and punitive damages.[102]

2.4 Universities' Liability in Negligence

2.4.1 Duty of Care

Section 323 of the Restatement (Second) of Torts, states that:

> One who undertakes, gratuitously or for consideration, to render services to another which he should recognise as necessary for the protection of the other's person or things, is subject to liability to the other for physical harm resulting from his failure to exercise reasonable care to perform his undertaking, if (a) his failure to exercise such care increases the risk of such harm, or (b) the harm is suffered because of the other's reliance upon the undertaking.[103]

In the modern setting, university-student relationships are largely governed by a dozen of U.S. cases.

2.4.1.1 Historical Perspective

Until the 1980s, universities were not held liable for any negligence of their staff towards their students. From 1960 to 1970 the court applied the *in loco parentis* doctrine, which made it difficult for students to sue the university for injuries or harm caused by hazing. The courts were not prepared to interfere with university-student matters. The university was in the same position as a baby-sitter. All punishments given by teachers were considered as reasonable unless there was a permanent injury or evidence of wicked motive on their part.[104]

---

[100] *See e.g., Estate of Chad Meredith v. Travis Montgomery and David May* (11th Judicial Circuit Miami-Dade County, Florida, 02-11335 CA02).

[101] *John v. MGN Ltd* [1997] QB 586.

[102] *Sutcliffe v. Pressadram Ltd* [1991] 1 QB 153; Punitive damages are available only if compensatory and aggravated damages are deemed insufficient punishment for the defendant. Aggravated damages are not design to punish the wrongdoer.

[103] Restatement (Second) of Torts (1965), § 323.

[104] Perry A Zirkel and Henry F Reichner (1986) 'Is the "In Loco Parentis" Doctrine Dead?', 15(3) *Journal of Law and Education* 271. p. 273–274. However, this position has changed due to the student rights movement in the 1960s. See Neil Jamerson (2013) 'Who Is the University: Birnbaum's Black Box and Tort Liability', 39 *Journal of College and University Law* 347. *See also Dixon v. Alabama*, 294 F. 2d 150 (5th Cir. 1961), where the validity of *in loco parentis* doctrine was questioned and the end of this doctrine was confirmed in *Bradshaw v. Rawlings*, 612 F.2d 135 (3d Cir.1979). *See also University of Denver v. Whitlock* 744 P.2d 54 (Colo.1987); *Fox v. Bd. of Sup'rs of La. State Univ.*, 576 So. 2d 978 (La. 1991); *Mcclure v. Fairfield University* 2003 Conn. Super. LEXIS 178.

An epoch-making case of 1961, *Dixon v Alabama State Board of Education*,[105] brought a sea change in courts' attitude toward the university's responsibility to students. "The Dixon court's decision eliminated blanket immunity for universities—which allowed universities to unilaterally discipline students under in loco parentis doctrine. This led to the beginning of a new body of case law defining a university's duties to its students".[106] The court, for the first time, required universities to provide students an opportunity to be heard before expulsion.[107]

From the 1970s the bystander principle was dominant. It implied that the university could not control students in a custodial sense.[108] There was a complete departure from the principle of *in loco parentis*. As young adults, students were free to choose their own path in their private matters and "universities—were [not] responsible for [students] misconduct injuring another student".[109] Ironically, whether it was the case of *in loco parentis* or bystander, the university was immune from any liability for students behaviour towards another student.

In *Bradshaw v. Rawlings*[110] the court regarded students as adults in almost every phase of community life. It thought that interfering with students' freedom to organise their private recreational and personal practice choices would produce a repressive and inhospitable educational environment, largely inconsistent with the objectives of modern thinking. It said that "the modern American college is not an insurer of the safety of its students"[111] and students were legally responsible adults who could take care of themselves.

Beach v. University of Utah[112] followed the *Bradshaw* ruling observing that the imposition of a custodial relationship between the university and its adult students would be inconsistent with the objectives of a modern education[113] and it would

---

105 294 F.2d 150, 159 (5th Cir. 1961).

106 Cori Smith (2021) 'The Civil Rights Approach to University Negligence Liability Arising Out of Studenton-Student Misconduct', 126(1) *Penn State Law Review* 243, p. 249.

107 Ibid.

108 This development was particularly pronounced in injuries caused to students in alcohol related students. See Robert D Bickel and Peter F Lake (1997) 'The Emergence of New Paradigms in Student-University Relations: From In Loco Parentis to Bystander to Facilitator', 23(4) *Journal of College and University Law* 755, p. 756; Peter F. Lake (1999) '*The Rise of Duty and the Fall of In Loco Parentis and Other Protective Tort Doctrines in Higher Education Law*', 64(1) Missouri Law Review 1, p. 16. See also *Bradshaw v. Rawlings*, 612 F.2d 135 (3d Cir. 1979); *Baldwin v. Zoradi* 176 Cal Rptr.809 (Cal. Ct. App. 1981); *Rabel v. Illionis Wesleyan University* 514 N.E. 2d 552 (III. App. Ct. 1981); *Beach v. University of Utah*, 726 P.2d 413 (Utah 1986).

109 Smith (n 106) p. 250.

110 612 F.2d 135 (3d Cir.1979). For the criticism of this case, see Robert D. Bickel & Peter F. Lake (1994) 'Reconceptualizing the University's Duty to Provide a Safe Learning Environment: A Criticism of the Doctrine of in Loco Parentis and the Restatement (Second) of Torts', 20 *Journal of College and University* 261, p. 273–76.

111 *Bradshaw v. Rawlings*, 612 F.2d 135 (3d Cir.1979), 138.

112 726 P.2d 413 (Utah 1986).

113 *Beach v. University of Utah* 726 P.2d 413 (Utah 1986). For a detailed analysis of the case, *see* William A. Kaplin & Barbara A. Lee, The Law of Higher Education: Student Version 16–17 (Jossey-Bass, 4th edn., 2007). *See also Mintz v. New York*, 47 A.D.2d 570, 362 N.Y.S.2d 619

be impossible for any university to babysit its students.[114] *Baldwin v. Zoradi*[115] emphasised that only by giving responsibilities to students they could grow into responsible adulthood. In *Denver v. Whitlock*[116] the court endorsed the social policy of fostering an educational environment of student autonomy and independence.

2.4.1.2 Present Position

The present position of a university vis-a-vis student has very much changed. It has been realised that students, especially new students or freshers, cannot manage everything by themselves. They need guidance and active support of their institution. Modern universities have a very close relationship with their students. They do not only carry out curricular activities, but their relationship goes much further afield. They are "very much involved in the well-being of students. They provide leadership and governance. Universities facilitate the maturation of young adults. All aspects of student life bear the imprimatur of the university".[117]

The bystander approach began to be abandoned in the early 1980s. And the courts began to impose liability on the university on three grounds: premises liability, assumption of responsibility and special relationship.

Premises Liability

In hazing and other cases, the courts rely on premises liability if they are under the university's control and a student is injured. This is based on section 343 of the Restatement (Second) of Torts:

> A possessor of land is subject to liability for physical harm caused to his invitees by a condition on the land if, but only if, he (a) knows or by the exercise of reasonable care would discover the condition, and should realize that it involves an unreasonable risk of harm to such invitees, and (b) should expect that they will not discover or realize the danger, or will fail to protect themselves against it, and (c) fails to exercise reasonable care to protect them against the danger.[118]

In *Mullins v. Pine Manor College,*[119] the victim was a first-year student at a women-only college and lived in the college dormitory. An intruder entered her locked room and forcibly took her to the college refectory and raped her. This

---

(1975); *Rubtchinsky v. State University of New York*, 46 Misc.2d 679, 260 N.Y.S.2d 256 (1965) (where the court refused to impose liability on the University for failure to supervise a push ball game as there was no duty to supervise students).

114 The court also quoted Restatement (Second) of torts, § 314(A).

115 176 Cal Rptr.809 (Cal. Ct. App.1981).

116 744 P2d. 54, 61 (Colo. 1987).

117 D K Srivastava, Aashish Srivastava, and Neerav Srivastava (2018) '"A Hazy Shade of Liability": Duty of Care of Universities to Prevent Hazing', 25(1) *Torts Law Journal* 25, p. 32.

118 Restatement (Second) of Torts § 343 (AM. L. INST. 1965). Similar analysis is found in Restatement (Third) of Torts § 40 (AM. L. INST. 2012) for non-university landlord.

119 389 Mass. 47, 449 N.E.2d 331, p. 335.

happened because there were insufficient numbers of security guards, and fencing and locks were inadequate. The court held the college liable. It predicated the college's liability on the principle that the university is a business-landlord and its students business-invitees.[120]

Assumption of Responsibility

In *Furek v. the University of Delaware*,[121] the plaintiff, Furek, attended the University of Delaware on a full football scholarship, including tuition, room and board. He joined the local Chapter of the Sig Ep fraternity (the local fraternity) at the University of Delaware. The university had leased land to the local fraternity on which it constructed its house. Members of the local fraternity were permitted to occupy the house during their stay. Furek participated in the hazing rituals known as 'Hell Night' with other students seeking membership to the fraternity. As part of the hazing ritual, pledges were paddled, forced to do callisthenics and ordered to eat food out of a toilet bowl. A fellow student, Donchez, poured oven cleaner over Furek's face and neck, which burnt and permanently scarred him. The university had clear policies against hazing and had issued strongly worded letters to students in 1977, 1979 and 1980, respectively, after hazing incidents. However, the university did not tell campus security about the hazing policies, and it did nothing to stop it.[122] Furek sought damages against the local fraternity, its national affiliate, the university and Donchez. During the trial, the court dismissed the complaint against the local fraternity on jurisdictional grounds, and no liability was found against the national fraternity. After trial, a jury awarded damages for $30,000, 93% to be paid by the

[120] A business-invitee is a person who is on the land of another for a purpose directly or indirectly connected with the business of the land owner. *See* Restatement (Second) of Torts (1977), § 332. The Restatement (Second) of Torts imposes liability on both a private landowner as well as a commercial landowner under certain circumstances for injury caused to any person on its land (§§ 343–44). See also R Brian Crow and Scott R Rosner (2002) 'Institutional and Organizational Liability for Hazing in Intercollegiate and Professional Team Sports', 76 St John's Law Review 87. *Stockwell v. Board of Trustees,* 64 Cal App 2d 197, 148 P 2d 405 (Cal Ct App, 1944). dormitory); *Nero v. Kansas State University,* 861 P 2d 768 (Kan, 1993) (male student, who had pending rape case against him, allotted accommodation in co-educational hall); *Peterson v. San Francisco Community College District,* 685 P 2d 1193 (Cal, 1984) (previous attacks had taken place in part of campus that had untrimmed foliage and hardly any light but no warning of danger; cf. *Rigdon v. Kappa Alpha Fraternity,* 256 Ga App 499, 568 SE 2d 790 (Ga App, 2002); *Modbury* (2000) 205 CLR 254). *Miller v. New York,* 62 NY 2d 506 (NY, 1984) (reports of rape, criminal trespass, robbery and burglary in dormitories by non-students but dormitory doors never closed; foreseeable that intruders could enter for criminal activities) and similar approach in *Cutler v. Board of Regents,* 459 So 2d 413 (Fla Ct App, 1984) (university told students' dormitory safe; fresher raped in her own room by three armed assailants); Douglas R Pearson and Joseph Beckham (2005) 'Negligent Liability Issues Involving Colleges and Students: Balancing the Risks and Benefits of Expanded Programs and Heightened Supervision', 42(4) *NASPA Journal* 460, p. 461, 464 and 466.

[121] 594 A.2d 506 (Del. 1991).

[122] See J Vivenzio, 'Kappa Delta Rho Whistleblower's case 'Sharply Narrowed'', *Centre Daily Times* (online 13 December, 2016) http://www.centredaily.com/news/local/education/penn-state/article120609988.html, where hazing claims against the university in negligence for its failure to enforce its established anti hazing policies and procedures were not taken up but the matter is against the fraternity is pending before the court.

university and 7% by Donchez. In a post-trial ruling, the Superior Court dismissed the claim against the university, leaving Donchez liable for the entire judgment. On appeal from this judgment, the broad question before the Supreme Court of Delaware was whether the university was under a duty to students to make and enforce policies that might protect them from harm occasioned by third parties who functioned under the auspices of the university. The court said that while the university's duty is a limited one, it cannot be said that none existed. It held that tort law provided:

> a sufficient basis for the imposition of a duty on the University to use reasonable care to protect resident students against acts of third parties. While…there is no duty on the part of a college or university to control its students based merely on the university-student relationship, where there is direct university involvement in, and knowledge of, certain dangerous practices of its students, the university cannot abandon its residual duty of control.[123]

The importance of *Furek* lies in the fact that it clearly states that liability can be imposed on a university for injuries caused to a student due to hazing.[124] The court said that section 323 of the Restatement (Second) of Torts offers a persuasive rationale to impose liability on the university for hazing. It stated that "The duty is owed by one who assumed direct responsibility for the safety of another through the rendering of services in the area of protection".[125]

In *Morrison v. Kappa Alpha Psi Fraternity*,[126] the Appellate Court of Louisiana stated that "universities which allow and regulate fraternal organizations have a duty toward their students to act within reasonable bounds to protect against illegal and proscribed hazing".[127]

McClure v. Fairfield University,[128] illustrates how assumption of responsibility by the university play out in other situations. There the university had an anti-alcohol policy that applied to all underage students. The university knew that the underage students go to a nearby beach area for drinking. The university was concerned with their safety and introduced a "Safe-Rides" program run by volunteer students between the campus and the beach area. One night, after drinking a student was walking back to the campus as he could not find a safe-rides program van. He was hit by a car and suffered injuries. Basing its decision on the *Restatement of Torts*,[129]

---

[123] *Furek v. University of Delaware* 594 A.2d 506 (Del.1991) (Supreme Court of Delaware), p. 520.

[124] Views similar to *Furek* court were expressed 25 years ago in *Chappel v. Franklin Pierce School* 71 Wn.2d 17 (1967). However, that case concerned a high school student. In *Chappel* the High School authorities were sued for hazing of a 16-year-old student. An off-campus initiation stunt was organised by students with knowledge and help of a School advisor. The initiation stunt resulted in injury to students. The court said that a connection existed between the School and off-campus hazing rituals, if the School had some control over the event and held the School liable.

[125] The *Furek* court agreed with Prosser's statement that "if one takes charge and control of [a] situation, he is regarded as entering into a relation which is attenuated with responsibility". See William Prosser and Page Keeton, *Prosser and Keeton on the Law of Torts* (St. Paul, Minn, 5th ed. 1984).

[126] 738 So. 2d 1105 (La. Ct. App. 1999).

[127] 738 So. 2d 1105 (La. Ct. App. 1999), p. 1115.

[128] 2003 Ct. Sup. 8050 (Conn. Super. Ct. 2003); 35 CLR 69.

[129] § 323.

Connecticut Superior Court said that the university, by offering shuttle services, had assumed responsibility for the plaintiff's safety while travelling between the beach area and the campus and held the university liable.

In *Peterson v San Francisco Community College District*,[130] a student was raped in the college near a parking lot which had untrimmed foliage and trees. Despite such attacks in the past at the same place the college had failed to warn students of the danger.[131] The court held the institution liable.

Where the university, by its own conduct, assumes the duty to protect students from the criminal conduct of others but fails to do so, the odds are against the university. In *Cutler v Board of Regents*,[132] the university authorities had told students that the dormitory was safe and no safety measures were required to be taken. Despite such assurance, a fresher was raped in her room by three armed assailants. The court held the university liable.[133]

In the event of a university appointing its own employees to supervise fraternity events, there is no doubt that the university has assumed responsibility for the failure of its employees to carefully supervise its students.[134] Negligence or failure by them would expose the university to liability. A striking example of university employees' negligence is furnished by *Coghlan v. Beta Theta Pi Fraternity.*[135] There an underage student at Idaho university was served alcohol at two fraternity parties while under supervision of university employees. The student became highly intoxicated and later fell down from the third floor of the building sustaining permanent injuries. The Idaho Supreme Court stated that since the university had "assumed a duty to exercise reasonable care to safeguard the underage plaintiff from the criminal acts of third persons, i.e., furnishing alcohol to underage students [at two fraternity events], of which the University employees had knowledge [was negligent and wrong]"[136] for which the university must be liable.

The university is not vicariously liable where it has transferred possession and control of a house to a fraternity. This has been confirmed by *Yost v Wabash*

---

[130] 36 Cal.3d 799 (Cal. 1984); 685 P.2d 1193.

[131] Cf. *Rigdon v. Kappa Alpha Fraternity* 256 Ga.App.499(Ga. Ct. App. 2002); *Modbury Triangle Shopping Centre Pty Ltd v. Anzil* (2000) 205 CLR 254.

[132] 459 So. 2d 413 (Fla. Dist. Ct. App. 1984).

[133] A similar approach by the court is evident in *Miller v. State of New York* 62 N.Y.2d 506 (N.Y. 1984). The plaintiff was blindfolded and raped twice at knife point in the laundry room of her dormitory. There were reports of rape, criminal trespass, robbery and burglary in the dormitories by non-students but the dormitory doors to all entrances were never closed. The court held that it was foreseeable that intruders could enter the dormitory for criminal activities, and that as a landlord, the University breached its duty.

[134] "[I]t is possible to create a duty where one previously did not exist. If one voluntarily undertakes to perform an act, having no prior duty to do so, the duty arises to perform the act in a nonnegligent manner". *Featherston v. Allstate Ins. Co.*, 125 Idaho 840, 843, 875 P.2d 937, 940 (1994) (citing *Bowling v. Jack B. Parson Cos.*, 117 Idaho 1030, 1032, 793 P.2d 703, 705 (1990)).

[135] 987 P.2d 300 (Idaho 1999).

[136] 987 P.2d 300 (Idaho 1999), p. 304.

College.[137] The plaintiff, Yost was a freshman and a pledge at the Phi Kappa Psi Fraternity (Indiana Gamma Chapter), located at Wabash College. As part of a hazing ritual, fraternity brothers held Yost forcibly under a shower. He lost consciousness when they dropped him. The fall caused him a head injury. The Supreme Court of Indiana held that Wabash College owed no duty to Yost as it had given the local fraternity complete control and possession of the leased property. For the same reason, the Supreme Court also said that even the national fraternity could not be held liable.

Special Relationship

One of the most recent cases, *Regents of the University of California v Superior Court of Los Angeles County*,[138] took an expansive view of when a university would be liable to its students for negligence. It talks about the special relationship between a university and its students. In *Regents*, a student at the University of California suffered from auditory hallucinations. He stabbed a fellow student. He was also involved in several other violent activities. Considering the unique features of the collegiate environment, the court held that "universities have a special relationship with their students and a duty to protect them from foreseeable violence during curricular activities".[139] Special relationships have an aspect of dependency: students depend on the university for their protection. Also, duty is owed to a limited class of students who are vulnerable. The *Regents* court said:

> Students are comparatively vulnerable and dependent on their colleges for a safe environment... Colleges do not have a special relationship with the world at large but only with their enrolled students. The population is limited as is relationship duration... Colleges generally have little say in how students behave off campus or in their social activities unrelated to school... Colleges are in a special relationship with their enrolled students only in the context of school-sponsored activities over which the college has some measure of control.[140]

The *Regents* court examined seven factors to determine the existence of a special relationship between the university and its students. These are as follows:

(1) the foreseeability of harm to the plaintiff,
(2) the degree of certainty that the plaintiff suffered injury,
(3) the closeness of the connection between the defendant's conduct and the plaintiff's injury,
(4) the moral blame attached to the defendant's conduct,
(5) the policy of preventing future harm,
(6) the extent of the burden on the defendant and consequences to the community of imposing a duty to exercise care with resulting liability for breach, and
(7) the availability, cost, and prevalence of insurance for the risk involved.[141]

---

[137] 3 N.E.3d 509 (Ind. 2014); see also *University of Denver v. Whitlock* 744 P.2d 54 (Colo. 1987).

[138] 4 Cal.5th 607, 230 Cal. Rptr. 3d 415, 413 P.3d 656 (Cal. 2018).

[139] 4 Cal.5th 607, 230 Cal. Rptr. 3d 415, 413 P.3d 656 (Cal. 2018), p. 660.

[140] *Regents of the Univ. of Cal. v. Superior Court of L.A. Cnty.*, 4 Cal.5th 607, 230 Cal. Rptr. 3d 415, 413 P.3d 656 (Cal. 2018), p. 625.

[141] *Regents of the Univ. of Cal. v. Superior Court of L.A. Cnty.*, 4 Cal.5th 607, 230 Cal. Rptr. 3d 415, 413 P.3d 656 (Cal. 2018), p. 626 citing *Rowland v. Christian*, 69 Cal.2d 108, 70 Cal. Rptr. 97, 443 P.2d 561 (Cal. 1968), p. 113.

We analyse three (foreseeability, policy considerations, and moral blame) of the seven factors as these are the most important factors and have been applied in a number of cases including *Mullins* and *Furek*.

- *Foreseeability*

The existence of a special relationship is determined by the foreseeability of harm to the plaintiff. Where a reasonable person in the position of the defendant foresees that the defendant's conduct would cause harm to the plaintiff, the defendant would be liable. The Restatement (third) of Torts[142] does not consider that foreseeability is vital in determining whether a duty exists. However, foreseeability often determines whether the defendant acted reasonably under the circumstances or caused injury to the plaintiff. A student's injury would be foreseeable if the university or a fraternity or sorority knows or ought to know the risk of such injury.[143] McGlone and Schaefer said that the university could foresee and recognise the possible risks associated with hazing more than the general student body.[144] *Chappel v. Franklin Pierce School*[145] emphasised that physical injuries were foreseeable when unsupervised initiation ceremonies involved physical ordeals on the part of the freshers.

Another important hazing case in this context is *Knoll v Board of Regents of the University of Nebraska*.[146] There, as part of 'the pledge sneak event', a fresher was abducted and taken outside the campus to a fraternity house. He was forced to consume vast quantities of alcohol and handcuffed on the third floor to a toilet pipe. The fresher attempted to escape but he fell and suffered severe injuries. The court found the university liable as fraternity houses were considered university housing. The university was aware of prior hazing incidents and could have reasonably foreseen "the pledge sneak event", including extreme intoxication and abductions,[147] even though the fraternity failed to disclose them.

Kleinknecht v. Gettysburg College[148] (not a hazing case) analyses when a students' injury would be foreseeable. A healthy student with no history of any heart problems while playing lacrosse at the college campus suffered cardiac arrest and died. The Court of Appeal held the college liable for its failure to provide adequate medical facility to the deceased. The court was of the view that the college should have

---

[142] Restatements (third) of Torts, § 7 (2010).

[143] *See also Brueckner v. Norwich* [1999] No. &30 A.2d 1086, where an institution was held liable for negligent supervision of student that resulted in injury to another student. See also *Fu. v. State* 643 N.W.2d 659 (2002).

[144] George R Schaefer (2016) 'After The Haze: Legal Aspects of Hazing', 6(1) *Entertainment and Sports Law Journal*. See also *Kleinknecht v. Gettysburg College* (1993) 989 F 2d 1360 (3d Cir.), discussed in James F Shea (1995) 'Duty of Care Owed to University Athletes in Light of Kleinknecht', 21(3) *Journal of College and University Law* 591.

[145] 71 Wn.2d 17 (1967).

[146] 258 Neb. 1, 601 N.W.2d 757 (1999).

[147] *Knoll v. Board of Regents of the University of Nebraska* 258 Neb. 1, 601 N.W.2d 757 (1999).

[148] 786 F. Supp. 449 (M.D. Pa. 1992).

foreseen such emergencies and reasonably prepared for handling them.[149] Likewise it is common knowledge that some students unable to bear hazing ordeals commit suicide. That being the fact university must take steps to protect the freshers from going in that direction.[150]

Policy Considerations

The courts often refer to legal policy and public policy.[151] Over the years, liability in negligence has been denied on the grounds of legal policy, such as a decision in favour of the plaintiff would open the floodgates of claim, lead to indeterminate liability to an indeterminate class and have a ripple effect on a chain of parties.[152] Here policy considerations refer to public policy.

Under public policy, courts look at social, economic and financial factors to determine whether any liability should be imposed. Many factors interplay: the ideas of morality and justice; where the loss should fall; the mores of the community; and whether the wrongdoer is insured against the liability. How wide the sphere of the duty of care in hazing cases would be depend on the demands of society for the protection of university students. Policy considerations are not static: they change with new developments and with the change in people's attitudes. Pre-*Mullins* and *Furek* judicial decisions (during the bystander era) adopted very different policy considerations regarding the universities' liability to their students. In *Bradshaw v. Rawlings,*[153] the court regarded students as adults in almost every phase of community life. It said that "the modern American college is not an insurer of the safety of its students"[154] and that students were legally responsible adults who could care for themselves.[155]

Now the emphasis is on increasing the university's accountability. Pearson and Beckham state that the "Furek decision reflected changing societal attitudes towards hazing and suggest that institutions are not free from all obligations to protect their students. Viewed from the perspective of public policy the court found the likelihood of injury during hazing activities occurring on university campuses greater than the

---

[149] See also *Blake v. Fried*, 173 Pa. Super. 27, 95 A.2d 360 (Pa. Super. Ct. 1953); *Nova Southeastern University, Inc. v. Gross*, 758 So. 2d 86 (Fla. 2000); *Harrington v. Louisiana State Board of Elementary & Secondary Education*, 714 So. 2d 845 (La. Ct. App. 1998).

[150] See *Schieszler v. Ferrum College* 236 F. Supp. 2d 602 (W.D. Va. 2002).

[151] Tettenborn (n 77) p. 428.

[152] *Ultramares Corp. v. Touche* 255 N.Y. 170, 174 N.E. 441 (1931); *Spartan Steel & Alloys Ltd v. Martin & Co (Contractors) Ltd* [1973] 1 QB 27.

[153] *Bradshaw v. Rawlings*, 612 F.2d 135 (3d Cir.1979). For the criticism of this case, see Robert D. Bickel & Peter F. Lake (1994) 'Reconceptualizing the University's Duty to Provide a Safe Learning Environment: A Criticism of the Doctrine of in Loco Parentis and the Restatement (Second) of Torts', 20 *Journal of College and University Law* 261, p. 273–76.

[154] *Bradshaw v. Rawlings*, 612 F.2d 135 (3d Cir.1979), 138.

[155] See also *Beach v. University of Utah* 726 P.2d 413 (Utah 1986); *Baldwin v. Zoradi 13 Cal App. 3d 275, 176 Cal Rptr.809 (Cal. Ct. App.1981); Denver v. Whitlock,* 744 P.2d 54 (Colo. 1987).

utility of university inaction".[156] According to *Mullins,*[157] parents, students, and the community expect universities to take reasonable care to protect their students from foreseeable harm on their campuses. Universities are in a far better position to provide campus security than students. Moreover, the universities do not provide their services to students gratuitously: they charge students tuition fees.

Peters, referring to the U.S. higher educational system, argues that the expansion of university services, high tuition fees, and decreased students' autonomy have increased the need for institutional accountability.[158]

The decision also reflects a more modern view of universities.

Whether Moral Blame Attaches to the Universities' Conduct

It is clear that there is a) a special relationship between a university and its students;[159] b) f reshers are very much vulnerable; and c) the university is in the best position to protect them.It is, therefore, just, fair and reasonable to impose liability on universities to protect students from hazing. Statutes have been passed in 44 out of 50 states to prevent and punish hazing. Such statutes direct universities to adopt robust anti-hazing policies and penalize those found guilty of hazing.[160] Universities are in the best position to prevent hazing. In *Mullins,*[161] noted before, the court held the college liable for the rape of a resident student. The liability of the college was based on the fact that rape happened due to the failure of the college to provide adequate security. By the same token, it would be fair, just and reasonable to impose a duty on the university to protect freshers from cruelty and violence on its campus.

2.4.2 Breach of Duty

Once the plaintiff has proved that a duty exists, the next step for the court is to decide if the defendant breached that duty.[162] While the existence of a duty is a legal question, the breach of that duty is a question of fact. The court examines if the defendant took reasonable care.[163] Whether the defendant took reasonable care is based on the defendant's actual or constructive knowledge.[164] The court will accord

---

156 See Pearson & Beckham, (n 120), p. 466.

157 *Mullins v. Pine Manor College* 389 Mass. 47, 449 N.E.2d 331 (1983) (Supreme Judicial Court of Massachusetts).

158 Kristen Peters (2007) 'Protecting the Millennial College Student', 16(2) *Southern California Review of Law and Social Justice* 431.

159 *Regents of the University of California v. Superior Court of Los Angeles County* 29 Cal.App.5th 890 (Cal. Ct. App. 2018).

160 As discussed in Sect. 2.2 (Anti-Hazing Legislation in the U.S.).

161 389 Mass. 47, 449 N.E.2d 331 (1983).

162 *Meany v. Meany*, 94-0251 (La. 07/05/94), 639 So.2d 229.

163 See *Dobson v. Louisiana Power Light Co.*, 567 So. 2d 569 (La. 1990).

164 *Meany v. Meany*, 94-0251 (La. 07/05/94), 639 So.2d 229; *Regents of the Univ. of Cal. v. Superior Court*, 29 Cal.App.5th 890, 240 Cal. Rptr. 3d 675 (Cal. Ct. App. 2018).

great deference to the facts of the case and the inference drawn from those facts.[165] If, after that, the court finds that the defendant failed to take reasonable care, the defendant would be considered to have breached the duty of care.[166]

In *Morrison v. Kappa Alpha Psi Fraternity*,[167] Morrison brought a suit for hazing related injuries caused by the Kappa Alpha Psi chapter at Louisiana Tech University. The question before the court was whether the university and the national fraternity had a duty of care to Morrison, which they had breached. The court said both the university and the national fraternity had actual knowledge of hazing at the Kappa Alpha Psi chapter, but their response was inadequate. They failed to exercise reasonable care that other universities and national fraternities would have done in their position. Thus, both the university and the national fraternity had breached their duty of care.[168]

In *Estate of Chad Meredith v. Travis Montgomery and David May*,[169] a student was subjected to a hazing ritual that included drinking copious amounts of alcohol and swimming across a frozen lake. He drowned and died. The court found that a 'special relationship' existed between the fraternity and the deceased and that the fraternity failed in its duty to safeguard the deceased from harm. The fraternity compensated the parents of the deceased and paid $12.6 million.

In *Ballou v. Sigma Nu General Fraternity*,[170] during the Fraternity's Hell Night event, Ballou and other pledges of the fraternity were encouraged to drink large amounts of alcohol. Ballou passed out after excessive drinking. Fraternity members tried to wake him up, but when he didn't, they left him on the couch. Ballou was found dead the next morning. The South Carolina Court of Appeals found that the local chapter of the fraternity had breached its duty of care to prevent the pledges from physical harm. It endorsed the statement made in *Ibach v. Jackson* that:[171]

> [T]he administration of alcohol by one person to another "in such quantities as to cause death, is a breach of duty and a tortious act…".[172]

A distinction was made in *Fraternity v. Tootle*,[173] where the plaintiff, Fair, became intoxicated by drinking his own beer that he brought at a party organised by the

---

[165] *Boykin v. Louisiana Transit Company, Inc.*, 96-1932 (La. 03/04/98), 707 So.2d 1225.

[166] *Regents of the Univ. of Cal. v. Superior Court*, 29 Cal.App.5th 890, 240 Cal. Rptr. 3d 675 (Cal. Ct. App. 2018).

[167] 738 So. 2d 1105 (La. Ct. App. 1999).

[168] See also *Furek v. University of Delaware* 594 A.2d 506 (Del. 1991). Cf. *Walker v. Phi Beta Sigma Fraternity* (RHO Chapter), 96-2345 (La.App. 1st Cir. 12/29/97), 706 So.2d 525.

[169] See More Law verdicts available at http://www.morelaw.com/verdicts/case.asp?s=FL&d=27242.

[170] 291 S.C. 140, 352 S.E.2d 488 (S.C. Ct. App. 1986).

[171] 111, 35 P. (2d) 672, (1934).

[172] 111, 35 P. (2d) 672, 680 (1934), p. 680.

[173] 473 S.E. 2d 213 (1996); In another case *Rothbard v. Colgate University* 235 A.D.2d 675 the court passed the verdict of no liability because the student had voluntarily consumed a large quantity of alcohol and got injured when he fell out of the fraternity house window. See also *Booker v. Lehigh University* 800 F. Supp. 234 (E.D. Pa.1992); *Albano v. Colby College* 822 F. Supp. 840 (D. Me. 1993).

fraternity. While driving back home, he killed another person. The Georgia Court of Appeals held that the fraternity was not liable for his death. However, it went on to say that the position would have been otherwise had the fraternity sold Fair the alcohol, despite knowing that Fair was in a noticeable state of intoxication and that he was going to drive in that state.[174]

2.4.3 Causation

The breach of duty is dependent upon causation. The test to determine causation is the 'but for' test. It must be established that the plaintiff's injury would not have occurred 'but for' the defendant's negligent conduct.[175] To determine the matter the courts apply a reasonable person's test: whether a reasonable person in the position of the defendant would have acted in the same or different way as the defendant. If a reasonable person would have acted in the same way, then the defendant would not be liable. The point is the courts seek to find whether the university's breach of duty, in fact, proximately caused the plaintiff's injury. Proximate causation is established when a court determines that the plaintiff's injury was foreseeable.[176]

In *Regents of the Univ. of Cal. v. Superior Court* (Regents II) the court said:

> where a [student's] erratic behavior demonstrated that he presented a foreseeable threat to his co-students…this evidence is sufficient to support a rational inference that the university should have foreseen [that the student] posed a threat [to other co-students].[177]

In *Furek*, there was no doubt that the test of proximate causation was satisfied. The university knew of the prevailing hazing activities on the campus and publicly condemned such behaviour.[178]

In *Mullins*,[179] *as* discussed before, a girl was taken away from her dormitory and raped. The court examined in detail the cause of the girl's rape, whether it was the negligence of the college or anyone else. After noting that the boundary walls of the college were not high enough to prevent an intruder's access to the dormitory and there were insufficient number of guards to prevent trespassers from entering into the residential area, the court concluded that prima facie the girl's rape was a failure on the part of the college to provide a safe and secure residential place.

---

[174] A similar view was taken y the court in *Alumni Ass'n v. Sullivan*, 524 Pa. 356, 572 A.2d 1209 (1990).

[175] *Fowler v. Roberts*, 556 So.2d 1 (La. 1989); *Stroik v. Ponseti*, 96-2897 (La. 09/09/97), 699 So.2d 1072; *Roberts v. Benoit*, 605 So.2d 1032 (La. 1991).

[176] *Palsgraf v. Long Island R.R. Co.*, 162 N.E. 99, 101 (N.Y. 1928).

[177] *Regents of the Univ. of Cal. v. Superior Court* (Regents II), 29 Cal.App.5th 890, 240 Cal. Rptr. 3d 675 (Cal. Ct. App. 2018).

[178] *Furek v. University of Delaware* 594 A.2d 506 (Del.1991) (Supreme Court of Delaware), p. 521–22; *Knoll v. Board of Regents of University of Nebraska* [1999] 601 N.E. 2d 757.762–65.

[179] *Mullins v. Pine Manor College*, 389 Mass. 47, 449 N.E.2d 331 (1983).

It may be interesting to contrast *Mullins* with *Hall v BD. Of Sup'rs Southern University.*[180] There a university student was shot while she was waiting for an elevator. She sued the university for damages. Her action failed. The Louisiana Court of Appeal said that even the utmost security precautions could not have prevented an attack on the plaintiff.[181]

2.4.4 Injury

Injury to the plaintiff is not by itself sufficient to impose liability on the defendant. As stated before, the injury must be a legal injury, and it must also be established that the defendant's negligence was the cause or one of the legal causes of the plaintiff's injury. The damage must not be too remote. The injury could be physical or emotional, or both.[182] Sometimes a person may suffer only physical injury, and sometimes both physical and emotional injury. The Restatement (Third) of Torts defines physical harm to include "physical injury, illness, disease, impairment of bodily function, and death"[183] and emotional harm as "impairment or injury to a person's emotional tranquillity".[184]

In *Vega v. Sacred Heart Univ., Inc.*[185] a female student was kidnapped and physically abused by members of her sorority. She suffered injuries in various parts of her body. During the investigation, it was found that she also received threatening phone calls and abusive comments on her Facebook page, which caused her anxiety and emotional distress.[186]

2.4.5 Vicarious Liability of the University and Organisations (Fraternities and Sororities) for Hazing

There are certain circumstances in which the law holds a person responsible for another person's fault, whether reckless, negligent or intentional. Such liability is called vicarious liability.[187] The underlying basis of vicarious liability is the same

---

[180] 405 S. 2d 1125 (La. Ct App. 1981).

[181] See also *Pennington v. Church's Fried Chicken Inc.*, 393 So. 2d 360 (La. Ct. App. 1980); *Grant v. Flint-Goodridge Hospital of Dillard University* 359 So. 2d 279 (La. Ct. App. 1978).

[182] *Regents of the Univ. of Cal. v. Superior Court* (Regents II), 29 Cal.App.5th 890, 240 Cal. Rptr. 3d 675 (Cal. Ct. App. 2018).

[183] Restatement (Third) of Torts: PHYS. & EMOT. HARM § 4 (Am. L. Inst. 2010).

[184] Restatement (Third) of Torts: PHYS. & EMOT. HARM § 45 (Am. L. Inst. 2010).

[185] 836 F. Supp. 2d 58, 60 (D. Conn. 2011).

[186] See also Cori Smith (n 106), p. 256.

[187] *Rowell v. Carter Mobile Homes, Inc.*, 500 So.2d 748 (La. 1987); *Henry v. Taco Tio, Inc.*, 606 So.2d 1376 (La.App. 2d Cir. 1992).

as that of an enterprise. Since the enterprise derives benefit due to activities carried on by a person who is an integral part of it, it must also pay for the risk created by such person.[188] "The tenor of recent judicial decisions is to give vicarious liability a broader remit".[189]

Vicarious liability is an instance of strict liability and arises where a particular type of relationship exists, for example, master-servant, principal-agent and employer-employee.[190] As far as hazing is concerned, there is no doubt that in the U.S., universities, fraternities and sororities owe a duty to prevent hazing. Universities have committees to draft anti-hazing policies and implement those policies through university employees. Failure by a university employee to enforce these policies can cause injury to a student. In such circumstances, the university may be vicariously liable. It may be noted that when the courts are examining whether a case is an instance of vicarious liability, they look at the general activities of the employee rather than the specific duties. It was clarified in *Emoakemeh v. Southern University*[191] that:

> the focus is on the general activities at the time of the tort, rather than the specific tortious act, the fact that the act is forbidden or is done in a forbidden manner does not remove it from the scope of employment….[192]

The Ohio Anti-Hazing Act provides that where a university staff knew or ought to have known of the hazing activities and did not take reasonable steps to prevent such activities, the university could be vicariously liable.[193]

The national fraternity of a local chapter is not vicariously liable for the wrongful acts of the hazer of a local chapter[194] unless the national fraternity was aware of hazing activities at its local chapter but failed to take any preventive action. In *Ballou*,[195] the Court of Appeals of South Carolina stated:

> Because it was within [the fraternity's] interest that new members be received, we are satisfied that the local chapter in conducting hell night and in requiring the pledges to participate in hell night as a condition of membership in [the fraternity] acted within the scope of the apparent authority conferred on it by [the fraternity].

---

188 See Neerav Srivastava, Aashish Srivastava & D.K. Srivastava (2019) 'A Million Winslows: Private Liabilities of Universities for Ragging in India', 19(2) *Oxford University Commonwealth Law Journal* 227, p. 251

189 Ibid.

190 *Schroeder v. Board of Supervisors* 540 So. 2d 380 (La. Ct. App. 1989).

191 654, So.2d 474 (LaCt app1995).

192 654, So.2d 474 (LaCt app1995) at 477; *Ermert v. Hartford Insurance Company*, 559 So.2d at 479; *Campbell v. Mouton*, 412 So. 2d 191, 195 (La.App.3d Cir.).

193 Ohio Revised Code § 2307.44. See also *Nova Southern University v. Gross* 758 S.2d 86 (Fla.2000); *Harrington v. Louisiana State Board*, 714 So.2d 845 (La.App.1998).

194 *Morrison v. Kappa Alpha Psi Fraternity*, 738 So. 2d 1105 (La. Ct. App. 1999) p. 1120.

195 291 S.C. 140, 352 S.E.2d 488 (S.C. Ct. App. 1986). See also *Derrick v. Sovereign Camp W.O.W*, 115 S.C. 437, 106 S.E. 222 (S.C. 1921) *Supreme Lodge of W.L.O.M. v. Kenny*, 198 Ala. 332, 73 So. 519 (1916); *Mitchell v. Leech*, 69 S.C. 413, 48 S.E. 290, 66 L.R.A. 723 (1904).

[The fraternity], then, was bound by the acts of its local chapter in this instance since they were performed within the apparent scope of its authority.[196]

2.4.6 *Defences:*[197] *Voluntary Assumption of Risk and Contributory Negligence*[198]

Where a danger in the university premises is known or obvious, but the student does not guard against it, the student could be deemed to have assumed the risk of injury to himself.[199] In other words, it means that the student has voluntarily assumed the risk. Where a fresher voluntarily drinks alcohol with other students at the fraternity house and becomes very sick he may not be able to recover any damages for his sickness from the fraternity, its members or the university. The fresher is the author of their own misfortune.[200] Contributory negligence relates to a situation where the plaintiff's fault directly or significantly contributed to the plaintiff's injury. In such cases, the damages provided to the plaintiff will be proportionally reduced.[201] It is the defendant's obligation to satisfy the court that the plaintiff voluntarily assumed the risk or was contributorily negligent.

Where a student does not have knowledge of the exact risk, the student cannot consent. In such a situation, the defendant cannot rely on the defences of voluntary assumption of risk or contributory negligence. In *Furek,* both the defences (voluntary assumption of risk and contributory) were unsuccessful. There the hazee anticipated that hazing would happen but had no precise knowledge that caustic substance would be poured over his head.[202]

The test of voluntary assumption of risk by the plaintiff is not easy to determine as it is a subjective one.[203]

---

[196] 291 S.C. 140, 352 S.E.2d 488 (S.C. Ct. App. 1986), p. 152.

[197] The authors have already examined the defence of consent to criminal hazing. See section on Consent to criminal hazing discussed earlier in the chapter.

[198] See generally Christensen v. Royal Sch. Dist. No. 160, 124 P.3d 283 (Wash. 2005); *Capitano v. CSX Transp.*, Inc., 698 So.2d 652 (Fla. Dist. Ct. App. 1997); *Merida v. Cardinal*, 749 N.E.2d 605 (Ind. Ct. App. 2001). Kenneth W. Simons, The Puzzling Doctrine of Contributory Negligence, 16 Cardozo L. Rev. 1693, 1705–1709 (1995).

[199] *Turcotte v. Fell*, 510 N.Y.S.2d 49 (App. Div. 1986).

[200] Peter F Lake and Joel C Epstein (2001) 'Modern Liability Rules and Policies Regarding College Student Alcohol Injuries: Reducing High-Risk Alcohol Use through Norms of Shared Responsibility and Environmental Management', 53(4) *Oklahoma Law Review* 611.

[201] *Weller v. College of the Senecas* 635 N.Y.S.2d 990 (App. Div. 1985).

[202] *Furek v. University of Delaware* (n 123) (referring *LEVINE v. LAM*, 226 A.2d 925 (Del. 1967).

[203] *Yankanwich v. Wharton*, Del.Supr., 460 A.2d 1326, 1330 (1983).

In *Ballou*,[204] also discussed above, the court held that the deceased accepted a portion of the risk but cannot be said to have voluntarily accepted the entire risk of extreme intoxication.

> As we view the evidence in the instant case, [Ballou] voluntarily assumed the risk of the dangers imposed by a situation involving verbal and physical hazing and consumption of alcohol to the point of intoxication; however, he did not as a matter of law freely and voluntarily with full knowledge of its nature and extent incur the risk of the dangers created by [the fraternity's] action of promoting extreme intoxication.[205]

In the *Estate of Chad Meredith v Travis Montgomery and David May*,[206] fraternity members forced a pledge to consume excessive alcohol and swim across a frozen lake. This resulted in his death. Fraternity members argued that the pledge's action was voluntary, and that they did not have a duty to protect the deceased. The jury found that the pledge was negligent to the extent of 10%, for his death and the defendants were liable for the remaining 90%.

In King v. University of Indianapolis (S.D.Ind. 2002),[207] not a hazing case, there was a question of the university's negligence towards a student who suffered a heat stroke during his participation in a university football practice game. The university employees treating him were negligent, and the student died. The deceased had signed a form exempting the university from liability for the risk inherent in the game of football. But, this exemption clause, it was held, was not broad enough to cover the negligence of university employees who treated the deceased.

2.5 University Liability to Students in Contract

Modern universities are different from the universities of the past. Until the 1960s, universities were considered to be in the same position as parents *vis-a-vis* students: the *in locus parentis* doctrine applied. When students were sent to universities, the latter assumed a parental role over their students. If any dispute occurred between the university and its students, the question would be whether the university breached its obligations or transgressed its powers and rights? It was only in exceptional cases that a student had an action against their university. Now the courts are veering around the view that university-student relationships are largely contractual. Kerry B. Melear said:

---

[204] *Ballou v. Sigma Nu General Fraternity*, 291 S.C. 140, 352 S.E.2d 488 (S.C. Ct. App. 1986), p. 153. See also *Derrick v. Sovereign Camp W.O.W*, 115 S.C. 437, 106 S.E. 222 (S.C. 1921) *Supreme Lodge of W.L.O.M. v. Kenny*, 198 Ala. 332, 73 So. 519 (1916); *Mitchell v. Leech*, 69 S.C. 413, 48 S.E. 290, 66 L.R.A. 723 (1904).

[205] 291 S.C. 140, 352 S.E.2d 488 (S.C. Ct. App. 1986), p. 151.

[206] The Associated Press, 'UM Fraternity Members Liable in Hazing Death', *Herald-Tribune* (online, 7 February 2004) https://www.heraldtribune.com/story/news/2004/02/07/um-fraternity-members-liable-in-hazing-death/28787263007/.

[207] NA 01-233-C-B/H (S.D. Ind. Oct. 3, 2002). See also *Avila v. Citrus Community College District* 111 Cal.App.4th 811 (Cal. Ct. App. 2003).

> the relationship between institutions of higher learning and their students has shifted from a theoretical perspective of *in loco parentis*, in which the university wielded strict control over the lives of students, to a consumer orientation. This contemporary characterisation of students-as-consumer was precipitated by the application of the lens of contract theory by the judiciary in scrutiny of the foundation of the institution-student relationship.[208]

Liethen clarified that "publications describing policies, procedures, and offerings as evidence of the terms of the general bargain reached by the student and the college".[209] In the U.S., there are standard university-student contracts. Offer, acceptance, and consideration in university-student contracts can be found in a student's application for admission to the university, university catalogues, student handbooks and bulletins and oral statements made by university authorities such as the vice chancellor, pro-vice chancellor and deans. The common examples of university-student relationship are contract to lease university housing, to provide food services and rules and regulations of the university. Where any dispute arises between the university and its students, the university-student contract is the primary basis and source of legal guidance for the resolution of the dispute. Contractual terms could be express or implied. A promise by a student to pay tuition and other fees and by the university to offer courses at an appropriate level are their respective consideration. If a student does not pay their fees, the university may be justified in terminating the student's contract.[210] University "publications describing policies, procedure, and offerings" are construed as evidence of express terms of the general bargain reached by the student and the college.[211] Student handbooks have been considered as binding contracts in many cases.[212] Some university-student contracts contain a disclaimer clause which allows the university to negate its obligations. In *Tobias v. The University of Texas at Arlington*[213] the court ruled that the alleged contract was not legally binding because it included the statement:

> The provisions of this catalog do not constitute a contract, expressly or impliedly, between any applicant, student, or faculty member and The University of Texas at Arlington or The University of Texas system.

---

[208] Kerry B Melear (2003) 'From In Loco Parentis to Consumerism: A Legal Analysis of the Contractual Relationship Between Institution and Student', 40(4) *NASPA Journal* 124, p. 124.

[209] M. A. Liethen, 'Institutional Liabilities' In J. W. Peltason & M. V. Massengale (Eds.), *Students and their Institutions: A Changing Relationship* (American Council of Education, 1978) p. 43–51.

[210] Srivastava et al (n 188), pp. 5, 6.

[211] Liethen (n 209) p. 45–51.

[212] Sara Kupferer, Walter Parrish, and Dennis Gregory (2011), 'Student Handbooks: Are They Legally Binding Contracts?', *Campus Safety & Student Development* p. 11–14. See also *Millien v. Colby College*, 2005 ME 66, 9, 874 A. 2d 397; *Jones v. Howe Military School*, 604 F. Supp. 122; 1984 U.S. Dist. LEXIS 24423 (1984); *Southwell v. University of the Incarnate Word*, 974 S.W.2d 351; 1998 Tex. App. LEXIS 3296 (1998); *Schaer v. Brandeis University*, 432 Mass. 474; 735 N.E.2d 373; 2000 Mass. LEXIS 576 (1996).

[213] 506 U.S. 1049; 113 S. Ct. 966. Cf. *Southwell v. University of the Incarnate Word*, 974 S.W.2d 351; 1998 Tex. App. LEXIS 3296 (1998); *Schaer v. Brandeis University*, 432 Mass. 474; 735 N.E.2d 373; 2000 Mass. LEXIS 576 (1996).

Hazing concerns the safety and security of students. Anti-hazing statutes obligate universities to protect their students by drafting anti-hazing policies. There is a reasonable and equitable obligation on the university to look after its students. Preventing hazing by a university is thus an implied term of university-student contract.[214] Where there is any breach of this contract by the university, it would be liable to the student for any injury or damage suffered by the student.

2.6 Conclusion

Hazing has been in the U.S. for centuries. The object of hazing was noble, to help new students to settle in the new university environment. Over the years, this goal has been completely forgotten. What happens is not a happy situation. The worst side of human being comes out during hazing. Despite 44 out of 50 states in the U.S. passing anti-hazing legislation, loss of life, permanent disability, rape, sodomy, and unthinkable mental and physical torture continue unabated.

Some state statutes (Massachusetts, Ohio and Pennsylvania) mandate that universities create an anti-hazing policy that provides punishments for students, staff and organisations (fraternities and sororities) for breaking this policy. Fraternities and sororities can be suspended or expelled for encouraging hazing. States such as Ohio and Pennsylvania require universities to have a publicly available record (last five years) of incidents involving violations of their anti-hazing policy or the anti-hazing statute. Consent is not a defence to hazing in most state statutes (except Alabama). A couple of states[215] provide immunity to a student from liability if they report the hazing incident to the concerned authorities or seek urgent medical attention to prevent death or serious bodily injuries to another student. In Massachusetts, the Anti-Hazing statute imposes a fine on a witness of a hazing incident who fails to report it.[216]

One-major lacuna with state statutes is that they lack uniformity. An activity or behaviour by a university student may be hazing in one state but not in another.[217] The quantum of punishment also differs from one state to another state. As hazing is prevalent across all the U.S. states, it is high time that federal legislation is drafted

---

[214] See Qi Li (n 65).

[215] Pennsylvania and Texas.

[216] However, the law provides that such punishment will only be imposed if the witness could have done so without endangering themselves or others. MASS. GEN. LAWS ANN. ch. 269, § 18.

[217] See Sussberg (n 2).

to tackle the problem.[218] The benefits of having a federal law are numerous. First, federal legislation on hazing will create greater consistency.

Second, since fraternities and sororities have local chapters in different states, they have to abide by the anti-hazing law of the state in which they are located. A federal legislation would be easy as they would have to follow just the federal law. Also, both a national fraternity/sorority and their local chapters situated across the U.S. would be required to follow one and the same law.

Third, federal legislation would also clarify to students what activities constitute hazing, especially those studying at a university not located in their home state. Currently, "students have a narrow definition of hazing, including only extreme forms like being tied up, beaten or raped".[219]

Finally, federal legislation can mandate all universities to have an anti-hazing policy, which will be consistent across all the U.S. universities.

While the statute provides for punishment, a victim of hazing can also bring an action in tort for damages. In fact, almost half of all court cases on hazing are about tort liability and negligence.[220] We have analysed several cases where a plaintiff suffering physical or mental injury has brought an action in intentional torts (assault, battery, false imprisonment and defamation) as well as in the tort of negligence against a university, fraternity and sorority. In negligence cases, courts have relied on the doctrines of premises liability, assumption of responsibility and special relationship to impose a duty.[221] A university, fraternity or sorority is negligent if it has breached its duty of care towards a student. A pledge who suffers injury from a breach of duty by the university, fraternity or sorority is entitled to damages. U.S. courts also found universities and national fraternities vicariously liable for injury caused to a pledge at a local chapter of the fraternity where the university or fraternity knew of hazing but failed to take any preventive action.

In many cases, before the court decides a to ward damages, the universities have paid large sums of money to settle the matter with the parents of the student who died

---

[218] Note that a bill [REACH (Report and Educate About Campus Hazing) Act] has been introduced on 15 the march 2021 before the Senate. REACH Act purpose seeks to: have an inclusive definition of hazing; amend 485(f)(7) of the Higher Education Act of 1965 to require universities to disclose hazing incidents; and amend Section 485(f)(8)(B)(i) of the Higher Education Act of 1965 requiring universities to have an educational program on hazing that includes information on hazing awareness, hazing prevention, and policies on hazing. See Congress. Gov, S.744 - Report and Educate About Campus Hazing Act at https://www.congress.gov/bill/117th-congress/senate-bill/744/text?r=8&s=5.

[219] Campo, Poulos and Sipple (n 6).

[220] Qi Li (n 65), p. 65.

[221] See, e.g., *Furek v. Univ. of Del.*, 594 A.2d 506, 520 (Del. 1991); *Knoll v. Bd. of Regents of Univ. of Neb.*, 601 N.W.2d 757, 762–65 (Neb. 1999), abrogated by *A.W. v. Lancaster Cnty. Sch. Dist.* 0001, 784 N.W.2d 907 (Neb. 2010); *Vega v. Sacred Heart Univ., Inc.*, 836 F. Supp. 2d 58, 62 (D. Conn. 2011).

due to hazing.[222] Universities, fraternities and sororities should focus on preventing hazing rather than paying compensation to the victim and moving on as if nothing happened. No amount of money can bring the deceased back to his parents.

[222] King (n 61); 'Hazing Victim's Family to Receive Nearly $1M from Virginia School', *NBC News* (online, 19 September 2022) https://www.nbcnews.com/news/us-news/hazing-victims-family-receive-nearly-1m-virginia-school-rcna48318.

Chapter 3
Hazing in India

"Ragging" [Hazing] is a systematised form of Human Rights' abuse as embodied under the Constitution of India as well as other Constitutions of the World.
—The Supreme Court of India (University of Kerala v Council of Principals of Colleges of Kerala AIR 2009 SC 2223 [8])

Hazing (called ragging)[1] is one of the biggest challenges facing the higher education sector in India.[2] It has led to suicide, attempted suicide, murder, rape, sodomy, sexual abuse, assault, physical and mental torture, and humiliation. The hazing situation is so bad that a university in February 2022 hired bouncers to protect its new students (freshers) from hazing.[3] The bouncers escorted the freshers when travelling between classes and their university-provided residences (referred to as hostels).[4]

Senior university students (seniors) in India haze freshers because they derive sadistic pleasure by showing off their power, authority and superiority.[5] They believe that since they were hazed, they have a right to haze too, and it is the only way to make freshers integrate into the institutional environment. Furthermore, many universities are apathetic towards the plight of freshers, and their complaints are often not taken seriously by the authorities. Almost every week, the media reports one or two severe hazing cases that have resulted in death or serious injury.[6] In November 2022, a fresher jumped off the second floor of the hostel to protect himself from

[1] Hereinafter the term hazing has been used instead of ragging for consistency.

[2] Mohan Rao et al. (2015) 'Psychosocial Study of Ragging in Selected Educational Institutions in India', https://www.ugc.ac.in/pdfnews/7661310_Psychosocial-Study-of-Ragging.pdf.

[3] IANS, 'Bouncers to Protect KGMU Medical Students from Ragging', *National Herald* (online, 14 February 2022) https://www.nationalheraldindia.com/national/bouncers-to-protect-kgmu-medical-students-from-ragging.

[4] Known as halls of residence in some countries.

[5] *Vishwa Jagriti Mission through President v. Central Government through Cabinet Secretary & Ors* AIR 2001 SC 2793.

[6] Priyesh Mishra, 'The Disease of Ragging Is Not Stopping in the Country, 4696 Cases Registered in Seven Years', *Amar Ujala* (online, 13 June 2019) https://www.amarujala.com/india-news/ragging-in-educational-institute-4696-cases-registered-in-last-7-years-in-ugc; Tanya Saighal, 'Ragging Complaints Doubled at Universities and Higher Educational Institutions over Last 3 Years: HRD

A. Srivastava et al., *Hazing (Ragging) at Universities: A Legal Perspective*,
https://doi.org/10.1007/978-981-99-5215-1_3

seniors suffering severe injuries to his hands, legs and ribs.[7] However, the prime accused in this case has now been granted bail.[8] Around the same time, at another university, a fresher committed suicide because of hazing.[9] In both cases, the victims had previously complained to the concerned authorities that seniors were harassing them.

The Supreme Court of India in the *University of Kerala v. Council of Principals of Colleges of Kerala*[10] said that

> [Hazing]in essence is a human rights' abuse.... In present times shocking incidents of [hazing] have come to the notice.... The student is physically tortured or psychologically terrorised. All human beings should be free to claim, as a matter of right in the society in which they live, for life of dignity but when it is intentionally or recklessly damaged or departed then the person's human right is abused; in that sense [hazing] is the best example of human rights' abuse.[11]

In the same order, the Supreme Court, for the first time, defined hazing as:

> any disorderly conduct whether by words spoken or written or by an act which has the effect of teasing, treating or handling with rudeness any other student, indulging in rowdy or undisciplined activities which causes or is likely to cause annoyance, hardship or psychological harm or to raise fear or apprehension thereof in a fresher or a junior student or asking the student to do any act or perform something which such student will not do in the ordinary course and which has the effect of causing or generating a sense of shame or embarrassment so as to adversely affect the physique or psyche of a fresher or a junior student.[12]

This chapter begins by giving figures on hazing and by describing gruesome incidents of hazing. It also explains why hazing is still a big menace despite anti-hazing policies and regulations. Many students commit suicide and are subjected to unimaginable atrocities. The next section examines the legal development that occurred in the last 25 years. We then examine the relevant provisions of the University Grants Commission (UGC)[13] Anti-hazing regulations and criminal law, including

---

Data', *India Today* (online, 24 July 2018) https://www.indiatoday.in/education-today/news/story/ragging-complaints-doubled-universities-hei-last-three-years-1294416-2018-07-24.

[7] Saurabh Gupta, '"They Torture Me Entire Night": Assam Ragging Horror, Student Critical', *NDTV News* (online, 28 November 2022) https://www.ndtv.com/india-news/dibrugarh-assam-student-jumps-off-hostels-second-floor-allegedly-to-escape-ragging-critical-5-arrested-3559274#pfrom=home-ndtv_topscroll.

[8] 'Prime Accused of Dibrugarh University Ragging Case Granted Bail', *Pratidin Time* (online, 14 February 2023) https://www.pratidintime.com/latest-assam-news-breaking-news-assam/prime-accused-of-dibrugarh-university-ragging-case-granted-bail.

[9] 'West Bengal: Student Dead, Ragging Complaint against 9 Seniors', *The Times of India* (online, 30 November 2022) https://timesofindia.indiatimes.com/city/kolkata/west-bengal-student-dead-ragging-complaint-against-9-seniors/articleshow/95868715.cms.

[10] Civil appeal no. 887 OF 2009.

[11] *University of Kerala v. Council of Principals of Colleges of Kerala* AIR 2009 SC 2223 (Kerala) para 12.

[12] Ibid, para 24.

[13] University Grants Commission (UGC) was formed in 1945 to oversee the work of the three Central Universities of Aligarh, Banaras and Delhi. After Indian Independence, it was entrusted

state anti-hazing statutes and the Indian Penal Code (IPC). The following section looks into judicial decisions related to hazing. The remaining parts deal with tortuous liability, including intentional tort, negligence and vicarious liability. The last section is conclusion.

3.1 Sociological Background

Prof. Rao and his colleagues dwelling upon the psychosocial issues responsible for hazing said:

> Corporal punishment by parents and teachers, the use of violent means to maintain law and order by police, to chastise wives by spouses, to redress 'honour' in honour crimes, to punish 'offending' groups in cases of caste and religious violence, to reform those who offend the 'moral police' are commonplace. Indeed violent action is valorised if the justifications are 'moral' enough. It is not surprising then for physical violence to be a part of [hazing], especially when it is 'to teach a lesson' to the junior or for the junior's 'own good'.[14]

Various kinds of discrimination have existed in India for centuries based on caste,[15] religion, region, sex, age, and the like.[16] Despite the constitutional provisions granting every person equality before the law and equal protection of the law,[17] acceptance of the social hierarchy is still a norm and has wide social acceptance and repercussions. Calling senior students or seniors as 'sir' or 'ma'am' by freshers is part of that ingrained social hierarchy. Hazing is rampant in Indian universities, primarily because of the social hierarchy, which is the product of India's past and centuries of caste system and religious discrimination. Further, educational institutions show ambivalence towards hazing, and there is silent support of teachers, parents, and university management like the Vice-Chancellor, Deans, Professors and senior academics. In one incident, Dalit[18] students were not allowed to participate in the Republic Day flag hoisting ceremony. The institution's faculty and management belonging to the higher caste failed to act against the perpetrators, who were also of the higher caste.[19]

---

with the responsibility of reporting current and future needs of education and suggest as well as implement provisions to improve the educational system of all the universities in India. For details, *see* www.ugc.ac.in.

[14] Rao et al. (n 2) p. 26.

[15] Maya Pramod (2016) 'Is Caste the Ideology that Underlies 'Ragging'', *Savari,* https://www.dalitweb.org/?p=3326.

[16] Rao et al. (n 2) p. 21.

[17] See Constitution of India, Art 14.

[18] Historically, Dalits belong to the lowest caste in the hierarchy of castes existing in India. Sometimes hazing also occurs on the basis of discrimination. Such discrimination may be on the ground of race, religion, caste, place of birth, color, nationality, gender, language and so on.

[19] RK Raghavan et al. (2007) 'The Menace of Ragging in Educational Institutions and Measures to Curb It', https://dos.iitd.ac.in/anti-ragging/menace.pdf, (Annexure III) p. 119.

According to the Raghavan Committee Report, discussed in the next section, freshers have been forced to strip and parade naked in front of seniors, watch pornographic movies, imitate sex acts, masturbate in public, participate in oral and group sex, drink excessive alcohol and bathe in their urine.[20] A student hiding under a goods train because of fear of hazing lost his arms and one leg when the train suddenly started moving. There have also been cases of seniors extorting money from the freshers as part of hazing.[21] In some cases, freshers have left the educational institution and returned home.[22] A student who could not bear the month-long atrocities by seniors, which included doing 100 sit-ups,[23] decided to leave the institution. On the other hand, some students undergo extreme psychological treatment because they were subjected to public abuse by senior students for six months. Constant hazing has driven freshers to a state of shock and speechlessness; many require psychiatric treatment.[24] The Supreme Court of India has said that "[t]he act[s] by the seniors is a 'fist of steel against ice', and likewise by doing so, they shatter the ambition, aim and object of freshers".[25]

Proponents of hazing believe that it makes freshers disciplined and respectful towards seniors, helps them create friendships, builds confidence, sheds inhibitions, makes them mentally tough and prepares them to deal with the real-world situations. In addition, it forges long-lasting relationships with seniors who can help them in their studies, future careers and job placements.[26]

On the other hand, opponents of hazing believe that hazing makes it harder for freshers to settle well and negatively affects their self-confidence and studies. It also makes them fear seniors who have abused and assaulted them. For some freshers, it has long-lasting emotional impacts, including shame, anxiety and depression.[27]

According to a study, almost half (46.9%) of the students believe that seniors haze because it is a college tradition. An equal number (46.2%) said that hazing makes seniors feel powerful and in control. Those seniors who haze are considered tough and powerful in their batch. Almost one-third (33.7%) believe that hazing helps seniors overcome their own trauma of hazing as freshers. Studies show that victims of hazing are more likely to haze freshers because of an inbuilt desire to take revenge.[28]

There are reasons why freshers comply with hazing. First, most freshers feel insecure: it is for the first time they are not living with their parents and family. Second, freshers need to be accepted by their new family members (batchmates and seniors), who are critical constituents of this family. Third, freshers fear that not only

[20] Ibid. (Annexure IX).

[21] Ibid. (Annexure IX).

[22] Ibid. (Annexure IX).

[23] Ibid. (Annexure IX).

[24] Ibid. (Annexure IX).

[25] *Kerala* (n 11), para 10.

[26] Rao et al. (n 2) p. 72, p. 77.

[27] Ibid, p. 72, p. 81.

[28] Ibid, p. 89, p. 91.

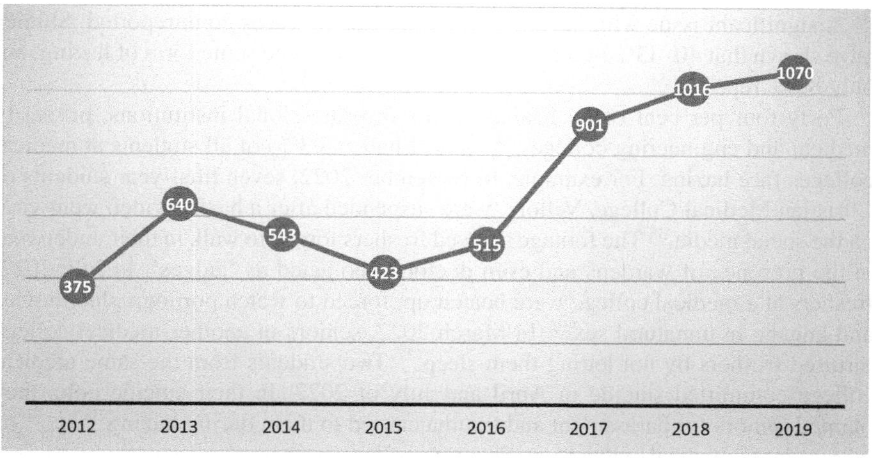

Fig. 3.1 Hazing complaints made by victims to the UGC anti-ragging helpline (2012–2019)[32]

seniors but also their batchmates will ostracise them if they do not undergo hazing. On the other hand, if they put up with hazing, they will get support from others, including seniors.

The UGC has reported that between 2011 and 2019, hazing was responsible for 54 suicides. The National Medical Commission of India (NMCI) is deeply concerned with the number of suicide cases because of hazing in medical colleges. In September 2022, it directed all medical colleges to submit data on suicides and dropouts over the past five years. According to the National Crime Records Bureau (NCRB), 13,123 students committed suicide in 2021.[29] However, there are no data on how many died because of hazing.

The UGC Anti-hazing Helpline received 5843 hazing complaints between 2012 to 2019. As shown below in Fig. 3.1, there has been an upwards trend in hazing complaints over the years.[30] In December 2021, the Union Minister of State (MoS) for education told the Lok Sabha in a written response that since 2018, the Anti-ragging [hazing] Helpline has received 2790 complaints. However, action had been taken in less than half (1296) of the total complaints. In 22% (616) cases, hazers were let off with a warning. In 620 instances, they were suspended, and in 17, they were rusticated.[31]

[29] National Crime Record Bureau (2021) 'Accidental Deaths and Suicides in India 2021', https://ncrb.gov.in/sites/default/files/ADSI-2021/ADSI_2021_FULL_REPORT.pdf.

[30] However, in 2020 and 2021, hazing complaints to the helpline fell to 219 and 533, respectively, as most students attended classes online because of the Covid-19 pandemic and were not physically present on university campus.

[31] Lok Sabha, 'Government of India, Ministry of Education, Department of Higher Education; http://164.100.24.220/loksabhaquestions/annex/177/AU3519.pdf.

[32] Adapted from https://amanmovement.org/registration/public/amanmovement/reportsyr.php.

A significant issue with hazing is that most hazing cases go unreported. Studies have shown that 40–43% of university students experience some form of hazing, but only 8.6% report it.[33]

Forty-four per cent of all hazing occurs in professional institutions, primarily medical and engineering colleges.[34] Almost half (48.3%) of all students at medical colleges face hazing. For example, in November 2022, seven final-year students of Christian Medical College, Vellore, were suspended after a hazing video went viral on the social media.[35] The footage showed freshers forced to walk in their underwear in the presence of wardens and even doctors who acted as 'judges'. In July 2022, freshers at a medical college were beaten up, forced to watch pornographic movies and engage in unnatural sex.[36] In March 2022, seniors in another medical college tortured freshers by not letting them sleep.[37] Two students from the same medical college committed suicide in April and July of 2022. In their suicide note, they blamed seniors for harassment and trauma caused to them during hazing.[38]

Similar to medical colleges, engineering college freshers are also prone to hazing. Two out of five (44.5%) students in engineering courses face hazing.[39] Freshers are required to run errands for seniors and do their assignments. Some of them are blindfolded, slapped and made to do sit-ups.[40] Freshers at engineering colleges who cannot bear hazing have committed or attempted to commit suicide after authorities failed to take any action on their complaints. In October 2022, seven students of an engineering college were suspended and fined Rs 50,000 each for hazing freshers.[41]

---

[33] Rao et al. (n 2) p. 13; Archana Panchal, 'Fresher's Experience, Awareness and Opinion about Ragging on University Campus' (Thesis; Maharaja Sayajirao University, 2013).

[34] Raj Kachroo, 'Progress Report of Monitoring the Ragging Prevention Program (Oct–Dec) 2020' (2021) https://amanmovement.org/registration/public/amanmovement/Reports/progressreport/PROGRESS_REPORT_-__4th_Quarter_2020.pdf; Rao et al. (n 2) p. 3.

[35] Arun Janardhan, 'Ragging Video on Social Media, 7 Students of CMC Vellore Suspended', *The Indian Express* (online, 10 November 2022) https://indianexpress.com/article/cities/chennai/cmc-vellore-suspends-7-final-year-mbbs-students-for-ragging-juniors-8259153/.

[36] Bobbins Abraham, 'Ragging Horror In Indore Medical College, Students Forced To Do Unnatural Sex, Slap Each Other', *IndiaTimes* (online, 27 July 2022) https://www.indiatimes.com/news/india/ragging-in-indore-mgm-medical-college-575799.html.

[37] Anu Kuruvilla, 'Ragging Continues to Ravage Kerala Campuses as Prevention Mechanisms Come under Lens', *The New Indian Express* (online, 21 March 2022) https://www.newindianexpress.com/states/kerala/2022/mar/21/ragging-continues-to-ravage-kerala-campuses-as-prevention-mechanisms-come-under-lens-2432335.html.

[38] Anil Kumar Tiwari, 'Sleep Deprivation, Slapping, Miming Sexual Acts: Inside The Murky World Of Ragging In Indian Colleges', *Article 14* (online, 14 September 2022) https://article-14.com/post/sleep-deprivation-slapping-miming-sexual-acts-inside-the-murky-world-of-ragging-in-indian-colleges-6321389fe534f.

[39] Rao et al. (n 2) p. 44.

[40] Ibid, p. 52.

[41] '7 Engineering Students Suspended for Ragging Juniors at Kanpur University', *India Today* (online, 18 October 2022) https://www.indiatoday.in/india/story/engineering-students-suspended-for-ragging-juniors-at-kanpur-university-2286781-2022-10-18.

Hazing is also prevalent in other professional colleges. In October 2022, a 19-year-old fresher studying Bachelor of Business Administration (BBA) was sodomised by five seniors. First, the seniors forced the fresher to undress and apply sanitiser, honey and powder on his anus. After that, they inserted a pencil and toothbrush into his anus. The torture and humiliation continued for three hours.[42]

Half of all hazing occurs in university hostels or in private accommodations outside the university campuses.[43] These places are breeding grounds for hazing as seniors and freshers stay in the same block. Seniors consider themselves higher in the social hierarchy and expect freshers to undergo initiation rituals. In hostels and private accommodations, there is a lack of regular surveillance by university officials. Seniors believe they are immune from punishment or prosecution.[44]

3.2 Hazing and Legal Development

The issue of hazing in Indian universities was brought in the limelight in 1998 by a non-government organisation (NGO)—the *Vishwa Jagriti Mission*. The NGO filed a public interest litigation (PIL) before the Supreme Court, highlighting the plight of freshers and the failure of measures taken by the government and educational institutions.[45] The NGO sought directions from the Supreme Court on how to curb the menace of hazing.

In 1999, the Supreme Court directed the UGC to adopt a more proactive view and frame appropriate guidelines to combat hazing. The UGC constituted a committee, under the chairmanship of Prof. K. P. S. Unny (hereinafter the Unny Committee), to frame the guidelines in the matter. In 2000, the Unny Committee submitted a detailed report suggesting a three-pronged approach to tackle hazing: prohibition by law, prevention through guidelines and punishment when required.[46]

In 2001, the Supreme Court, in the *Vishwa Jagriti Mission through President v. Central Government through Cabinet Secretary & Ors*,[47] stated that universities

[42] 'Gujarat Shocker, 'Toothbrush, Sanitiser Inserted in College Student's Private Parts in Ragging Case', *Zee News* (online, 22 October 2022) https://zeenews.india.com/india/gujarat-shocker-toothbrush-sanitiser-inserted-in-college-students-private-parts-in-ragging-case-2525531.html.

[43] Rao et al. (n 2) p. 13.

[44] Ibid, p. 48.

[45] *Vishwa Jagriti Mission through President v. Central Government through Cabinet Secretary & Ors* (n 5).

[46] The Unny Committee recommended drafting hazing-specific statutes at the federal and state levels that treat hazing as other serious offences, such as rape and atrocities against lower caste persons, and prescribe suitable punishment (imprisonment and/or fine) for those involved. The Unny Committee also recommended a few guidelines to prevent hazing in universities. These include universities informing prospective students through admission brochures that it prohibits hazing and obtaining a written undertaking from the applicant that they will not indulge in any such activity.

[47] *Vishwa Jagriti Mission through President v. Central Government through Cabinet Secretary & Ors* (n 5).

should initiate the anti-hazing movement from the time of advertisement for admission. The Supreme Court delineated the types of punishment that educational authorities could award to those involved in hazing. These include expulsion or suspension from the institution or classes for a period of time; there is also a provision requiring a student to pay a fine and tender a public apology.[48] The Supreme Court also outlined consequences for institutions that fail to stop hazing:

> Failure to prevent [hazing] shall be construed as an act of negligence in maintaining discipline in the institution on the part of the management, the principal and the persons in authority of the institution. Similar responsibility shall ...be fixed on hostel wardens/superintendents... If an institution fails to curb [hazing], the UGC/Funding Agency may consider stoppage of financial assistance to such an institution ....University may consider disaffiliating a college or institution failing to curb [hazing].[49]

Despite such constructive directions by the Supreme Court, until 2006, there was no decrease in hazing. Therefore, in 2006, the Supreme Court in the *University of Kerala v The Council of Principals of Colleges* appointed another committee, the Raghavan Committee, to investigate the problem of hazing in universities and recommend measures to tackle it.[50]

On 7 May 2007, the Raghavan Committee submitted its report stating that most Indian universities failed to implement the Unny Committee's recommendations (prohibition, prevention and punishment) to tackle hazing.[51] The Raghavan Committee stated that university functionaries considered hazing a non-academic issue and were either indifferent to it or lacked the commitment to prevent it. Failure to implement the Unny Committee recommendations has resulted in adverse consequences. Hazing continues as before and perhaps more. "[P]hysical assaults, wrongful confinement, use of criminal force, threats, intimidation and denial of basic human rights"[52] are common place.

According to the Raghavan Committee Report (RCR), to tackle hazing, nine factors need to be considered, including the following: placing the primary responsibility for curbing [hazing] with academic institutions; providing incentives to institutions for curbing the menace, and disincentives for failure to do so; not immunising university students from the penal provisions of the law; taking a concerted action at the level of the school, higher educational institution, district administration, university, state and central governments to make any anti-hazing measures effective; and involve media and civil society in the anti-hazing exercise.[53]

---

[48] The punishment may also take the shape of (i) withholding scholarships or other benefits (ii) debarring from representation in events (iii) withholding results (iv) suspension or expulsion from hostel or mess, and the like. *Vishwa Jagriti Mission through President*, above n 5, p. 2795.

[49] *Vishwa Jagriti Mission through President* (n 5) p. 2795.

[50] The Committee was chaired by Dr. R.K. Raghavan, former director of the Central Bureau of Investigation.

[51] RK Raghavan et al. (n 19).

[52] Ibid, 4.15.

[53] Ibid, p. 4 [Foreword].

In addition, the RCR made 50 recommendations to contain hazing. The Supreme Court, vide its order dated 16 May 2007, directed that eight of the 50 recommendations must be immediately adopted.[54]

3.3 UGC Anti-hazing Regulations

On 8 May 2009, the Supreme Court directed that the Draft Regulations on Curbing the Menace of Ragging [hereafter the UGC Regulations], formulated by the UGC, should be urgently implemented. The UGC Regulations came into effect on 4 July 2009. It applies to all institutions within the definition of a university as per the UGC Act 1956.[55] Under the UGC Regulations, it is the general and collective responsibility of all staff (temporary or permanent) of a university to prevent hazing and act promptly to any incident of hazing that comes to their notice.[56]

3.3.1 Definition of Hazing

The definition of hazing in the UGC Regulations is the same as that mentioned by the Supreme Court in the *University of Kerala v Council of Principals of Colleges of Kerala,* stated above.[57] In addition, the UGC Regulations give examples of actions that can constitute hazing when committed against a fresher or any other student. These include seniors: (a) teasing, treating or handling with rudeness a fresher or any other student; (b) indulging in rowdy or indisciplined activities causing annoyance, hardship, physical or psychological harm or raising fear or apprehension in a student; (c) asking any student to do any act that causes a sense of shame, torment or embarrassment; (d) preventing, disrupting or disturbing the regular academic activity of a student; (e) exploiting the services of a student for completing academic tasks; (f) extorting money from a student or forcing them to pay on the seniors behalf; (g) participating in sexual abuse, homosexual assaults, stripping, forcing obscene and lewd acts, gestures, causing bodily harm or any other danger to a student; (h) abusing, humiliating or publicly insulting a student by spoken or written words (including in electronic form) to derive perverted pleasure, vicarious or sadistic thrill; and (i) doing

---

[54] *University of Kerala v. Council of Principals of Colleges of Kerala*, order dated May 16, 2007 [Petition(s) for Special Leave to Appeal (Civil) No(s). 24295/2004]. See infra Conclusion, p. 45.

[55] Under sec. 2 (f) of the UGC Act 1956 "University" means a University established or incorporated by or under a Central Act, a Provincial Act or a State Act, and includes any such institution as may, in consultation with the University concerned, be recognised by the Commission in accordance with the regulations made in this behalf under this Act. It also includes institutions deemed to be a university under s. 3 of the University Grants Commission Act, 1956.

[56] Regulations on Curbing the Menace of Ragging in Higher Educational Institutions in 2009, r 6.4 (n) (Regulations).

[57] Above n 12.

any act that affects the mental health and self-confidence of a student with or without an intent to derive a sadistic pleasure or showing off power, authority or superiority over any student.

In June 2016, the UGC Regulations were amended to include physical and mental abuse based on ethnicity, caste, religion, colour, regional background, linguistic identity, nationality and sexual orientation.[58] The amendment became necessary because students from Northeast India and African nations were harassed using derogatory words regarding their regional background.[59]

3.3.2 *Universities must Prohibit and Prevent Hazing*

The UGC Regulations mandate that universities must take steps to prohibit and prevent hazing within and outside the campus.[60] First, all public notifications (in print or electronic form) of the institution must expressly provide that hazing is a serious offence prohibited in their institution. Those guilty of hazing and/or abetting hazing must be punished under the UGC Regulations and applicable penal law.[61] Second, a student (and their parents) seeking admission to a university must file an affidavit that they would not participate in any hazing activities.[62] In spite of such an affidavit, if a student is involved in any hazing activity, the university might expel or debar such student from the institution or take any other strict action.[63] Third, universities must launch a publicity campaign against hazing through posters/leaflets prominently displayed on notice boards of buildings such as academic departments, cafeterias and hostels.[64] The poster must contain details of the anti-hazing helpline so that students can report hazing incidents immediately to the concerned authorities.[65] In addition, to check if there is any hazing, the university must conduct discreet

---

[58] Regulations (n 56), r 3 (j).

[59] Vishwas Kothari, 'New UGC Rules to Bolster Fight against Ragging', *The Times of India* (online, 7 July 2016) https://timesofindia.indiatimes.com/city/pune/new-ugc-rules-to-bolster-fight-against-ragging/articleshow/53088309.cms.

[60] Regulations (n 56), r 5.

[61] Ibid.

[62] A student seeking admission to a hostel forming part of the institution, or seeking to reside In any temporary premises not forming part of the institution, including a private commercially managed lodge or hostel, shall have to submit additional affidavits countersigned by his/her parents/guardians in the form prescribed in Appendixes A and B to these Regulations, respectively along with his/her application. Regulations on Curbing the Menace of Ragging in Higher Educational Institutions in 2009, r 6.1 (g).

[63] Regulations (n 56), r 6. The format of the affidavit both for student and parents has been provided in Appendixes A and B.

[64] Ibid, r 6.1 (i) and (m); r 6.2(a).

[65] Ibid, r 6.1 (i) and (m); the universities must also have a joint sensitization programme and counselling of both freshers and senior students on the ills of hazing, Regulations on Curbing the Menace of Ragging in Higher Educational Institutions in 2009 r 6.2(e).

random surveys among freshers every fortnight during the first three months of the academic year.[66]

3.3.3 Role of the Anti-ragging [hazing] Squad (ARS) and Anti-ragging [hazing] Committee (ARC)

Universities must, according to the UGC Regulations, form an anti-ragging [hazing] squad (ARS) and an anti-ragging [hazing] committee (ARC), and their details provided to students.[67] The ARS is required to be constituted by the head of the institution with such representatives as are necessary for maintaining vigil, oversight and patrolling functions to prevent hazing. The ARC must have a diverse mix of members, including representatives from the civil service, police administration, local media, parents and students.[68] It must oversee any hazing complaints and punish the wrongdoer by imposing a fine or by suspending or rusticating them.

Although the quantum of punishment is within the discretion of the punishing authority, it should not be disproportionate to the offence.[69] Punishment is required to be proportionate to the gravity of the misconduct.[70]

An ARC's decision to suspend a student because another student has filed a police complaint against the former is invalid, as such a complaint does not establish a prima facie case of hazing.[71] However, if the police, after an investigation, criminally charge the student, the ARC will be justified in suspending that student.[72]

The ARC must follow all procedural formalities and should not punish any student accused of hazing without a proper hearing,[73] otherwise, its action would violate the principles of natural justice guaranteed under the Constitution of India.[74] Where an ARC suspends a student pending an inquiry; this action would not violate the principles of natural justice so long as the ARC has provided a show cause notice to the student.[75]

---

[66] Ibid, r 6.4 (l). The institution may design its own methodology of conducting such surveys.

[67] Ibid, r 6.3. The UGC Regulations also require academic institutions to constitute a Mentoring Cell consisting of senior students volunteering to be mentors for freshers [r 6.2(f)].

[68] Ibid, r 6.3 (a)–(c).

[69] *Ranjit Thakur v. Union of India* AIR 1987 SC 2386. WA No 328.

[70] *Divisional Controller, NEKRTC v. H Amaresh* [JT 2006 (6) SC 428], para 10, *Bhagat Ram v. State of Himachal Pradesh* AIR 1983 SC 454.

[71] *Alpha Jose v. State of Kerala* (2006) 3 KLT 886.

[72] *Rahul Pandurangji Khadatkar and Others v. State of Maharashtra and Others* AIR 2002(2) Bom 312; see also Maharashtra Prohibition of Ragging Act 1999, s 6.

[73] *Shakul Prakash Kaushik v. Anti-Ragging Committee* C/SCA/19145 of 2016.

[74] Constitution of India, Art 14 and 21. *See R. Karthik v. The Dean* (2004), *available at* https://indiankanoon.org/doc/858001/; *Nirav Bhulabhai Patel v. State of Gujarat & Ors* C/SCA/1958/2014 (9.2), *available at* https://indiankanoon.org/doc/135749792/.

[75] *Rohit Kumar Singh Mara v. Union of India* Writ Petition No. 19771 of 2014.

Where the ARC fails to provide the accused student with an opportunity to explain or defend himself or proceed in the matter with a predetermined mind,[76] its action would violate the principles of natural justice guaranteed under the Constitution of India.[77] In the *State of Bihar and Ors v Vivek Kumar & Ors*,[78] the ARS, after investigation of a hazing complaint, reported the matter to the ARC, which recommended the College's Officer on Special Duty (OSD) to expel the petitioner from the institution. The Court held that both the recommendation made by the ARC and the order passed by the OSD were untenable: expelling the petitioners on a mere report of the ARS (without giving an opportunity to the petitioner to explain or defend) was against the principles of natural justice.

In *Kolli Madhav Sairam Reddy v Union of India*,[79] the Gujarat High Court held that a student found guilty of hazing must be allowed to present their defence regarding the proposed penalty and its quantum otherwise, "the proposed punishment would, ordinarily, amount to hollow formality or a mere eyewash and would not qualify as inquiry in accordance with the principles of natural justice".[80]

However, the ARC does not violate any principles of natural justice by not allowing the accused student to defend himself, provided: the student has been found guilty of violating discipline and punished on one or more occasions in the past; and the guilty student was allowed to appeal against the ARC's decision, which after due consideration was rejected.[81]

In *Sk Nur v Director College of Engineering and Management and Ors*,[82] the court pointed out that different punishment for different hazers does not amount to discrimination. The principle is that each accused case is decided on its own merits. It could be suspension for some accused and expulsion for others. Expelling one student by the ARC and suspending five others was perfectly in order as the student expelled was involved in various incidents of misconduct in the past, and nothing but expulsion could stop him from committing the grave offence of hazing.

Where hazing occurs outside the university campus, it is difficult for the university authorities to deal with such situations, although the UGC Regulations covers such situations. The head of the institution is required to provide details of such hostels/lodges to local police and authorities. It is the duty of the ARS to ensure vigil in such locations to prevent the occurrence of hazing.[83] In July 2022, four senior dental college students staying in a privately managed hostel were charged with hazing a

[76] *Oryx Fisheries Private Ltd. v. Union of India & Ors* (2010) 13 SCC 427.

[77] Art 14 and 21 Constitution of India. *See R. Karthik v. The Dean* Writ Petition No. 620 of 2004; *Nirav Bhulabhai Patel v. State of Gujarat & Ors* C/SCA/1958/2014.

[78] Civil Writ Jurisdiction Case No. 1378 of 2012.

[79] 2011 (1) GLR 481.

[80] 2011 (1) GLR 481, para 12.3.

[81] *Rajendra Prasad v. The Vice Chancellor Rajasthan Agriculture University & Anr* 2010 SCC Raj 1295 (Rajasthan High Court).

[82] WP No 199 (W) of 2005, Kolkata High Court.

[83] The Head of the institution shall also inform the local police and authorities with details of every privately commercially managed hostels or lodges used for residential purposes by students enrolled in the institution.

fresher residing in the same hostel. Their fault was that they forced the fresher to drink alcohol and urinate in his trousers.[84]

There are some other duties for the universities under the UGC Regulations. These include i) the appointment of a full-time warden residing in each hostel to prevent any incident of hazing;[85] ii) filing of a First Information Report (FIR) with the police within 24 hours of a hazing incident if the head of the institution considers that it involves breaches of one or more penal law provisions;[86] and iii) mentioning in the Migration/Transfer Certificate of a student leaving the institution that he/she was punished for committing or abetting hazing.[87]

3.3.4 *Sanctions Against Recalcitrant Universities*

Those institutions that fail to follow the above steps may not be eligible for any UGC grant or assistance[88] and may be declared as not possessing the minimum academic standard required to function as a university. Whether all institutions follow the UGC Regulations is hard to say, as no data are available at this point.[89]

3.3.5 *All India Council for Technical Education (AICTE) and the National Medical Commission of India (NMCI)*

The All India Council for Technical Education (AICTE)[90] and the National Medical Commission of India (NMCI)[91] have made anti-hazing regulations based on the

---

[84] 'Ragging Case on Four Navi Mumbai Dental Students', *The Times of India* (online, 12 September 2022) https://timesofindia.indiatimes.com/city/navi-mumbai/ragging-case-on-four-navi-mumbai-dental-students/articleshow/94139326.cms.

[85] Regulations (n 56) r 6.4 (c) - the security personnel posted in hostels shall be under the direct control of the warden.

[86] Ibid, r 7. The period of twenty-four hours start from the time hazing has been reported to the Head of Institution or has been recommendation by the ARS that it breaches penal law provisions.

[87] Ibid, r 6.4(m) – There reference to hazing must be separate to those relating to general conduct and behaviour.

[88] Ibid, r 9.4.

[89] However, see, e.g. OP Jindal Global University, 'Student Handbook - Anti-Ragging Regulations' https://jgu.s3.ap-south-1.amazonaws.com/student-hand-book.pdf, p. 162–169.

[90] AICTE, r 8(2). The AICTE Regulations, unlike the UGC and NMCI Regulations, require the university to file an FIR with the police for every hazing incident. Under the UGC and NMCI Regulations, FIR shall be filed only if hazing involves breaches of one or more penal law provisions.

[91] In *Maulesh G Shah v. Ministry of Health and Family* Case No CIC/LS/A/2013/001352-SS 27 [January 2014] a Right to Information (RTI) petition was filed by the appellant regarding failure of the Baroda Medical College to implement the Medical Council of India Anti hazing Regulations See also *Parth Prakashbhai Vala v. Anti-Ragging Committee* C/SCA/19143/2016.

UGC Regulations, which apply to universities imparting education to technical and medical colleges, respectively.[92]

Whether it is the UGC, AICTE or NMCI regulations, the purpose is to empower academic institutions to take administrative action to prevent hazing. If the institutional head or other responsible officers fail to discharge their duty, the regulations make them liable for their failure to act.

3.4 Anti-hazing Legislation

Fourteen (out of 28) states and one union territory (out of eight) have enacted an anti-hazing statute.[93] They are diverse and lack consistency, although the thrust of each piece of legislation is to prohibit hazing and prescribe punishment for hazing, abetment to hazing, and conspiracy to haze. University staff failing to discharge their duty to prevent hazing can be charged criminally under the state anti-hazing statute.

3.4.1 Defining Hazing

The Supreme Court and the UGC, as noted before, have defined hazing. States' anti-hazing statutes likewise also define hazing. Such definitions are similar (but not identical) to that provided by the Supreme Court and the UGC. Section 2(b) of *The Kerala Prohibition of Ragging [Hazing] Act 1998* states that hazing means:

> … display of disorderly conduct, doing of any act which causes or is likely to cause physical or psychological harm or raise apprehension or fear or shame or embarrassment to a student in any educational institution and includes—
>
> (i) teasing, abusing, threatening or playing practical jokes on, or causing hurt to, such student; or
>
> (ii) asking a student to do any act or perform something which such student will not, in the ordinary course, willingly, do.[94]

---

[92] All India Council for Technical Education (Prevention and Prohibition of Ragging in Technical Institutions, Universities including Deemed to be Universities imparting technical education) Regulations 2009; National Medical Commission (Prevention and Prohibition of Ragging in Medical Colleges and Institutions) Regulations, 2021.

[93] The States are: Andhra Pradesh, Assam, Chandigarh, Goa, Himachal Pradesh, Haryana, Jammu and Kashmir (was downgraded from state to a union territory on 5 August 2019), Karnataka, Kerala, Maharashtra, Tamil Nadu, Telangana, Tripura, Uttar Pradesh and West Bengal.

[94] (Kerala Act) (emphasis added). See also; The Uttar Pradesh Prohibition of Ragging in Educational Institutions Act 2010, s 2(d); The Goa Prohibition of Ragging Act 2008, s 2(e); The West Bengal Prohibition of Ragging in Educational Institutions Act 2000, s 2(4) (West Bengal Act); The Maharashtra Prohibition of Ragging Act 1999, s 2(c); The Jammu and Kashmir Prohibition of Ragging Act s 2(f).

The *Assam Prohibition of Hazing Act, 1998* provides a similar definition except that it also includes "causing social harm" in the definition.[95] The *West Bengal Prohibition of Hazing in Educational Institutions Act, 2000*, contains physiological harm in the definition of hazing.[96]

The *Chhattisgarh Anti-Hazing Act 2001* explicitly refers to using criminal force by hazers to physically restrain a fresher during hazing activities.[97] The *Himachal Pradesh Educational Institutions (Prohibition of Hazing) Act, 2009* also mentions 'indecent gestures and obscene behaviour' as hazing.[98] Under the *Andhra Pradesh Prohibition of Hazing Act 1997*, 'hazing' means 'doing an act which causes or is likely to cause insult, annoyance, fear, apprehension, threat or intimidation, injury to a student and outraging the modesty of a student.[99] A student can sue for mental distress caused due to hazing in some states but not others.[100]

Certain activities are hazing under the UGC Regulations but not in the state statutes. For example, "[e]xploiting the services of a fresher or any other student for completing the academic tasks assigned to an individual'[101] and 'any act of financial extortion or forceful expenditure burden put on a fresher"[102] are described as hazing in the UGC Regulations. Studies have shown that seniors exploiting freshers to complete their assignments is one of the most common forms of hazing.[103] A fresher was killed by a senior student for not completing his assignment.[104]

3.4.2 The Extent of Prohibition

Ten states prohibit hazing both within and outside educational institutions,[105] and three states prohibit hazing only within the boundaries of the educational institution.[106] It is hard to imagine that hazing perpetrated in any academic or social activities organised outside its campus will not attract any punishment if the event is organised under the auspicious of the educational institution. In a 2014 incident,

---

[95] Section (2)(c).

[96] This is in addition to physical and psychological harm: s 2(4).

[97] Section 2(a).

[98] Section 2(c)(iv).

[99] Sections 2, 4.

[100] For example, Maharashtra and Assam specifically mention that hazing involves any act that causes or is likely to cause psychological harm.

[101] Regulations (n 56) r.3.

[102] Rao et al. (n 2) p. 54.

[103] Kerala (n 11) [19]; Rao et al. (n 2) 54.

[104] *Inspector General of Police, Tamil Nadu v. John David* (2011)5SCC509.

[105] Andhra Pradesh, Goa, Haryana, Himachal Pradesh, Jammu and Kashmir, Kerala, Maharashtra, Tamil Nadu, Uttar Pradesh and West Bengal.

[106] Assam, Chhattisgarh and Karnataka. Tripura is silent as to whether ragging is forbidden within and/or outside the institution.

24 students were washed away while on an excursion trip from their university and died while taking photographs at a river bank.[107] The accident occurred because the water was suddenly released from the reservoir of a nearby hydropower project. The university authorities were held liable for failing to warn the students of the danger. Likewise, institutional authorities will also be responsible if hazing occurs at a social or educational event organised by them outside the university campus.

3.4.3 Penalty

Most states, in addition to suspension and expulsion of hazers, also provide for imprisonment for a term that may extend up to two years or a fine of up to Rs 10,000 or both. The lengthiest imprisonment any state provides for is up to five years or a fine of Rs 5000 or both.[108] There are provisions in a couple of states for imposing hefty fines of up to Rs 50,000.[109] On the other hand, several states have not made any provision for punishment for hazing, causing death or abetment to suicide.[110] Perhaps, the idea was that the general criminal law of the country would deal with such serious offences. Three states make hazing a non-bailable[111] offence,[112] and one state makes it a cognisable, non-bailable and non-compoundable offence.[113] The State of Assam declares hazing as a cognisable, bailable and compoundable offence. Several states are silent on this issue.

Haryana and Goa are lenient towards hazers and do not provide for any imprisonment or fine.[114] They only provide for disciplinary actions such as withholding results,suspension from the hostel and withdrawal of scholarships. Both these states also provide for expulsion and debarring of the wrongdoer from admission to any other educational institution for three years.

---

[107] *Court on its own motion v. State of Himachal Pradesh* 2017 ACJ1271. See also *Prabir Kumar Das v. State of Odisha and Others* 2013(I) OLR154.

[108] Chhattisgarh.

[109] Andhra Pradesh and Himachal Pradesh.

[110] Andhra Pradesh is an exception. There the punishment prescribed for causing death or abetting suicide by ragging is life imprisonment or up to ten years imprisonment and fine.

[111] A bailable offence is one, in which the arrested person has a right to be released on bail. Non-bailable offences are serious offences where the arrested person cannot be released on bail, but the court may order him to be released on a suitable bail.

[112] Himachal Pradesh, Chhattisgarh, and Tripura.

[113] Chhattisgarh.

[114] Haryana and Goa. Assam is also relatively lenient: it provides for imprisonment which may extend up to six months and fine of up to 10,000 rupees.

3.4.4 University Officials' Duties

Under state statutes, institutional authorities do not commit any offence for failing to prevent hazing proactively.[115] The duties of the head of the institution begin after the commission of hazing. The head of the institution is required to investigate the matter or appoint a committee for investigation.[116] Failure to do so is deemed to be an offence,[117] and the punishment is the same as that of the hazer.[118] If a prima facie criminal offence is found to have been committed by the hazer after investigation, it must be reported to the police.[119] In Himachal Pradesh, failure by the university head or the responsible authority to report hazing to the police is treated as culpable negligence.[120]

While educational institutions must be involved in prosecuting hazing, there is a serious issue of conflict of interest. *M Kavya v The Chairman, University Grants Commission*[121] is on the point. There hazing assumed a political dimension and had wide media coverage.[122] Rather than finding that there had been an incident of hazing, which would have undermined the university's position, the investigating authorities said that there was no hazing but a mere 'quarrel between students.' The High Court was unimpressed and overturned the institution's finding. It held that not only was

---

[115] Only the All India Council for Technical Education (Prevention and Prohibition of Ragging in Technical Institutions, Universities including Deemed to be Universities imparting technical education) Regulations 2009, s7(1) provide that any lapse on the part of the head of the institution and the concerned administrative authority to take adequate ragging prevention measures shall make them liable for criminal negligence. See. The UGC Regulations lists a number of measures to be taken to prevent ragging. However, it does not make failure to take such measures as an offence. See discussion above on UGC Regulations.

[116] Tripura is the only state that is an exception.

[117] Constitution of India, art. 311. See also *R. Karthik v. The Dean, Stanley Medical College and Ors* 2004 WritLR423.

[118] See Kerala Prohibition of Ragging Act 1998, ss 4, 7; The Jammu and Kashmir Prohibition of Ragging Act 2001, s 6; Maharashtra Prohibition of Ragging Act 1999, s 7; Tamil Nadu Prohibition of Ragging Act 1997 s 7; Andhra Pradesh Prohibition of Ragging Act 1997, s 7. Himachal Pradesh provides for a lesser punishment (two years imprisonment and/or fine of Rs. 25,000) compared to the ragger (three years imprisonment and/or fine of Rs. 50,000). See Himachal Pradesh Educational Institutions (Prohibition of Ragging) Act 2009, s 3(2) and s. 5. Anti-ragging laws of Chhattisgarh, Haryana and Tripura are silent on this point.

[119] The Uttar Pradesh Prohibition of Ragging in Educational Institutions Act 2010, s 4(1); The Jammu and Kashmir Prohibition of Ragging Act 2001 s 5, and Kerala Prohibition of Ragging Act 1998, s 6; Himachal Pradesh Educational Institutions (Prohibition of Ragging) Act 2009, s 4(2). The State of Haryana requires police complaints to be made only if the ragging act is a criminal offence. See The Haryana Prohibition of Ragging in Educational Institution Ordinance 2012, s 7(3). See also Regulations (n 56) r. 9.

[120] Himachal Pradesh Educational Institutions (Prohibition of Ragging) Act 2009, 4(3).

[121] [2015] WritLR 141 (The High Court of Madras).

[122] The petitioners were members of the Students Federation of India.

there hazing of the fresher but the fresher was also subjected to 'secondary victimisation'.[123] In another case, a Dalit girl was forced to drink toilet cleaner, resulting in severe internal injuries to her stomach and intestine. The university officials tried to cover up the incident and said that it was a case of attempted suicide.[124] A hazer is often shielded where they have a close relationship with institutional staff holding a high position.[125]

3.4.5 *The Indian Penal Code 1860 (IPC)*

The IPC is the general penal law of the country: it is applicable throughout India. The perpetrators or abettors of hazing can be prosecuted and punished under the state anti-hazing legislation (if there is one),[126] the IPC, or under both. In fact, some states such as Andhra Pradesh, Telangana and Himachal Pradesh have provisions that state that the anti-hazing statute "shall be in addition to and not in derogation of any other law for the time being in force".[127] Thus, an action can also be brought against the hazer under the IPC. However, no person can be punished twice for the same offence.[128]

The provisions of the IPC that may apply to hazing incidents where hazers cause hurt[129] or grievous hurt,[130] cause grievous hurt by dangerous weapons,[131] or hazers are involved in kidnapping,[132] wrongful restraint,[133] wrongful confinement,[134] criminal intimidation (forcing a person to do something that the person is not legally bound

[123] '[S]econdary victimisation refers to the victimisation that occurs not as a direct result of the criminal act, but through the response of institutions and individuals to the victim': *M. Kavya v. the Chairman, University Grants Commission* 2015 WritLR141 [49].

[124] 'Shameless Cover-Up of Ragging? University Says Dalit Girl Tried to Commit Suicide', *Manorama* (online, 29 June 2016) https://english.manoramaonline.com/news/kerala/keralite-dalit-girl-ragging-gulbarga-university-cover-up.html accessed 23 December 2019.

[125] Ramendra Singh, 'AIIMS Brass Shielding Accused, Cry Ragging Victims', *The Times of India* (online, 3 October 2016) www.timesofindia.indiatimes.com/city/bhopal/AIIMS-brass-shielding-accused-cry-ragging-victims/articleshow/54662007.cms accessed 3 December 2019.

[126] Some anti-hazing statutes mention that it shall have effect notwithstanding anything inconsistent with any other enactment. See the Uttar Pradesh Prohibition of Ragging in Educational Institutions Act 2010, s 9; West Bengal Prohibition of Ragging in Educational Institutions Act 2000, s 9.

[127] Andhra Pradesh Prohibition of Ragging Act, 1997, s 8; Himachal Pradesh Educational Institutions (Prohibition of Ragging) Act, 2009, s 10.

[128] Indian Penal Code, s 5 (IPC).

[129] Ibid, s 321.

[130] Ibid, s 322.

[131] Ibid, s 324.

[132] Ibid, s 359.

[133] Ibid, s 339.

[134] Ibid, s 340.

to do), abetment to suicide,[135] sexual harassment,[136] rape (including sodomy),[137] culpable homicide not amounting to murder,[138] and murder.[139]

In *Yelchur Monahar v State of Andhra Pradesh*,[140] a male student, as part of hazing, brutally attacked a female student and hacked her to death. The accused was convicted of murder under section 302 of the IPC and the *Andhra Pradesh Prohibition of Ragging [Hazing] Act, 1997* and was sentenced to life imprisonment.[141]

In the well-known case of Aman Kachroo, four senior students of a medical college in Kangra, Himachal Pradesh, severely beat up and punched a 19-year-old fresher, Aman Kachroo, resulting in his death. The perpetrators were held guilty under sec. 304 (culpable homicide not amounting to murder), sec. 452 (assault), and sec. 342 (wrongful confinement) of the IPC.[142] In November 2022, 10 students were charged under various sections of the IPC and the Telangana Prohibition of Ragging [Hazing] Act.[143] The police also arrested six faculty members of the institution and charged them with negligence to prevent hazing.[144]

3.4.6 Defence of Consent

The Indian criminal law recognises a limited defence to a criminal act. However, section 90 of the IPC states that a consent is not a defence if

> the consent is given by a person under fear of injury, or under a misconception of fact, and if the person doing the act knows, or has reason to believe, that the consent was given in consequence of such fear or misconception; or if the consent is given by a person who, from unsoundness of mind, or intoxication, is unable to understand the nature and consequence of that to which he gives his consent.[145]

---

[135] Ibid, s 306.

[136] Ibid, s 354A.

[137] Ibid, s 375.

[138] Ibid, s 299.

[139] Ibid, s 302. In *Inspector General of Police, Tamil Nadu v. John David,* ss 302, 364, 342 and 201 of the IPC were pleaded.

[140] 2005 (2) ALD Cri 751, 2005 CriLJ 4593.

[141] *See also Puli Dinesh Babu v. The State of Telangana* 2015 (3) ALT (Crl) 366 (A.P); the position is similar in California. A victim of ragging can bring an action under the California Penal Code, s 245.6 as well as under any other provision of law; *see* http://codes.findlaw.com/ca/penal-code/pen-sect-245-6.html.

[142] Ss 304, 452, 34, 342.

[143] Sections 307 (murder attempt), 342 (wrongful confinement), 450 (trespass), 323 (voluntarily causing hurt) and 506 (criminal intimidation), read with section 149 of the IPC and sections 4(I), (II), and (III) of the Prohibition of Ragging Act of 2011.

[144] 'Six Arrested IBS Faculty Members Were Members of Anti-Ragging Squad', *Deccan Chronicle* (online, 17 November 2022) https://www.deccanchronicle.com/nation/crime/171122/six-arrested-ibs-faculty-members-were-members-of-anti-ragging-squad.html.

[145] IPC (n 128), s 90.

Any consent given by an intoxicated person is invalid because the person does not know the nature and consequences of the act for which they consented.[146] Furthermore, consent obtained under a misconception is also invalid if the person getting the consent knows or is aware of the misconception.[147]

The mere fact that a student feels compelled to give consent to hazing out of fear or was not free to excise his judgment does not amount to genuine consent; merely showing up at the location where hazing is likely to take place does not by itself establish that the victim has consented to hazing activities. Instead, it must be proved that the victim knew the danger and the nature and extent of the risk and, being fully aware of the risk, assumed it.

3.5 High Courts Varying Approach to Hazing Adoption of serious and reformatory approaches by the High Courts

Judicial decisions pertaining to anti-hazing regulations and anti-hazing legislation have already been discussed in the previous two sections. This section, especially focuses on High Courts' (state highest courts) varying approaches to hazing. The apex court of the country, the Supreme Court, as noted before, has repeatedly stressed that hazing is a systematised form of human rights abuse[148] and likened seniors as a 'fist of steel against ice'.[149] Some of the High Courts have followed this approach. *Shri Amlan Jyoti Borthakur v. Assam Engineering College,*[150] involved severe hazing of freshers by seniors. One of the victims suffered blood clotting in his brain. The appellant and the other student were debarred from academic activities and expelled from the hostel. The Chief Justice of the Assam High Court rejected the appellant's argument that they resorted to hazing because they wanted to maintain discipline and decorum in the hostel. The Chief Justice observed that "[n]o law of this country permits the appellant to physically assault and cause injury to junior students in the garb of moral policing in the hostel".[151]

Some of the Indian courts have been reluctant to grant bail to students accused of committing serious offences under the IPC and the anti-hazing law. Ankit *Patel v The State of Chhattisgarh,*[152] is a tragic story of a fresher who committed suicide

---

[146] Ibid, s 85.

[147] *Parshottam v. State*, (1962) 64 Nom LR 788. In *R v. Williams*, 1923 1 KB 340 a girl consented to having sexual intercourse with her music teacher because he said that that it would improve her voice quality. This consent was illegal and the teacher was charged with rape of the girl.

[148] Kerala (n 11) para 12.

[149] Ibid, para 10.

[150] WA No. 327 of 2017; *Abhinash Medhi v. The Assam Engineering College* WA No.328 of 2017. See also *Shakul Hameed v. State of Kerala* on 2 November 2012, WP (C) No 24871 of 2012.

[151] WA No. 327 of 2017.

[152] M Cr C No 6644 of 2014.

by hanging himself as he could not bear the physical and mental torture inflicted on him from time to time by seniors. The Chhattisgarh High Court looking into the seriousness of the offence and the probability that the accused may tamper with prosecution witnesses, refused to grant him bail. In another case, the Kerala High Court rejected the pre-arrest bail request of the petitioners who had committed grossly reprehensible acts against freshers.[153]

The serious response in the above cases seems to be at odds with reformatory approach adopted by a number of other High Courts.[154,155]

The Gujarat High Court in *Dr Nirav Bulabhai Patel v State of Gujarat & 4*[156] considered the young age and future career of the petitioners in setting aside the punishment (suspension for three years) given by their university. The Court said that the penalty in such cases ought to have a reformatory approach because the petitioners must have realised the ills of hazing and the need for discipline. In the interest of justice the punishment the petitioners had already undergone was considered sufficient.

The future careers of hazers were also aken into consideration by the Delhi High Court in giving its verdict. In *Akshay Chaudhary & Another v University of Delhi & Anor,*[157] the petitioners were involved in hazing and were expelled by the V.C. for three years. The court reduced their expulsion to one year and allowed them into the final year of their undergraduate course so that they could complete their degree and their future prospects were not hampered.[158]

---

153 Crime No 300 of 2017 of *Valancheri Police Station, Malappuran District v. Muhammad Sufail*, Kerala High Court.

154 When a student is rusticated and/or suspended by their institution for participating in hazing activities, they often file a writ petition under Art. 226 of the Constitution of India before the High Court of the state for setting aside or reducing the punishment. State High Courts have in most cases granted relief to the student by either setting aside or reducing the sentence.

155 Usually, an appeal lies to the Vice Chancellor or the head of the institution or a disciplinary committee or disciplinary board against an order made by the ARC. The courts are unlikely to intervene and go into the merits of the case unless the petitioner has exhausted such procedure. See *Shakul Hameed v. State of Kerala* on 2 November 2012, WP (C) No 24871 of 2012; *Philson Mathew & Ors v. Holy Cross College of Management & Technology & Anr* WP (C) No 20058 of 2013.

156 SCA No. 1958 of 2014.

157 WP (C) No 1897/2010 & CM No 9422/2010. The petitioners were final-year students found guilty of hazing a fresher under the UGC Regulations; the fresher also filed an FIR with the police authorities. As a result, the Vice Chancellor (VC) expelled the petitioners from the College and its hostel. After one academic year, the petitioners entered into a settlement with the victim; based on the settlement, the Court quashed the FIR as it was likely to mar the future career of the petitioners. The petitioners then requested the V.C. to confine their expulsion to one academic year and allow them to undergo the final year again. The V.C. refused. The High Court stated that allowing the V.C.'s expulsion to stand would nullify "what this Court had attempted to do by quashing the FIR...Not only would the petitioners remain without a Degree of Graduation, but their future prospects will also be seriously hampered".

158 Quote from paras 22, 23, 24 and 25.

The Karnataka High Court in *T.T. Chakravarthy Yuvraj v Principal, Dr. BR Ambedkar Medical College,*[159] said that the punishment imposed on the student should not result in retribution or give vent to a feeling of wrath. The Judge quoted Shakespeare that "Justice should be tempered with mercy,' particularly when the students are in the position of those about whom—Jesus Christ said—'They know not what they do. Forgive them'".[160]

Several High Courts have reduced the period of suspension awarded by the university to those found guilty of hazing freshers. We will briefly state the important points that emerge from those cases. In *Sarthak Sen Gupta v State of West Bengal & Ors*[161] the Calcutta High Court[162] modified the University's punishment given to the petitioner debarring him from two semesters to one semester. In *Basudev Sethi v State of Odisha and Another,*[163] the period of suspension given to the hazer by the ARC was also reduced. The Odisha High Court observed that university students are "children [who] are vulnerable, and they need to be valued, nurtured, caressed and protected".[164] Kerala[165] and Uttarakhand[166] High Courts showed a similar lenient approach to hazers.

In *Sk. Nur Alam v Director, College of Engineering and Management and Others,*[167] the hazer was expelled from the institution under the West Bengal anti-ragging law.[168] The transfer certificate issued to him by the College mentioned his offensive behaviour in the conduct column. The[169] Calcutta High Court held that the student had already suffered a harsh punishment in the form of expulsion and hoped "that the College issue the transfer certificate in such a manner that the future of

---

[159] AIR1997 Karnataka 261.

[160] AIR1997 Karnataka 261, para 18.

[161] W.P. No. 15604 (W) of 2013.

[162] The petitioner, on past occasions, was acquitted for hazing freshers on submission of an undertaking to the university. This time, the petitioner assaulted another student, who complained to the local police station and university authorities. The University authorities, in strict compliance with the AICTE Regulations and norms, permanently expelled the petitioner from the University hostel and debarred him from appearing in any examinations for two consecutive semesters.

[163] W.P. (C) No. 25002 of 2017 and W.P. (C) No. 25003 of 2017.

[164] W.P. (C) No. 25002 of 2017 and W.P. (C) No. 25003 of 2017 [18].

[165] *Fenil P Wilson v. The Director on 16 August 2016* WP (C) Nos 38867 of 2016 & 2016 of 2017.

[166] *Sandeep Panwar v. Govind Ballabh Pant University* WP (M/S) No 2914 of 2016. See also *Anil Singh Waldia v. Govind Ballabh Pant University* WP (M/S) No 2915 of 2016 and *Alankrit Bamrara v. Govind Ballabh Pant University* WP (M/S) No 2912 of 2016.

[167] *Sk. Nur Alam v. Director, College of Engineering and Management and Others* (2006)(3) CHN 291.

[168] West Bengal Prohibition of Ragging in Educational Institutions Act 2000, ss 6, 7.

[169] *Nirav Bhulabhai Patel v. State of Gujarat & Ors* C/SCA/1958/2014; 1958/2014, para 19.

the petitioner is not totally closed and he is not driven out of the main stream of the society."[170] This decision of the court is apparently against a UGC regulation.[171]

The Allahabad High Court in *Abhinav Kumar and Ors v Union of India,*[172] setting aside the suspension of 22 students of the prestigious Indian Institute of Technology Kanpur (IIT-K), said:

> Petitioners are not petty criminals. They are in a premier institute of this nation, which has been conferred the status of an institute of national importance. To get admission in such institutes is an arduous task and only the competent few...gain an entry. Such students are potential national assets.... a harsh decision may not only defeat the morale of such students but may also be a loss to the nation.[173]

3.6 Liability in Tort

A victim of hazing can sue the wrongdoer in tort law to claim compensation for their injuries, monetary loss, or both. Some wrongful acts, for example, assault and battery, by the wrongdoer expose him to liabilities in both criminal law and tort law. However, there are differences between criminal action and tort action. Under criminal law, the wrongdoer may be awarded a death sentence, a term of imprisonment and/or a fine. In tort, the victim receives monetary compensation and damages. An action in criminal law is brought against the wrongdoer by the public prosecutor, who must establish the case beyond all reasonable doubt. On the other hand, in tort law, the judge decides the case on the balance of probabilities. Tort law in India is primarily the English Common law of torts "as found suitable to Indian conditions".[174]

The primary source of tort law in India is therefore English judicial decisions. Hazing is as prevalent in India as in the U.S. The U.S. is also a common law country; its structure of the law is similar to England and India. There is a dearth of hazing cases in India. Therefore, we will discuss English and U.S. cases wherever relevant. First, we will discuss intentional torts and then tortious liability in negligence.

3.6.1 Intentional Torts

The common law as yet does not recognise the tort of hazing. As far as hazers are concerned, their conduct vis-à-vis freshers is often intentional. The conduct of

[170] *Sk. Nur Alam v. Director, College of Engineering and Management and Others* (2006)(3) CHN 291, para 14.

[171] Regulations on Curbing the Menace of Ragging in Higher Educational Institutions in 2009, r 6.4(m).

[172] Writ - C Nos. 584, 1419, 2554 and 2903 of 2018.

[173] *Abhinav Kumar and Ors v. Union of India,* Writ - C Nos. 584, 1419, 2554 and 2903 of 2018.

[174] Ratanlal and Dhirajlal, *Ratanlal & Dhirajlal The Law Of Torts (Justice G.P. Singh)* (Lexis Nexis, 27th ed, 2016), p. 1.

hazers could lead to physical injury or mental harm. The hazer could be liable for assault, battery, false imprisonment and defamation. Under Indian law, to succeed in an intentional tort, the victim must prove that the conduct of the wrongdoer was unlawful.[175]

- Assault and Battery (3.6.1.1)

A victim of hazing can sue the hazer in a suitable case in the torts of assault and/or battery. To succeed, the victim must prove that the offensive act of the hazer was intentional and without any lawful justification.[176] Assault consists of an attempt to strike the victim without touching.[177] If the hazer comes in physical contact with the victim, they are liable in battery. Blackstone defined assault as "an attempt or offer to beat another, without touching him; as if one lifts up his cane or his fist in a threatening manner at another; or strikes at him but misses him"[178] Actual physical contact is necessary to make the wrongdoer liable in battery, but it is not necessary for imposing liability in assault. However, it must be proved that the hazer had the intention to hit the victim immediately, as well as the ability to carry out the threat into effect.[179] Where a person accidentally touches another without any intention to harm, there is no battery. However, if the hazer touches the victim in a rude and revengeful manner, they are liable in battery.

In many cases, the wrongdoer is liable in both assault and battery. For example, in *W v Meah*[180] (not a hazing case), the Court awarded the plaintiff aggravated damages for her rape and vicious assault. During hazing, where freshers have been raped, sodomised, kicked, paddled, punched, and banged against an object by the hazer, they are liable in both assault and battery.

A recent hazing case is an excellent example of assault and battery. There, freshers at a medical college were beaten up and, among others, forced to have unnatural sex.[181] If the victim is subjected to rape, the hazer is liable not only in criminal law but also in the torts of assault and battery: assault occurs when the hazer, without touching the victim's body, threatens to have sex with the victim; battery occurs when the hazer actually touches the victim's body or have sex with the victim forcibly .

---

175 *Jai Bhagwan v. Suman Devi* 2011 185 DLT 29.

176 *Pratap Daji v. B.B.& C.I. Rly* (1877) ILR 1 Bom 52; *P. Kader v. K A Alagarswami* AIR 1965 mad. 438.

177 *Raghbinder Singh v. Bant Kaur* (2011) 1 SCC 106. Cf *Bavisetti Venkat Surya Rao v. Nandipati Muthayya* AIR 1964 A.P. 382.

178 William Blackstone, Commentaries on the Laws of England: Vol 2 iii, p. 120. See also William H Erickson (1967) 'What Constitutes an Assault', 16 *Clev.-Marshall Law Review* 14.

179 Blackstone (n 178) p. 248. *Stephens v. Myers* (1830) 4 C & P 349: 34 RR 811.

180 (1986) 1 All ER 835.

181 Abraham (n 36).

- False Imprisonment (3.6.1.2)

The word false means erroneous or wrongful.[182] False imprisonment is an intentional tort in which the victim can sue the hazer, provided two requirements are satisfied: (i) the hazer totally restrains the victim's freedom from movement for a period of time, and (ii) the imposition of restraint was without any lawful justification. The area of imprisonment may be small or large and could be constructive.[183]

False imprisonment is one of the most common torts committed by seniors during hazing. As part of hazing, one or more senior students would first forcibly enter the classroom or hostel room of freshers and bolt the room from the inside. Then, they would ask freshers to perform demeaning acts, such as stripping naked in front of other students (often of the opposite sex), watching pornographic videos and imitating sexual acts, and forcing freshers to have sex. Seniors often beat up freshers who refuse to comply, and freshers are not allowed to leave until the demands of the seniors have been satisfied. In a border line case, *Bavisetti Venkata Rao v Nandipati Muttayya*[184] the court refused to impose any liability on the defendant. There the plaintiff had not paid his land revenue. The defendant called a goldsmith to remove the plaintiff's earrings that the plaintiff was wearing. In the meantime, however, someone paid the plaintiff's land revenue. The plaintiff sued the defendant in assault and false imprisonment. The defendant was held not liable, as he had said nothing to put the plaintiff in fear of immediate or instant violence.

Another hazing incident is also worth mentioning. At a medical college, seniors forced a boy and a girl to strip naked and have sex. When they refused, seniors locked them in a room for three days without food or water.[185] In *Rahul Pandurangji khadatkar and Others v State of Maharashtra and Others*,[186] the hazers took a fresher to their residence and confined the fresher in a room for eight hours. The hazers asked the fresher offensive and disgusting questions. If the victim failed to answer their questions, hazers would beat him up with a stick. In this case, the tortious liability of the hazers was not only for false imprisonment but also for assault and battery: false imprisonment because the hazers restrained the fresher's liberty to move; assault was committed whenever any hazer lifted the stick, as it would have caused the fresher a reasonable apprehension of harm; and battery when the hazers hit the fresher without any lawful justification.

- Defamation (3.6.1.3)

The law of defamation seeks to protect one's reputation. Unfortunately, no single test exists to determine what is defamatory.[187] Whether a statement is defamatory

---

182 Ratanlal and Dhirajlal (n 174) p. 251.

183 Ibid.

184 AIR 1964 AP382.

185 Raghavan et al. (n 19) (Annexure IX).

186 AIR 2002 (2) Bom 312.

187 See C Sappideen and P Vines (Eds.), *Fleming's the Law of Torts* (Thomson Reuters, 10th ed, 2011).

or not is a question of fact. The right to reputation is an inherent personal right. A person's reputation is his property. Article 19(1)(a) of the Constitution of India guarantees every person a fundamental right to freedom of speech and expression. "The law relating to defamation is a reasonable restriction on [this] fundamental right"[188] To bring an action in defamation, a fresher must prove that the statement made by the seniors has lowered their reputation in the eyes of right-thinking people of society. Freshers have been forced to strip and parade naked in front of seniors.[189] Students from Northeast India and African countries were harassed by the use of derogatory words regarding their regional background.[190] Caste-based hazing, which is also widely prevalent in India, gives rise to an action by the victim for damages to his reputation.[191] Damages allowed in defamation are similar to those awarded for personal injuries.[192]

3.6.2 Universities' Liability in Negligence

To bring an action in negligence for hazing, against the university, the victim must prove that the university failed in its duty to take reasonable care to protect the victim. Next, such a duty must have been breached by the university, and the situation should be such that a reasonable person would think it is fair, just and reasonable to impose liability.[193]

University-Student Special Relationship

Generally, a duty of care does not include an affirmative duty to protect a third party unless there is a 'special relationship'. Certain recognised relationships, for example, parent and child, employer and employee, principal and agent, fall under such categories. To determine whether a duty exists on the university to protect its students, we have to look into whether the victim's injury and the manner in which it was caused was reasonably foreseeable by the university. Furthermore, policy considerations are vital to establish a duty in novel situations or a grey area.

As discussed in Chap. 2, the special relationship comes into play through the assumption of responsibility by the university for the safety of its students.[194] So far as the university-student relationship in India is concerned, judicial decisions discussed

---

[188] Ratanlal and Dhirajlal (n 174) p. 267.

[189] Raghavan et al. (n 19) (Annexure IV).

[190] Vishwas Kothari (n 59).

[191] Rao et al. (n 2) p. 114.

[192] *John v. MGM Limited* [1997] QB 586.

[193] *Caparo Industries plc v. Dickman* [1990] ALL ER 568, [1990] 2 AC 605.

[194] See Chap. 2, *Furek v. University of Delaware* 594 A.2d 506 (Del.1991) (Supreme Court of Delaware); *Davidson v. University of North Carolina at Chapel Hill* 142 N.C. App. 544 (N.C. Ct. App. 2001); *Mullins v. Pine Manor College* 389 Mass. 47, 449 N.E.2d 331 (1983) (Supreme Judicial Court of Massachusetts); *Regents of University of California v. Superior Court of Los Angeles County* 4 Cal. 5th 607, 413 P. 3d 656 (2018).

in Chap. 2 are relevant. Students in India are as vulnerable as U.S. students and depend on their universities for protection. Not all students reside in university-provided accommodations. For some university degrees, staying on campus is mandatory, and even if a student does not stay on a university campus, they spend much time together in class rooms, university libraries, sporting clubs, and cafeterias.

The "modern university provides a setting in which every aspect of student life is, to some degree, university guided".[195] The academic and career success of students are linked to the university's name and ranking.[196] Universities in India, under the UGC Regulations, are required to undertake several hazing prevention measures:educate students about hazing, establish ARS and ARC, and take a written undertaking from new students and their parents that the student has not in the past indulged in any hazing activity nor would they do so after joining the institution.[197] Taking such stringent measures prima facie indicates that Indian universities are well aware of the menace of hazing and how an unwary student could be a victim of it. Thus, it is clear that universities are responsible for protecting their students from hazing.[198]

The High Court in *Madhya Pradesh State Road Transport Corp v Basantibai,*[199] confronted with a new situation where there were no existing precedents, looked at the judicial decisions of England to decide the matter. The thrust of the decision was that in a new duty situation, the court can resolve the matter by following an incremental approach.

If there are no Indian or U.K. judicial precedents, the court may also look at the relevant U.S. precedents. In the U.S., the 'special relationship' between a university and its students took a long time to develop. Until the 1960s, the *in loco parentis*[200] rule was in vogue. Between the 1970 and mid-1980s, the bystander principle was dominant.[201] The bystander principle considered university students primarily adults and responsible for their own safety. Now the position is:

> Academic and career success of students are linked to the university's name and its ranking. Rankings have become more important in recent years. The higher the ranking, the more attractive a university will be to prospective students. The same also applies to its safety record. Students and alumni often wear clothing bearing the university logo. University advertisements often name successful alumni. Students help with research and a myriad university projects. In short, a university has a vested interest in the wellbeing of its students....Recently

---

[195] *Furek v. University of Delaware* (n 194).

[196] Neerav Srivastava, Aashish Srivastava and DK Srivastava (2019) 'A Million Winslows: Private Liability of Universities for Ragging in India', 19(2) *Oxford University commonwealth law journal* 227; See World University Rankings, https://www.timeshighereducation.com/world-university-rankings.

[197] A template has been provided by the UGC. See Appendix A at the end of the book.

[198] Srivastava et al. (n 196).

[199] ILR [1976] MP 508.

[200] Universities were free from liability and could not be held liable if a hazer causes injury or damage to the victim.

[201] Although there were some exceptions. For example, see *Mullins v. Pine Manor College* (n 194).

> 'pastoral care' — a concept that involves protection, strengthening and shielding the weak — has been used. That is illuminating.[202]

To impose liability in negligence on universities, three essential elements of negligence must be proved by the victim of hazing: (1) the university owed a duty of care to the victim; (2) the university breached this duty; and (3) the breach of the duty resulted in harm to the victim.

Duty of Care

The question of the existence of a duty on the university to protect its students from hazing depends on whether there are appropriate judicial precedents or relevant legislation. Hazing has not yet been recognised as a tort by any court in India. The structure of the common law of tort in India is largely based on the judicial precedents of the U.K. To create a new duty, one can look at *Caparo v Dickman.*[203] In that case, Lord Bridge laid down a threefold test for the determination of duty in a novel situation: foreseeability of damage, proximity between the parties, and the existence of just, fair, and reasonable circumstances. Lord Oliver, while endorsing these requirements, added policy considerations, i.e., social, economic and financial factors, to determine whether liability should be imposed or not in a novel situation.

i. *Foreseeability*

In determining foreseeability, the courts in India often take a liberal approach. The Supreme Court of India said that:

> The law of torts exists for the purpose of preventing men from hurting one and another… it would be primitive to…close…the ever-expanding and growing horizon of tortious liability. Even for social development, orderly growth of society and cultural refineness, the liberal approach to tortious liability by courts is more conducive.[204]

In *Madhya Pradesh Road Transport v Basanti Bai,*[205] there was a communal riot in the city; therefore, the authorities imposed a curfew. However, the appellant's driver was required to go through the curfew to join his duties. The driver was stabbed to death by a ruffian. The issue before the court was whether the appellant was negligent in not providing an adequate arrangement for the deceased's safety. The court said, "Normally, an employer owes no duty of care for the safety of his employee while the employee is proceeding to the place of employment from his house".[206] This principle, the court said, could not be applied where the situation was abnormal: a

---

[202] D K Srivastava, Aashish Srivastava, and Neerav Srivastava (2018) '"A Hazy Shade of Liability": Duty of Care of Universities to Prevent Hazing', 25(1) *Torts Law Journal* 25, p. 32.

[203] [1990] 2 AC 605 (HL).

[204] *Jay Laxmi Salt Works (P) Ltd. v. State of Gujarat* (1994) SSC [18].

[205] (1971) IILLJ 273 MP (Madhya Pradesh High Court); ILR[1976]MP508 (Madhya).

[206] Ibid, p. 512.

curfew had been imposed requiring citizens to be within doors, and it was reasonably foreseeable that the employee was likely to suffer injury at the hands of some ruffian unless the employer made an adequate arrangement. The court stated:

> requiring an employee to work in such a situation is itself such an act from which harm to the employee is foreseeable and the employer being closely and directly connected with the act of requiring him to join his work, the employer must have his safety in contemplation….They should have taken adequate care for the safety of the employee… either by providing safe transport or some person to accompany and guard him, In case it was not possible …the employer should have temporarily closed the business….It has also to be kept in view that the employee, in the instant case, unlike a police constable or a fireman, was not in such an employment where it was expected of him from the nature of employment to face the hazards of a riot.[207]

It is important to note that the court, after reference to leading English decisions on liability in negligence: *Donoghue v Stevenson*,[208] *Hedley Byrne & Co Ltd. v Heller and Partners Ltd*,[209] and *Home Office v Dorset Yacht Co Ltd*,[210] which brought into existence new duties stated that "These cases clearly establish that a new duty situation can be recognised…".[211]

Arguably, a university has a duty to control hazing on its campus and residential premises. The Sociological background, the UGC Regulations and the anti- hazing legislation sections, and the Supreme Court warnings clearly demonstrate that hazing is out of control in universities in India. All kinds of barbaric treatment is given to vulnerable freshers. It is foreseeable that if no proper care is taken of them by their university, more and more freshers are likely to suffer. A university should know or ought to know the problem facing freshers from hazing and the need to control the activities of seniors.[212]

---

207 Ibid, p. 512.

208 [1932] A.C. 562.

209 [1964] A.C. 465.

210 [1970] All E. R. 294.

211 Madhya Pradesh (n 205) p. 512.

212 See *Nero v. Kansas State University* 861 P. 2d 768–1993. There a male student was asked to leave a co-educational halls because of a pending rape case against him. However, due to shortage of space he was again allotted another co-educational hall of residence. At this hall, he raped a girl. The issue was whether the University was liable in negligence for not taking sufficient security measures to protect the girl. The court said that since the University knew about a pending rape case against the male student and it did not give any warning danger to the student, it was liable; the university's duty was to exercise reasonable care to protect the girl. See also *Peterson v. Francisco Community College District*, 685 P 2d 1193 (Cal. 1984); *Cutler v. Board of Regents* (459 SO. 2d 413 (Fla CT App 1984).

ii. *Proximity*

The test of proximity may be briefly described as foreseeability of a reasonable person.[213] A university and its students are in a proximate relationship. "For many students, college is the first time, they have lived away from home".[214] "Universities facilitates maturation of young adults…Admissions in India typically require a non-hazing declaration by the prospective student and their parents. Under legislation and regulations in India, university administrators and staff are required to take action to prevent hazing".[215] The proximity principle limits the persons to whom a duty is owed. They are those "who are so closely and directly affected by my act that I ought reasonable to have them in contemplation".[216] According to *Davis v Radcliff*[217] proximity refers to such a relation between the parties that renders it just and reasonable to impose liability in negligence.

iii. *Is it fair, just and reasonable to impose a duty on a university to prevent hazing?*

The concept of proximity is an artificial one. The question is whether it is just, fair and reasonable to impose a duty on the university to protect its students from hazing. In this context, we have to examine various factors, including the historical and sociological background of hazing in India, anti-hazing legislation and regulations, judicial decisions, and community attitude toward hazing. In spite of the fact that Art. 14 of the Constitution of India guarantees every person equality before the law, Indian society is still plagued with caste, religion, and gender-based discrimination. It is not just fair and reasonable to allow seniors to perpetuate hazing against freshers on the grounds of caste, region and religion. Thus, there is a duty on universities to protect their students. Both anti-hazing legislation and UGC Regulations mandate that universities must take all necessary measures to prevent and report hazing. The UGC Regulations mandate the following:

1. Every institution must constitute an ARC, ARS, Monitoring Cell and Mentoring Cell to control hazing.
2. The faculty of the institution and its non-teaching staff must be sensitised towards the ills of hazing, its prevention and the consequences thereof.
3. Every institution must obtain an undertaking from every employee (both teaching and non-teaching staff) that they would promptly report any case of hazing, which comes to their notice.
4. It must be the general collective responsibility of every employee (both teaching and non-teaching staff) to prevent or to act promptly against the occurrence of hazing or any incident of hazing that comes to their notice.

---

[213] Ratanlal and Dhirajlal (n 174) p. 469.

[214] *Regents of University of California v. Superior Court of Los Angeles County* (n 194).

[215] D K Srivastava, Aashish Srivastava, and Neerav Srivastava (n 202), p. 32.

[216] In *Donoghue v. Stevenson* 1932 AC 562 (HL), per Lord Atkin, p. 580. See also Ratanlal and Dhirajlal (n 174), 469.

[217] (1990) 2 ALL ER 536, p. 540 (PC).

Hazing being a human rights abuse,[218] imposing a duty on universities to protect their students cannot be unjust, unfair and unreasonable.

iv. *Policy Considerations*

Duty is also based on policy considerations. The courts primarily look at social, economic and financial factors to determine whether liability should be imposed in a given situation. In this exercise, courts would examine (i) whether the idea of morality and justice require the imposition of a duty; (ii) where should the loss fall; (iii) mores of the community; and (iv) whether the wrongdoer was insured against the loss. Policy considerations are not static. In the U.S., first, the policy was that university students were to be treated as adults with no need for any protection from the university. This was changed in *Furek v University of Delaware.*[219] There, the court said that certain student activities required university supervision: It emphasised that the "likelihood of injury during fraternity activities occurring on university campuses is greater than the utility of university inaction".[220]

Policy considerations in India would support the imposition of a duty in the tort of negligence on the university to prevent hazing. UGC Regulations, provisions of anti-hazing statutes and the Supreme Court describing hazing as human rights abuse clearly indicate that students and the community at large expect universities to protect their students from harm likely to be caused by hazing. Taking such care will cost universities money. Indian universities are not as rich as their U.S. counterparts. There are a few private universities that charge high fees. Public universities also charge fees, albeit not as high as private universities. Private universities can buy insurance to cover their costs. However, public universities can also buy insurance and spread the cost of insurance among their students.

v. *Incremental Approach*

In *Sutherland v Heyman Council,*[221] Brennan J of the High Court of Australia stated that "the law should develop novel categories of negligence incrementally and by analogy with established categories…".[222] It is clear from earlier discussions that it is fair just and reasonable that universities must be liable for failure to control hazing. There does not seem to be any policy consideration that would be in conflict with this approach. "Holding universities liable for a failure to take reasonable steps would be analogous to and an incremental development".[223]

---

[218] See Kerala (n 11).

[219] *Furek v. University of Delaware* (n 194).

[220] Ibid.

[221] (1985) 60 ALR 1.

[222] The incremental approach of Justice Brennan was approved in *Caparo Industries Plc v. Dickman* (n 193).

[223] Srivastava et al. (n 196) p. 245.

Madhya Pradesh Road Transport Corporation v Basanti Bai,[224] discussed before, clearly establishes that the employer's duty was extended by applying the incremental approach to provide a safe system of transport to its employees from their home to the work place in abnormal situations.

Breach of Duty

While the existence of a duty of care is a legal question, its breach a question of fact.[225] One needs to look into whether the "defendant omitted to do something which a reasonable and prudent man, guided by those considerations which ordinarily regulate the conduct of human affairs, would have done, or has done something which a reasonable and prudent man would not have done".[226] This eliminates "the personal equation and is independent of the idiosyncrasies of the particular person whose conduct is in question".[227] When it appears to a reasonable person from the circumstances of the case that certain consequences might occur or ought to occur, and in fact, those consequences do occur, the court should hold the defendant liable.[228] Sometimes a person may confront a dangerous situation, and various courses may be open to deal with it. The fact that the person opted not for the best option does not make the person negligent.[229] Often decisions are made in such circumstances in the heat of the moment.

In the U.S. universities, students are frequently hazed in fraternities and sororities. They die, commit suicide and experience life-threatening injuries. Students are coerced to drink an excessive amount of alcohol. U.S. institutions could foresee that failure to supervise freshers could result in hazing. India has no direct judicial decision on the breach in the context of hazing. Therefore, three U.S. cases on the issue of breach of duty are discussed.

In *Furek v University of Delaware*,[230] although the University had assumed responsibility for its students' safety, it failed to discharge this obligation. A fresher got burned and scarred due to oven cleaner poured on him by fraternity members. The university had anti-hazing policies, but they were not strictly enforced. The university was held liable. In *Mullins v Pine Manor College*,[231] an intruder entered a residential college and raped a student. The court found that college security was inadequate as a single key could open the commons building, dormitory and students' rooms and held the College liable. In the *Estate of Chad Meredith v Travis Montgomery and David May*,[232] a student died after fraternity members compelled him to consume

[224] 1971 ACJ 328.

[225] Ratanlal and Dhirajlal (n 174) p. 480.

[226] Ibid, p. 480.

[227] *Glasgow Corporation v. Muir* (1943) AC 447, 448. Ibid, p. 469.

[228] *Veeran v. Krishnamorthy* AIR 1966 Ker 172.

[229] *Indian Airlines v. Madhuri Chowduhri*, AIR 1965 Cal 252.

[230] 594 A.2d 506 (Del.1991).

[231] 389 Mass. 47, 449 N.E.2d 331 (1983).

[232] The Associated Press, 'UM Fraternity Members Liable in Hazing Death', *Herald-Tribune* (online, 7 February 2004). https://www.heraldtribune.com/story/news/2004/02/07/um-fraternity-members-liable-in-hazing-death/28787263007/.

excessive amount of alcohol and swim across a frozen lake. The court held that the fraternity had a duty to protect the deceased, which it breached. A large sum, $14 million, was awarded as damages to the deceased's parents. As discussed in the sociological background, freshers at hostels in India are most prone to hazing if adequate security measures are not in place.[233] In December 2022, a medical university in Assam decided to lodge freshers and senior students in separate hostels to prevent hazing.[234] Note that lodging freshers in a separate hostel from their seniors is a requirement under the UGC Regulations but may not be adhered to by universities.

Breach of Statutory Duty

Where legislation imposes responsibilities on an institution, they must be carried out effectively (not carelessly or negligently). A statutory duty is mandatory, not discretionary. It protects individuals as members of a specific class rather than the public at large. Breach of a statutory duty allows the victim remedy to sue the wrongdoer under criminal law. However, it does not close the option of a civil suit:

> The inference that there is a concurrent right of civil action is readily drawn when the predominant purpose is manifestly the protection of a class of workmen by imposing on their employers the duty of taking special measures to secure their safety.[235]

Finding liability for breach of a statutory duty is easier when there is a correlation between statutory obligation and the victims' harm. Thus, where any legislation, rules or regulations set out specific duties on universities to control hazing, such duties must be carried out diligently, not negligently.

In India, action for breach of a statutory duty is based on the same common law principles that have been developed in other countries, such as the U.S., the U.K. and Australia. Statutory duties have become part of negligence in the U.S. Indian courts are willing to impose a private duty for breach of statutory provisions designed to ensure personal safety. In *Vithaldas v Municipal Commissioner of Bombay,*[236] the court held the Municipality liable for leaving a trench open in a public lane. In *Punjab State Electricity Board v Zora Singh,*[237] failure to provide electricity resulted in private liability.[238]

A question that needs to be examined is whether the breach of subsidiary legislation, such as the UGC Regulations, could give rise to a private action for breach of a

---

[233] Rao et al. (n 2).

[234] IANS, 'Assam Institutes Keep Freshers in Separate Hostels to Prevent Ragging', *Mangalorean.com* (online, 8 December 2022) https://www.mangalorean.com/assam-institutes-keep-freshers-in-separate-hostels-to-prevent-ragging/.

[235] Ratanlal and Dhirajlal (n 174), p. 582.

[236] (1902) 4 Bom LR 914.

[237] (2005) 6 SCC 776.

[238] *Hawthorn Corp v. Kannuluik* [1906] AC 105 the corporation was found to be negligent in the planning of the original drains. In general, commentators encourage the Indian courts to proactively redress the complexities of the legislature and executive – see MC Mehta (2006) The Accountability Principle: Legal Solutions to Break Corruption's Impact on India's Environment', 21 *Journal of Environmental Law and Litigation* 141.

statutory duty. Like other subsidiary legislation in India, the UGC Regulations were formed under the UGC Act 1956 and approved by Parliament.[239] According to s. 20 of the UGC Act, the UGC "shall be guided by such directions on questions of policy relating to national purposes as may be given to it by the Central Government". The Act does not contain any explicit limit on private actions. The preamble to the UGC Regulations state that it was made pursuant to the 'directions' of the Supreme Court and 'the determination of the Central Government' to prohibit, prevent and eliminate hazing.

According to the UGC Regulations, educational institutions must take all necessary measures to achieve the object of eliminating hazing within and outside the institution[240]; properly illuminate and keep a close watch on all locations vulnerable to hazing[241]; tighten security at vulnerable places and intense policing by the anti-hazing squad[242]; and maintain round the clock vigil in hostel premises to prevent hazing. Furthermore, no institution should permit hazing or condone it.[243]

The universities are liable when there is any breach of the above obligations imposed on them by the UGC and a student is injured. Under the Indian law, a writ petition against the wrongdoer is maintainable when there is a breach of a statutory duty.[244] Thus, any student can approach the High Court under Art. 226 of the Constitution seeking a direction that the university must fulfil its anti-hazing obligations under the UGC Regulations.

Causation

After the plaintiff has successfully proved that the defendant owed the plaintiff an affirmative duty and that the defendant breached this duty, the plaintiff must also prove the causal connection of this duty or damage to the defendant's negligence.[245] A successful plaintiff is awarded compensation or damages by the court.[246] If the injury or damage to the plaintiff had happened anyway, there is no question of the defendant's liability.[247] Causation, like the breach of duty, is a question of fact; the victim must establish that the defendant's breach of duty, in fact, caused the plaintiff's harm.[248] To determine the cause-and-effect relationship between the university and

---

239 Under s. 28 of the UGC Act, regulations are laid before parliament for a period of 30 days.

240 UGC Reg 5(b).

241 UGC Reg 6(1)(k).

242 UGC Reg 6(1)(l).

243 UGC Reg 5(a).

244 See *Capital Bar Association and Ors. v. State of Odisha and Ors* W.P. (C) Nos. 18036 and 18312 of 2012.

245 In *Yadava Kumar v. Divisional Manager, National Insurance Company Limited* (2010) 10 SCC 341 the Supreme Court distinguished between compensation and damages. It said that "in the matter of computation of compensation, the approach will be slightly more broad based than what is done in the assessment of damages". See also *Branch Manager, New India Insurance Co. Ltd. v Malliga* (2012) 2 TN MAC 576; Ratanlal and Dhirajlal (n 174) p. 180–82.

246 Ibid.

247 *Barnett v. Chelsea Hospital Management Committee* [1968] 3 All ER 1068.

248 Ratanlal and Dhirajlal (n 174) p. 180.

student, the but-for test is used, which means that the harm to the victim would not have occurred but for the defendant's wrongful act. In the U.S. case of *Hall v Board of Supervisors Southern University*[249] (though not directly related to hazing), the inadequacy of the security argument was an issue. There, an assailant shot a student as she awaited an elevator. She sued the university for negligence, claiming it breached its duty to provide adequate security. The court rejected her argument and held that such an incident could have happened despite the utmost security precaution, and the university's negligence did not cause the plaintiff's injuries.[250]

Defences

Contributory Negligence

Contributory negligence means the plaintiff's own culpability contributed to the plaintiff's injury or damage. The plaintiff was a co-author of his own misfortune, and the plaintiff's damages are reduced by considering the extent of the plaintiff's fault.[251] The requirements for successfully establishing this defence are similar to those prevailing in the U.K., Australia and the U.S.[252] The U.K. passed the *Law Reform (Contributory Negligence) Act*, 1945, which lays down the rule for apportionment of damages when both the defendant and the plaintiff are negligent and have contributed to the plaintiff's damage or injury. Section 1(1) of the Act states that

> Where any person suffers damage as the result partly of his own fault and partly of the fault of another person or persons a claim in respect of that damage shall not be defeated by reason of the fault of the person suffering the damage, but the damages recoverable in respect thereof shall be reduced to such extent as the court thinks just and equitable having regard to the claimant's share in the responsibility for the damage.

India does not have a federal legislation like the U.K. on contributory negligence. However, one of its states, Kerala, passed the *Torts (Miscellaneous Provisions) Act* in 1976. Section 8 of the Act mirrors section 1(1) of the U.K.'s *Law Reform (Contributory Negligence) Act*, 1945.

The Supreme Court of India, while dealing with the issue of apportionment of damages for contributory negligence, stated that "it is now well settled that in the case of contributory negligence, courts have the power to apportion the loss between the parties as it seems just and equitable".[253] The courts, particularly the high courts of various states, follow the principle laid down in the U.K.'s Law Reform (*Contributory Negligence*) Act of 1945 for apportioning damages where both the plaintiff and

---

[249] 405 So 2d 1125 (La Ct App 1981).

[250] See also *Waters v. the University of England* [1998] NSWSC 248; *Mullins v. Pine Manor College* (n 194).

[251] D.K. Srivastava and A.D. Tenekone, *The Law of Tort in Hong Kong* (LexisNexis, Fourth Edition 2020 by Prof. Charu Sharma) p. 505.

[252] In the U.S. case of *Estate of Chad Meredith v. Travis Montgomery and David May* discussed above, the jury found that Meredith contributed to his death to the extent of ten percent, and the defendants were liable for the other ninety percent.

[253] *Municipal Corporation of Greater Bombay v. Laxman Iyer* AIR 2003 SC 4182.

defendant have contributed to the plaintiff's injury or damage.[254] There are several Indian cases on contributory negligence (not related to hazing) where the plaintiff's damages have been reduced according to the degree of the plaintiff's negligence.[255]

Voluntary Assumption of Risk

In contrast to the defence of contributory negligence, voluntary assumption of risk or *volenti non fit injuria* is a complete defence. In *Smith v Baker & Sons*, Lord Herschell said that the maxim *volenti non fit injuria* "is founded on good sense and justice. One who is invited or assented to an act being done towards him cannot, when he suffers from it, complain of it as a wrong".[256] Thus, where the victim of hazing voluntarily assumes all the risk, the hazer would go scot-free: there would be no liability on the hazer.

As the issue of hazing and voluntary assumption of risk has thus far not come up before Indian courts, it is worth examining how foreign jurisdictions, especially the U.S., deal with this question. In *People v Lenti (Lenti I)*,[257] the defendants argued that the freshers knew there would be physical abuse during hazing and warned of physical harm, to which they consented. The Court said that the freshers assumed the risk of some physical abuse but not the extent of physical harm that happened. A similar approach was taken by the court in *Furek v University of Delaware*,[258] discussed before. A student playing a game of cricket for the university may be aware of the general nature of risks in the game and cannot sue the university for any injury caused while playing. However, the university cannot plead voluntary assumption of risk if there is a deliberate injury caused to the student by another university player.[259]

Fear and coercion are significant factors why freshers at Indian universities consent to hazing. Freshers are aware that refusing hazing would lead them to being ostracised, punished, and beaten more severely than those who consent to hazing.[260] After all, who would freely consent to be physically tortured or receive severe injuries?[261] In the U.S. case *Quinn v Sigma Rho Chapter of Beta Theta Pi*,[262] the Court

---

[254] Ratanlal and Dhirajlal (n 174) p. 570–571.

[255] See for example Ibid. p. 571–72. *Rural Transport Service v. Bezlum Bibi* AIR 1980 Cal. 165; *Subhakar v. Mysore State Road Transport Corporation* AIR 1975 Kerala 73; *Vidya Devi v. M.P. Road Transport Corporation* 1974 M.P.L.J 573; AIR 1975 M.P. 89.

[256] [1891] AC 325. (1965) AC 656; *Branch Manager, National Insurance Co Ltd. v. Agilan* (2011) 2 TN MAC 429.

[257] *People v. Lenti*, 44 Misc. 2d 118, 253 N.Y.S.2d 9 (N.Y. Cnty. Ct. 1964).

[258] *Furek v. University of Delaware* (n 194).

[259] See *King v. University of Indianapolis, (S.D.Ind. 2002)*, NA 01-233-C-B/H (S.D. Ind. Oct. 3, 2002) where a student suffered a stroke while participating in football practice. He was treated by a university employee but died. The student had signed a form, assuming the inherent risk of the game of football. The court disregarded the consent form and held that the form contained language expressly addressing the risks inherent in the sport of football, but it nowhere mentioned the student's assumption of risk from possible negligence on the part of the university employee.

[260] Rao et al. (n 2) p. 98.

[261] D.K. Srivastava and A.D. Tenekone, *The Law of Tort in Hong Kong* (n 251) p. 46.

[262] 507 NE 2d 1193, 1198 (Ill. App. 1987).

rejected the *volenti non fit injuria* defence as the defendants coerced the plaintiff into joining hazing activities.[263]

If it is illegal to punch any person in his eyes or other vulnerable parts of his body, consent cannot legalise these wrongful acts.[264] Hazing in India often leads to assault, grievous hurt, wrongful confinement, and abetment to suicide, which are all illegal under the IPC and state anti-hazing legislation. Consent to such illegal acts is meaningless; it does not provide any defence of voluntary assumption of risk to the hazer. The IPC also states that consent given by a person under fear of injury, under a misconception of fact, or by an intoxicated person (hazee) is invalid.[265]

Vicarious Liability

Where a faculty member, administrative staff or an employee of a university is responsible for hazing, the university could be vicariously liable for their wrongs.[266] It does not matter whether the wrongful act has not been expressly or impliedly authorised by the university.[267] These days, the stress is on enterprise liability. The Supreme Court of India in *MC Mehta v Union of India*[268] and the House of Lords in *Cox v Ministry of Justice*[269] favoured enterprise liability theory, which is premised on the principle that one who benefits from another's work must also pay for the loss caused to the enterprise (or public body or corporation) by that person.

A university is also a public body or corporation. Therefore, to impose liability on the university, the employee must do the wrongful act in the course of his employment.[270] Next, both the employer and employee are joint tortfeasors. However, the action by the victim is invariably brought against the employer because the employer is in a better financial position to pay damages than the employee.

A university could also be liable for an intentional tort against the victim where there is a close connection between an employee's wrongful act and the university's employment.[271] In the English case of *Lister v Hesley Hall Ltd*,[272] the employer of a boarding house warden was held liable for the sexual abuse of boys residing there.

---

[263] *Samira Kohli v. Prabha Manchanda* (2008) 2 SCC 1, paras 48 to 50. In particular, the Supreme Court at length discussed the question of patient's consent in variety of situations. See also Ratanlal and Dhirajlal (n 174) p. 95–96.

[264] *Imperial Chemical Indutries v Shatwel* (1964) 2 All ER 222 (HL); Ibid, p. 97.

[265] Sec. 90 IPC.

[266] Although the employee can also be sued but that is only a theoretical possibility.

[267] Srivastava et al. (n 196) p. 251.

[268] (1987) 1 SCR 819 (SC1).

[269] [2016] UKSC 10.

[270] In *Court on its own motion v. Himachal Pradesh and Ors*, ACI 1271 (Himachal Pradesh High Court) 24 students were taken on an educational tour by a College. They were spending time near the bank of a river. While taking photographs, the water level of the river suddenly rose and all of the students were washed away. The College had not given any warnings to the students about such dangerous possibilities. The Court held the College 30% liable.

[271] See *Gayatari Balaswamy v. ISG Novasoft Technologies Ltd.* (2014) 5 LW 97 (Madras High Court).

[272] [2002] 1 AC 215. See also *Bazley v. Curry* [1999] 2 SCR 534.

The House of Lords found a close connection between the warden's work and his sexual abuse of the boys and held the employer vicariously liable.

A similar view was taken in the Indian case, *Chairman of the Railway Board v Chandrima Das*[273] (not on hazing). There a woman was gang raped by employees of the Railway Board. Rape being an intentional tort, the issue before the Supreme Court of India was whether the Railway Board was vicariously liable. The Supreme Court clarified that the fact that the tort was intentional did not take it out of the purview of the course of employment and held the Railway Board vicariously liable.[274]

The UGC Regulations provide that it:

> shall be the general collective responsibility of all levels and sections of authorities or functionaries, including members of the faculty and employees of the institution, whether regular or temporary and employees of service providers providing service within the institution, to prevent or to act promptly against the occurrence of [hazing] or any incident of [hazing] which comes to their notice.[275]

In India, there have been incidents where professors have participated in hazing. A professor at M S University of Baroda was arrested along with several senior students for hazing a junior student.[276] A video clip showing the hazing incident was provided to the police by the complainant. In such cases, the close connection test is apparently well-established. If the facts, as stated, are proved, the university could be held liable.

Where the university appoints senior students to train freshers, but they end up hazing them, the university could be vicariously liable. In the U.S. case of *Brueckner v Norwich University*,[277] the court ordered the university to pay $10,000 for emotional distress and $1.75 million in punitive damages to freshers hazed by senior students employed by the university. The court found that hazing activities were closely connected to the employment of senior students.

Given the modern context where courts are likely to take an expansive view of vicarious liability, it may be possible to hold the university liable. Where a student is part of the university's anti-hazing apparatus, the student "is an integral part of the framework by which the university regulates [hazing]: students are acting on behalf of the university".[278] For example, when the university pays a student union leader stipend to control hazing within the campus, but the leader fails to control hazing, the university could be vicariously liable. And it does not matter whether the act was deliberate or negligent.

---

[273] [2000] 1 SCR 480 (SC1).

[274] See also *Cox v. Ministry of Justice* [2016] UKSC 10, per Lord Reed; *Armes v. Nottinghamshire County Council* [2017] UKSC 60.

[275] Reg 6.4 (n).

[276] 'Baroda University Professor Held for Ragging Student', *India Today* (online, 21 October 2012) https://www.indiatoday.in/india/north/story/baroda-university-professor-held-for-ragging-student-119259-2012-10-20.

[277] 730 A 2d 1086 (Vt 1999) (Supreme Court of Vermont) (Vicarious liability was imposed on the University for hazing of students by upper classmen); see also *Emoakmeh v. Southern University* 654, So.2d 474 (LaCt app 1995).

[278] Srivastava et al. (n 196) p. 254. See also *Cox v. Ministry of Justice* [2016] UKSC 10.

3.7 Conclusion

It is abundantly clear from the regular episodes of hazing reported by the media that hazing was and is out of control, or there is no prospect of it being meaningfully controlled. Severe sentences have been imposed on hazers, yet, it continues. It is like any crime: the fact that it is punished does not mean that it can stop.

In 1998 the *Vishwa Jagriti Mission* brought the issue of hazing before the Supreme Court and sought its directions on how to save the victims of hazing. The Unny Committee, the Raghavan Committee, the Supreme Court directions, the UGC Regulations and the state anti-hazing legislation, all try to curtail hazing of freshers. Ironically, they have not had much success.

The Supreme Court of India has directed that hazing must be dealt with an iron hand. On the other hand, many cases decided by the High Courts have adopted a reformatory approach. It is worth repeating some of the remarks made by High Court judges: "Justice should be tempered with mercy, ... 'They know not what they do. Forgive them'".[279] Students are "vulnerable, ...they need to be valued, nurtured, caressed and protected".[280] Punishment should not "drive [students] out of the mainstream of the society".[281]

The Raghavan Committee Report made 50 very useful recommendations to contain hazing. In 2007, the Supreme Court, directed that some of those recommendations, stated below, must be immediately implemented without any further lapse of time.[282]

1. The punishment given to hazers must be exemplary and justifiably harsh so that it serves as a deterrent against future occurrences of hazing.
2. Every single incident of hazing where the victim or his parent/guardian or the Head of institution is not satisfied with the institutional arrangement for action, a First Information Report (FIR) must be filed with the local police. Any failure or delay in lodging the FIR should be construed as culpable negligence by the institutional authority.
3. Courts should ensure that cases involving hazing are taken up on a priority basis to send the correct message that hazing is not only to be discouraged but also to be dealt with sternness. Sri Lankan hazing legislation has similar provisions.
4. Schools must introduce hazing in their curriculum as part of the human rights subject to sensitise students early on about its evils.
5. The admission prospectus of universities must spell out that those involved in hazing in the past would not get admission and those already enrolled would be expelled from the institution.

---

[279] *T.T. Chakravarthy Yuvraj v. Principal, Dr. BR Ambedkar Medical College* AIR1997 Karnataka 261, para 18.

[280] W.P. (C) No. 25002 of 2017 and W.P. (C) No. 25003 of 2017 [18].

[281] *Sk. Nur Alam v. Director, College of Engineering and Management and Others* (2006)(3) CHN 291, para 14.

[282] Kerala (n 54) order dated May 16, 2007.

6. Central and State governments must launch a wide publicity about the menace of hazing and that serious consequences would follow in case any student is detected to have been involved.
7. It shall be the collective responsibility of the authorities and functionaries of the concerned institution and their role must also be open to scrutiny for the purpose of finding out whether they have taken effective steps for preventing hazing. In case of their failure, action must be taken; for example, denial of any grant-in-aid or assistance.
8. All universities must form anti-hazing committees (ARC) and anti-hazing squads (ARS) to prevent hazing.

These recommendations seem to offer some solutions to reduce hazing cases. However, the tragedy is that the recommendations were made 16 years ago and have not yet been properly implemented by academic institutions. Hazing still continues, and there is no reason to believe that any decrease in the incidents of hazing is possible in the near future. While we are writing the concluding part of this chapter, news has just come in that an engineering student in Andhra Pradesh and a medical student in Telangana, unable to bear the pain of hazing, committed suicide.[283]

[283] 'Student Commits Suicide Due to Ragging in Nellore', *ap7am.com* (online, 20 February 2023) http://www.ap7am.com/lv-371058-student-commits-suicide-due-to-ragging-in-nellore; 'Telangana Medical Student Dies Days After Attempting Suicide Over "Ragging"', *NDTV* (online, 27 February 2023) https://www.ndtv.com/india-news/telangana-student-who-attempted-suicide-over-harassment-by-senior-dies-3817286.

Chapter 4
Hazing in Sri Lanka

Student harassment, gender violence, and inhuman 'ragging' [hazing] must be condemned and eradicated from all universities.
—(National Education Commission (Sri Lanka), National Education Policy Framework (2020–2030) (June 2022))

Hazing (ragging) in Sri Lankan universities[1] has become increasingly vicious in the past four to five decades. In November 2022, the Higher Education State Minister told the media that unless drastic measures were adopted, extreme forms of hazing would not stop in Sri Lankan universities.[2]

Many senior students perceive hazing as part of socialisation and a way of initiating freshers into a new world.[3] According to them, it is a sub-culture (*Upa Sanskruthiya*) of higher education. However, on the pretext of familiarising freshers with the sub-culture of higher education, senior students commit atrocities and criminal activities against them.[4] Hazing has been responsible for many deaths, suicides, rapes, grievous hurt,[5] and severe mental health issues such as depression, anxiety and chronic stress.[6]

---

[1] The term "university" in this chapter refers generally to all institutions of higher education.

[2] Yoshitha Perera, 'Causes of University Rights Abuses Deep-Rooted', *The Sunday Times, Sri Lanka* (online, 6 November 2022) http://www.sundaytimes.lk/221106/news/causes-of-university-rights-abuses-deep-rooted-500930.html.

[3] Siri Gamage (2017) 'Psychological, Sociological, and Political Dimension of Ragging in Sri Lankan Universities', 1(7) *Social Affairs* 34; Hemamalie Gunatilaka, Dushan Jayawickrama, and Ananda Rathnayake (2022) 'Prevalence of Ragging and Sexual and Gender Based Violence in Sri Lankan State Universities', *UNICEF* https://www.unicef.org/srilanka/media/2431/file/Prevalence%20of%20Ragging%20and%20Sexual%20and%20Gender%20Based%20Violence.pdf, p. 1.

[4] Shatara Jayasinghe, 'Ragging Perpetuated under the Guise of Promoting University "Sub-Culture"', *DailyMirror* (online, 14 February 2017) https://www.dailymirror.lk/news-features/Ragging-perpetuated-under-the-guise-of-promoting-university-sub-culture/131-123786.

[5] Ibid.

[6] Anula Wijesundere, 'Menace of University Violence', *The Island Online* (online, 18 October 2021) http://island.lk/menace-of-university-violence/.

A. Srivastava et al., *Hazing (Ragging) at Universities: A Legal Perspective*,
https://doi.org/10.1007/978-981-99-5215-1_4

Hazing often takes place on university premises: it could be near lecture halls, tutorial rooms, student canteens, university roads and parks.[7] Freshers who are lucky get away with benign forms of hazing, such as reading a book upside down, following a dress code set by seniors, kneeling in front of senior students and approaching a person of the opposite sex to say something silly. However, in most cases, freshers suffer from brutal and abusive hazing. For example, male students have been forced to drink alcoholic cocktails, take off their clothes and be naked in front of others, masturbate in front of seniors and engage in pseudo-sexual acts.[8]

Sexual hazing,[9] sex and gender-based violence are mainly perpetrated against female and underprivileged students from remote areas.[10] They "are severely traumatised by the hazing experience, as many are unable to cope with the vulgarity, humiliation, sadism, obscene language, mental torture and cruelty perpetrated on them".[11]

Politics also plays a significant role in the hazing of freshers.[12] A study commissioned by the National Education Commission (NEC) in 2014 named Janatha Vimukthi Peramuna (JVP) as the political party responsible for hazing in universities.[13] Also, without naming JVP, the Vice-Chancellor (V.C.) of the University of Ruhuna stated that hazing was a political enterprise used by a particular political party to recruit students for demonstrations, picketing, and raising funds. In 2002, a third-year university student and an anti-hazing campaigner at the University of Sri Jayewardenepura was killed in a brutal attack by pro-hazing supporters and JVP members. The President of the General Students Union of the University affiliated

[7] Gunatilaka et al., (n 3) p. 10.

[8] Ibid.

[9] Hemantha Senanayake, '"Ragging" Is Dragging Sri Lanka Down', *DailyFT* (online, 10 June 2020) https://www.ft.lk/columns/Ragging-is-dragging-Sri-Lanka-down/4-701376; IG Premadasa, N C Wanigasooriya, L Thalib and A N B Ellepola (2011), 'Harassment of Newly Admitted Undergraduates by Senior Students in a Faculty of Dentistry in Sri Lanka,' 33(10) *Medical Teacher* 556, pp. 5, 6.

[10] Wijesundere (n 6). See also Gunatilaka et al. (n 3).

[11] Premadasa et al. (n 9). See also Wijesundere (n 6) p. 3 (A mathematics teacher at a university was tortured).

[12] *It's Not New, It's Corruption Itself (a Revelation from Ruhunu Chancellor) Talk With Chathura* (online, directed by Talk with Chatura, 28 September 2019) https://www.youtube.com/watch?v=idUG1dI3n5g; Wijesundere (n 6).

[13] Sujata Gamage, 'Ragging Is Responsible for the Misogynistic and Anti-Intellectual Culture in Our Universities', *Daily FT* (online, 11 June 2020) https://www.ft.lk/Columnists/Ragging-is-responsible-for-the-misogynistic-and-anti-intellectual-culture-in-our-universities/4-701438.

with the JVP (known as the 'Three Percent')[14] crashed a heavy computer monitor on the victim's head, fracturing his skull into tiny pieces. When other students tried to take the victim to the hospital, the party followers blocked all roads preventing the vehicle from reaching the hospital. Two days later, the victim died.[15]

Sri Lanka has taken various measures to control hazing. The *Prohibition of Ragging and Other Forms of Violence in Educational Institutions Act* (Anti-Hazing Act) was passed in 1998 to eradicate hazing in universities. The Anti-Hazing Act defines hazing as "any act which causes or is likely to cause physical or psychological injury or mental pain or fear to a student or a member of the staff of an educational institution".[16] In January 2010, the University Grants Commission of Sri Lanka (UGC-SL) issued Guidelines to curb the menace of hazing in universities.[17] The UGC-SL Guidelines require universities to take prescribed measures to prevent hazing and punish those involved in it. It also requires universities to set up anti-hazing helplines and report hazing cases to the relevant police station. In 2017, UGC-SL set up a 24 hour hazing helpline for students to call in case they face distress or violence.[18] Despite 3500 hazing complaints made to the helpline and the police in the past five years, investigations were made in only a few cases.[19] Unfortunately, professionals, such as Vice-chancellors and other senior university staff, despite being aware of hazing, accept it as an everyday occurrence of university life and ignore it.[20] UGC-SL Guidelines, the Anti-Hazing Act and the 24 hour helpline have also failed to stem the tide of hazing in universities.

This chapter begins with sociological background on hazing. It also analyses a few hazing cases to indicate the gravity of the problem and how this practice has spoiled the future of higher education students. We will then examine in detail the UGC-SL Guidelines, which outline measures to control hazing. The Guidelines were prepared to facilitate strict immediate implementation of the provisions of the Anti-Hazing Act 1998. Next, we analyse the Anti-Hazing Act, which requires universities to adopt strategies to prevent hazing, set out the procedures to be followed in dealing with it, and punish those involved in it. Next, we look at the judicial response to

---

[14] The General Students Union of University of Sri Jayewardenepura affiliated to the Inter University Students' Federation (IUSF), which was in the clutches of the Janatha Vimukthi Peramuna (JVP) known as the 'Three Percent', defended hazing. IUSF is now under JVP-breakaway faction, the Frontline Socialist Party. See Gagani Weerakoon, 'Samantha's Verdict a Watershed Moment', *Ceylon Today* (online, 11 June 2022) https://ceylontoday.lk/2022/06/11/samanthas-verdict-a-watershed-moment/.

[15] Nadira Gunatilleke, 'The Dark Side of Ragging in State Universities', *Sunday Observer* (online, 6 November 2022) https://www.sundayobserver.lk/2022/11/06/opinion/dark-side-ragging-state-universities.

[16] *Prohibition of Ragging and Other Forms of Violence in Educational Institutions Act, No 20 of 1998* (section 17) (Prohibiton Act).

[17] *Guidelines to be Introduced to Curb the Menace of Ragging in the Universities or Higher Educational Institutes (HEIs) [2010] 2010 (Guidelines).*

[18] Gunatilaka et al. (n 3).

[19] Perera (n 2).

[20] Wijesundere (n 6) p. 5.

hazing. A criminal case decided in 1998 shows that the attitude of the courts is likely to be tough against hazers.[21] We then look into the possibility of a civil action in tort. Sri Lanka is a common law country, so tort actions like assault, battery, false imprisonment, defamation and negligence should be available to a victim of hazing. Finally, we make some observations in the conclusion section of this chapter.

4.1 Sociological Background in Sri Lanka

Sri Lanka "is a multicultural, multilingual country consisting of an ethnoreligious blend of Sinhalese (75%), Sri Lankan Tamils (11%), Moors (Muslims) (9%) and other groups (5%).[22] Its official languages are Sinhala, Tamil and English". A drastic change happened in Sri Lanka after the cessation of colonial rule in 1948. While during the colonial rule, the power was vested in the elitist class and students from this class overwhelmingly went for higher education. After independence, every person, rich or poor, was welcome to the university. Thus, the demography of the university changed. "The majority of English-speaking urban upper and the middle class was replaced by Sinhalese and Tamil speaking lower classes from lesser privileged backgrounds".[23] The medium of instruction was also changed from English to Sinhalese and Tamil. Senior students from lower socio-economic backgrounds saw the elite students as enemies who needed to be tamed and put in their place.[24]

However, hazing was not reported as a problem in the early phases of post-independent Sri Lankan higher education. The first two cases of hazing were reported in 1975. The first case concerned hazing of teachers in government schools attending a diploma course at a university. The second case was quite serious. A 22-year girl was inhumanely harassed. She jumped from the top floor of Peradeniya University Building to escape from hazers. Unfortunately, she was severely injured and became permanently disabled. She lived her miserable life for 27 years but then committed suicide.[25]

---

[21] *Priyangani Navraten and Ors v. Chandrasena* (1998) 1 Sri L.R.170.

[22] *Department of Census and Statistics. Census of Population and Housing 2011* http://www.statistics.gov.lk.

[23] Ayanthi Wickramasinghe, Pia Axemo, Birgitta Essén and Jill Trenholm (2022) 'Ragging as an Expression of Power in a Deeply Divided Society; a Qualitative Study on Students Perceptions on the Phenomenon of Ragging at a Sri Lankan University *Plos One* https://journals.plos.org/plosone/article?id=10.1371/journal.pone.0271087, p. 2.

[24] Gamage (n 3) p. 37.

[25] Saleem Marsoof et al. (2020) 'Redressing Victims of Ragging and Providing a Regulatory Mechanism to Prevent Ragging in Sri Lankan Universities', https://www.academia.edu/44968993/Redressing_Victims_of_Ragging_and_Providing_a_Regulatory_Mechanism_to_Prevent_Ragging_in_Sri_Lankan_Universities, p. 5.

Hazing has become deep-rooted in the past four to five decades.[26] From 1974 to 2022, approximately 25 undergraduate students have died because of hazing.[27] In October 2022, the Court of Appeal upheld the death sentence given to the accused, who, as part of hazing, was responsible for the murder of a fresher at Peradeniya University in 1997.[28] In addition, hazing rituals have made students permanently disabled.[29] In March 2022, a student was descending the stairs when a group of senior students threw a tractor tyre down the stairs. It hit the student and he fell on the ground with his head hitting the floor, causing severe damage to his brain. The doctors said he was physically paralysed and would never be able to recover fully.[30]

According to a study, 57% of university students face hazing.[31] More than half (51%) go through psychological hazing, one-third (34%) physical hazing and 17% sexual hazing.[32] In 2014, a student and his friend were hospitalised for severe injuries caused by sexual abuse during hazing. The student later committed suicide.[33] According to a media report dated 3 May 2020, around 20 university students have committed suicide because of hazing.[34]

The most common effect of hazing is that students give up their higher education. The Ministry of Education informs that approximately 2000 students drop out of universities every year because of hazing.[35] Those victims of hazing who manage to stay back, unfortunately, become future aggressors.[36]

The UGC-SL Committee interviewed many students and provided some relevant details of those interviews.[37]

---

[26] Perera (n 2).

[27] Gunatilleke (n 15).

[28] 'Engineering Faculty Student's Murder in 1997 Following Severe Ragging: Appeal Court Upholds Death Sentence for Convict' *Daily Mirror* (online, 28 October 2022) https://www.dailymirror.lk/breaking_news/Engineering-faculty-students-murder-in-1997-following-severe-ragging-Appeal-Court-upholds-death-sentence-for-convict/108-247643.

[29] Himaya Perera and Asiri Ekanayake, 'Tradition vs Trauma: Hazing in Universities Worsen', *The Sunday Times* (online, 3 May 2020) https://www.pressreader.com/sri-lanka/sunday-times-sri-lanka/20200503/282664689550934.

[30] Ibid.

[31] Ayanthi Wickramasinghe et al. (2022) 'Ragging, a Form of University Violence in Sri Lanka—Prevalence, Self-Perceived Health Consequences, Help-Seeking Behavior and Associated Factors', 19(14) *International Journal of Environmental Research and Public Health* 8383, p. 7.

[32] Gunatilaka et al. (n 3).

[33] Gunatilleke (n 15).

[34] Perera and Ekanayake (n 29).

[35] Senanayake (n 9).

[36] Wijesundere (n 6).

[37] A student said there was no hazing in the first week of orientation; hazing began a week after; initial hazing was in the form of verbal abuse, which later changed to hard physical hazing. The new students were assaulted and beaten by senior students. They could not attend most of their lectures due to injuries or pass their examinations; A male student was asked to perform obscene sexual acts as a rapist and masturbate. He was assaulted for not following seniors' orders promptly. In one incident, the blow was so hard that he fell to the ground, his knees dislocated, and his spine damaged. He was taken to the therapy room. Although a senior student applied some oil or cream

4.2 UGC-SL's Guidelines to Curb the Menace of Hazing

The UGC-SL in its circular (No. 919) dated 15 January 2010 acknowledged that the level of hazing in universities is simply alarming. It causes death, permanent physical and mental disability and includes cruel, criminal, inhumane torturing of freshers like animals. Further, the universities have not profitably used the powers vested in them under the Anti-Hazing Act 1998.[38] All this prompted the UGC-SL to issue Guidelines to curb the mence of hazing. The UGC-SL Guidelines explain what acts constitute hazing against any student or a member of staff (victim). The UGC-SL Guidelines detail forms of hazing, prevention measures, procedures to be followed in the event of hazing and punishment to those found guilty of hazing under the Anti-Hazing Act.

Forms of Hazing:

1. Sexual harassment or causing grievous hurt to the victim.
2. Threatening (verbally or in writing) to cause injury to the victim's person, reputation or property or another person in whom the victim is interested. Compelling the victim to do any act which the victim is legally not required to do or to omit to do any act which the victim is entitled to do.
3. Restraining the personal liberty and the freedom of movement of the victim; or another person in whom the victim is interested without lawful justification and for the purpose of forcing the victim to take a particular course of action.
4. Unlawfully obstructing the victim from proceeding in any direction in which such victim has the right to proceed.
5. Unlawfully restraining the victim in such a manner as to prevent him from proceeding beyond certain circumscribed limits.

---

on his legs and backside, they "continued to abuse him sexually"; A female student was attacked with rotten eggs, and she left the educational institution soon after this incident; Freshers were required to pass on a salivated toffee to other students from mouth-to-mouth; Freshers were asked to write the names of 100 batchmates within a short period of time. If a fresher made any mistake, he had to write all the names again. Freshers as a part of hazing were forced to consume alcohol and not allowed to drink water. In one incident hazers forcibly shaved a fresher until his face started bleeding. They also made him spend all the money on unnecessary things. Although he complained to the authorities, but nothing happened. Some academic staff also favoured hazing; A monk who was a student explained his plight. He had to bathe naked with 64 other monks and sleep in the same tiny room as others. He could defecate but was allowed to use only a tiny bit of water to clean himself; A hazed student was required to memorise 250 batchmate names. She was also ordered to serve drinks to male students until 4 am in the morning; A fresher was raped on three occasions, the last occasion by six senior students. His hands and legs were tied to the bed. He felt he was going to die. Seniors also penetrated him with an iron rod which made him bleed profusely from his anus. He complained to the university's security office and police, but they did nothing; A student wanted to move to a different university because of hazing. However, the Vice Chancellor instructed her to make a formal request without disclosing hazing as the reason for changing the university. See Marsoof et. al. (n 25).

[38] *Guidelines* (n 17).

6. Unlawfully occupying any premises under the management or control of an educational institution.
7. Causing any mischief in respect of any property of or under the management or control of an educational institution.[39]

Measures Universities Must Take to Prevent Hazing

The UGC-SL Guidelines state that all the possible steps must be taken by the university to prevent hazing. The idea is to create a university environment free of hazing. University staff, (academic and non-academic) have an obligation to control hazing. The UGC-SL Guidelines require universities to:

1. take an undertaking from new students[40] that they will not "aid, abet, participate in any form of hazing or violence"; the template is also required to be countersigned by the student's parent or guardian.[41]
2. appoint an Anti-hazing Committee, both at the university and faculty level.[42]
3. prepare a handout detailing acts constituting hazing and punishments for such acts.
4. appoint an academic staff as Temporary Student Counsellor for a period of three months or more from the beginning of the academic year.[43]
5. educate heads of departments, unit heads, parents and new entrants on all aspects of hazing and the Anti-Hazing Act.
6. display anti-hazing posters in prominent places and brief security staff on the measures to be taken to prevent hazing.
7. inform senior students of the consequences of hazing.
8. conduct an orientation programme, especially for freshers and educate them on possible hazing locations and procedures to be followed if subjected to hazing.
9. inform local police of the places and periods of time when hazing is most likely to occur.
10. make the media aware of measures taken to curb hazing and create public awareness.
11. encourage the presence of student counsellors and sub-wardens for longer hours on campus on a voluntary and roster basis.
12. initiate student-friendly and safer innovative programmes or activities to familiarise freshers with the educational environment and culture.[44]

---

[39] Ibid.

[40] See Appendix B.

[41] Ibid.

[42] The Committee shall consists of Vice-Chancellor, Deputy Vice-Chancellor, Deans, one Council member representing the UGC and several other staff and University Medical Officer.

[43] The Guidelines state that no counsellor should deal with more than 20–25 students.

[44] *Guidelines* (n 17) No. 1.1–1.16.

Procedure Universities Must Follow in the Event of Hazing

1. Record all complaints relating to hazing; follow the procedure prescribed in the Anti- Hazing Act and report the matter to the relevant police station.
2. Encourage the victims of hazing to provide as much evidence as possible, including details of injuries, names of witnesses and photographs or videos, etc.
3. Refer the victims of hazing for medical or psychiatric examination and request for a medical report, if necessary.
4. In case of grievous injuries to the victim or any punishable act by the wrongdoer under the Penal Code and the Convention against Torture and Other Cruel, Inhuman or Degrading Treatment or Punishment Act, No 22 of 1994, report to the police.
5. Obtain details of damage caused to the university or public property as a result of hazing.
6. Report all incidents of hazing and the punishments meted out to the wrongdoer (under the Anti-Hazing Act) to the UGC.[45]

It came to the notice of the UGC-SL that universities were using different procedures concerning student disciplinary matters. To correct that, the UGC issued on 2 November 2011 a Circular (Number 946) providing a new procedure for dealing with a charge of misconduct/indiscipline against a student. The circular empowers the head of an institution to impose an out-of-bounds declaration on students whose infringement of discipline was so severe that it amounted to an offence.[46]

Punishment to the Wrongdoer

The UGC-SL Guidelines emphasise that hazing is a serious offence under the Anti-Hazing Act 1998. Several offences under this Act are non-bailable. Apart from these punishments, a student could also be expelled from the institution and made to pay compensation for any damage to property due to hazing and for injuries caused to the victim.

Other Measures Taken by the UGC to Control Hazing

The UGC has established a Centre for Gender Equity and Equality to help student victims of hazing. A special unit at the Centre deals with hazing complaints. The UGC has also established a 24 × 7 emergency hotline. On this hotline, students can report about hazing incidents, sexual harassment and bullying. After making a complaint to the educational authorities about the hazing incident, the victims should lodge a complaint with the local police station.[47]

---

[45] Ibid, No. 2.1–2.8.

[46] Abdul Raheem Mohamed Zulfi (2021) 'A Critical Review of Legal Interventions for Combatting Ragging in Sri Lankan Universities: A Case Study of South Eastern University of Sri Lanka' in *2nd Asia International Conference on Multidisciplinary Research 2020,* http://ir.lib.seu.ac.lk/handle/123456789/5314.

[47] Ibid.

Further, a Mobile App was launched in 2017 for state university students, enabling them to instantly inform the authorities of hazing incidents. The Mobile App can be used by students 24 hour of the day to call in case they face distress or violence.[48] The UGC is required to monitor student complaints, identify students' current location and the address of the local police station. In case the UGC receives a distress call from a student about ongoing hazing the local police station must be immediately alerted.[49]

4.3 Legislation on Hazing

Hazing can be punished under the Universities Act, No 16 of 1978 (The Universities Act); the Convention Against Torture and Other Cruel, Inhuman or Degrading Treatment or Punishment Act, No 22 of 1994; the Penal Code 345 of 1995; and the Prohibition of Hazing and other forms of Violence in Educational Institutions Act No 20 of 1998 (Anti-Hazing Act).[50]

4.3.1 Universities Act 1978

Under section 131 of the Universities Act, where the presence of any person on the precincts of a university is undesirable, the head (Vice Chancellor) of that institution, after giving such person an opportunity of being heard, prohibit them from entering or remaining on such precincts or part of such precincts as specified. Thus, a student who is involved in hazing may be refused entry to their university by the Vice Chancellor. A similar action can also be taken by the Vice Chancellors or Heads of other universities if they feel that the presence of such a person is undesirable in their university. According to the Act, such prohibition remains in force until withdrawn. Disobeying prohibition is treated as an offence, and the wrongdoer may be asked to pay a fine of one hundred rupees per day or part thereof.[51] The offender can also be separately sued for hazing.

---

[48] Gunatilaka (n 3).

[49] Ibid.

[50] This Act was gazetted after a student in 1997 committed suicide due to hazing.

[51] Section 131 of the Universities Act 1978. See also Mohamed Zulfi (n 46).

4.3.2 Convention Against Torture and Other Cruel, Inhuman or Degrading Treatment or Punishment Act (Anti-torture Act)

The Constitution of Sri Lanka recognises the fundamental right of a person not to be tortured or subjected to inhuman or degrading treatment or punishment.[52] Under the Anti-Torture Act, any person torturing or intentionally inflicting severe pain and suffering on a person (that frequently happens in hazing cases) must be awarded imprisonment for a period, "not less than seven years but not more than ten years".[53] The offences committed under this Act are non-bailable.

Some of the examples of torture explicitly focus what hazers do to freshers. Freshers have been asked to imitate a rapist, masturbate, and inflict hard blows to themselves resulting in dislocation of knees and damage to their spine. A freshers was raped by six senior students while his hands and legs were tied to the bed. Seniors also penetrated his anus with an iron rod which made him bleed profusely. Even monks, as noted before, have not been spared. 64 monks were forced to sleep in the same tiny room and not allowed to clean themselves properly after defecation.

4.3.3 Penal Code 345 of 1995

Sexual and Gender Based Violence (SGBV) can be dealt with under the Penal Code 345 of 1995. If a student is raped, their remedy lies under s. 363 of the Penal Code.[54] In addition, the Constitution of Sri Lanka enables a person to seek punishment for hazing for their human rights violations.[55]

4.3.4 Prohibition of Hazing and Other Forms of Violence in Educational Institutions Act No 20 of 1998 (Anti-hazing Act)

The Anti-Hazing Act was specifically enacted to prevent and punish hazing. Hazing is now a distinct offence under this Act. The provisions of the Anti-Hazing Act are not affected by the Universities Act 1978, the Convention Against Torture and Other Cruel, Inhuman or Degrading Treatment or Punishment Act, No 22 of 1994 or any other law. This is so because the provisions of the Anti-Hazing Act are in addition

---

[52] Constitution of Sri Lanka, Art 11.

[53] Convention Against Torture and Other Cruel, Inhuman or Degrading Treatment or Punishment Act (Sec. 2).

[54] *Penal Code (Ordinance No. 2 of 1883)* s. 363.

[55] *Constitution of the Democratic Socialist Republic of Sri Lanka 1978* (Art. 126).

to and not in derogation of the provisions of any other law.[56] The Anti-Hazing Act states, "Every Court shall give priority to the trial of any person charged with any offence under this Act...".[57] All offences under the Anti-Hazing Act are deemed cognisable.[58] It means that the police can arrest the accused without any warrant.

Under the Anti-Hazing Act any person who commits or participates in hazing within or outside an educational institution is guilty of an offence. After a summary trial before a magistrate, the hazer can be sentenced to rigorous imprisonment for a term not exceeding two years and ordered to pay compensation to the victim.[59]

The Act also criminalises sexual harassment that sometimes occurs during hazing. In addition, the Act criminalises hostage-taking, wrongful restraint, and unlawful confinement. Section 2(2) of the Act provides that a person who, whilst committing hazing, causes sexual harassment, or grievous hurt to any student or a member of the staff, is liable to a term of imprisonment and compensation as determined by the court. Sexual harassment or infliction of grievous hurt are considered serious offences: the maximum term of imprisonment for such offences is ten years on conviction after a summary trial, and bail cannot be granted to the accused except by a judge of the High Court.[60] It should be noted that provisions of the Anti-Hazing Act protect not only a student but also a member of staff.

The Anti-Hazing Act forbids criminal intimidation within or outside an educational institution.[61] A number of activities within and outside an educational institution against any student or staff member are considered criminal intimidation. These include threatening (verbally or in writing), causing injury to any person (student or staff) or damage to their reputation or property. Criminal intimidation action can also be brought against a hazer for damaging another person's reputation or property in whom the victim is interested. The hazer in the above situations can be liable to rigorous imprisonment for a term not exceeding five years.

Depriving a student or a member of staff, or another person on the educational premises or any other premises of their liberty and freedom without lawful justification is an offence under Anti-Hazing Act.[62] The hazer, on conviction, can be awarded rigorous imprisonment for a term not exceeding seven years.

Wrongful restraint or unlawful confinement of any student or staff by the hazer is also an offence under the Anti-Hazing Act. For wrongful restraint, the hazer can be liable for rigorous imprisonment for a term not exceeding seven years.[63] On the other hand, for unlawful confinement within a certain limit, the punishment is for a term not exceeding seven years.[64]

---

[56] *Prohibition Act (n 16)* s 14.

[57] Ibid, s 15.

[58] Ibid, s 11.

[59] Ibid, s 2.

[60] Ibid, s 9.

[61] Ibid, s 3.

[62] Ibid, s 4.

[63] Ibid, s 5.

[64] Ibid, s 6.

Forcible occupation of any premises by a person under the management or control of an educational institution is an offence under the Anti-Hazing Act. Such activities may not be regarded as hazing, but since an educational institution's property is involved, the Anti-Hazing Act makes them punishable. The punishment mandated is imprisonment for a term not exceeding ten years, a fine not exceeding ten thousand rupees, or both imprisonment and fine.[65] Likewise, if a person causes mischief (i.e. loss, destruction or any damage to property: sec 408, Penal Code of Sri Lanka) in connection with any property under the management or control of an educational institution, such person commits an offence. The punishment for such mischief is imprisonment for a term not exceeding twenty years and a fine of five thousand rupees or three times the amount of loss or damage caused to such property, whichever amount is higher.[66] Where a person convicted is a student of an educational institution, they can be expelled from the institution. If the person convicted is a staff member, they could be dismissed by the educational institution.[67]

If a person, while committing hazing, also sexually harasses or causes grievous hurt to any student or member of staff or is suspected of committing the crime of hostage-taking, the wrongdoer cannot be released on bail except by a judge of the High Court.[68] Where a person is convicted for such an offence (sexual harassment, grievous hurt, hostage-taking) under the Anti-Hazing Act,[69] and an appeal is preferred against the conviction, the appellate court may, by taking into consideration the gravity of the offence and the antecedents of the offender, either release or refuse to release the offender on bail.[70]

Section 10 of Anti-Hazing Act states that where a person is convicted for sexual harassment, grievous hurt, or hostage-taking under the Anti-Hazing Act, the provisions of sec. 303 and sec. 306 of the Code of Criminal Procedure Act, No.15 1979 do not apply. Section 303 allows the court to impose suspended sentences of imprisonment in some cases, and sec. 306 of the Code also empowers the court to conditionally release the offenders.[71] It seems that the underlying reason for such strict provisions in section 10 is not to soften the rigour of the Anti-Hazing Act.

---

65 Ibid s 7(1).

66 Ibid, s 7(2).

67 Ibid, s 8.

68 Ibid, s 9(1). See also Art. 154P of the *Constitution of the Democratic Socialist Republic of Sri Lanka 1978*; Bail Act (No. 30 of 1997).

69 Ibid, s 2(2) and s 4.

70 Ibid, s 9.

71 See also Mohamed Zulfi (n 46).

4.4 Supreme Court's Approach to Hazing

An interesting case on hazing decided by the Supreme Court of Sri Lanka is *Priyangani Navaratne and others v. Chandrassena.*[72] Eight petitioners (three females and five males) were found guilty of hazing. They were enrolled in a teachers training programme at a college. One day seniors (petitioners) and freshers were playing at the college playground. After a while, petitioners put freshers into a separate group, and all kinds of atrocities were committed by the petitioners on the freshers. No petitioner was in any way less guilty than the other. The President of the College, the respondent, informed the petitioners that the Disciplinary Committee of the College had found them guilty of hazing freshers and that their internships were terminated for one month in the case of females and two months in the case of males. The Secretary to the Ministry of Higher Education amended the Disciplinary Code to include hazing and gave the College power and responsibility with respect to hazing offences. In the meantime, there was a further investigation by the Disciplinary Committee of the College and the punishment of all the petitioners was enhanced: the male petitioners were expelled from the College and the female petitioners' termination of internship was extended for a further period of one year. The petitioners objected to the second punishment. They argued that the enhanced punishment violated their constitutional rights under Article 12 (1) of the Constitution. The petitioners explained that the amended provisions of the Code by which the petitioners' punishment was enhanced was a second punishment for the same offence as the amended provisions were sought to be given retrospective operation and, therefore, unconstitutional. The court, having found that the petitioner's conduct constituted severe hazing, said it was wholly inequitable to grant them any relief. The court observed:

> The petitioner's conduct is extremely serious....hazing is sometimes sought to be justified as being a necessary part of orientation....Such hazing may be tolerated, if at all, if it is clean fun; but it is totally unacceptable if it causes pain or suffering, physical, mental or emotional distress, to the victims....It was cruel, inhuman and degrading to ill-treat or torment persons to the point of pain and exhaustion requiring hospitalisation.[73]

The court further said that "the public interest demands deterrent, rather than lenient punishment for admitted or proven misconduct. and in my view the punishments first imposed were wholly inadequate for what the petitioners did. To restore those punishments would be to condone the violation of the rights of the newcomers".[74]

The court held that no relief should be granted to the petitioners. The petitioners' offence was so serious that they could have also been given the same enhanced punishment the first time.

---

[72] (1998) 1Sri LR 170.

[73] (1998) 1Sri LR 170, p. 173.

[74] (1998) 1Sri LR 170, p. 174.

4.5 Liability in Tort Law

Sri Lanka's common law of tort is the Roman-Dutch law but at the same time English law concepts of tort law have been infused. Tort law is part of 'delict' and refers to an actionable wrong. Delict, known as, "damnum injuria datum" was created by the *Lex Acquillia* in 287 B.C., a remedy for pecuniary loss (damnum) wrongfully caused (injuria datum). It covers injury or damage to a person, their property and dignity. The plaintiff will be required to prove that the defendant breached its duty of care or statutory duty.[75] Prof. R.G. McKerron, defines delict as:

> The breach of a duty imposed by law, independently of the will of the party bound, which will ground an action for damages at the suit of any person to whom the duty was owed and who has suffered harm in consequence of the breach.[76]

The principle *Lex Aquilian* and *Actio Injuriaurum* are the foundation stone of the law of delict. Where a hazer, intentionally or negligently causes any harm to the victim, the latter can sue for intentional or negligent tort. The tort law also endorses liability for other's action where the necessary criteria for the imposition of vicarious liability can be established. Under the vicarious liability where a university employee has breached its duty to protect its students, the university can be vicariously liable.[77]

4.5.1 Intentional Torts

In England the torts of assault, battery and false imprisonment were created to prevent breaches of the peace. For a smooth and peaceful environment it was considered that violence should be controlled by the state. In this context all these torts were considered appropriate to make defendant liable for their conduct of inflicting harm or threatening to do so.

- Assault and Battery

Under the Roman-Dutch law, the plaintiff can file a civil action against the defendant for assault in the same way as in English law.[78] "The wrong of assault of another without any justification constitutes a delict".[79] Physical contact with the body of the plaintiff assaulted is not necessary for a claim in assault. It is sufficient that the acts or gestures of one party puts another in a reasonable fear of immediate violence.[80]

---

[75] Evidence Ordinance (sec. 101) provides that "Whoever desires any court to give judgment as to any legal right or liability dependent on the existence of facts which he asserts, must prove that those facts exist".

[76] See R G McKerron, *The law of Delict* (6th Platinum reprinted, August 2009) p. 5.

[77] In the modern Roman Dutch law, English law doctrine of vicarious liability has been adopted.

[78] See UL Abdul Majeed, *A Modern Treatise on the Law of Delict (Tort)* (self-pub, 2017) p. 527.

[79] Wijeyadasadasa Rajapakshe, *The Law Of Delict* (self-pub, 2022) p. 77.

[80] Ibid, p. 77.

Throwing a missile at the plaintiff which does not touch the plaintiff or shaking one's fist or pointing a gun or another dangerous fire arm at the plaintiff is an assault. The bodily movement of the defendant must cause a reasonable apprehension in the mind of the plaintiff that the use of force against the plaintiff is imminent.[81] Where the defendant assaults the plaintiff in self defence, no action in tort would lie.[82]

In contrast to assault, battery means direct and intentional application of force to another without that person's consent and without any legal justification. For battery, it is not essential that there must be any actual physical contact between the defendant and the plaintiff. For example, it is battery if a stone thrown by the defendant strikes the plaintiff, although there was no actual physical contact between between the plaintiff and the defendant.[83]

During hazing seniors are often involved in various activities that would constitute the torts of assault and battery. Where hazers use foul language or rude gestures, creating a reasonable apprehension in the fresher's mind that use of force against them is imminent, such behaviour would give rise to an action in assault. Making threatening telephone calls to a fresher could amount to assault. Likewise, sending threating email or WhatsApp messages which cause reasonable apprehension in the mind of a fresher that violence would be perpetrated against the fresher is also assault. On the other hand, beating, kicking, punching, or grabbing a fresher from the fresher's hair amounts to battery.[84] It would also be battery to physically or sexually violate a fresher without the fresher's consent. Kissing a girl without her express or implied consent is battery.[85] Lastly, in serious cases of battery (for example rape and sodomy) aggravated and punitive damages could also be awarded.[86]

The Sri Lankan Federation of University Teachers Association has remarked that hazing incidents involving beating, bucketing, forcing freshers to perform vigorous exercises or wear particular clothes frequently happens in the guise of hazing.[87] A study conducted at the University of Colombo found that one in five (20.7%) medical students face physical violence and 5.0% sexual violence during their time at the university. All such affected students have a case in the torts of assault and battery. When the plaintiff gets grievous injures due to the defendant's vehicle running into him or the plaintiff is beaten with iron rods, the plaintiff has a case in battery.[88]

---

[81] Majeed (n 78). pp. 526, 527. See also *R v. Jolly* 1923 A D 176 at 179. See also *R v. Umfaan* (1908) TS 62; In *Barton v. Armstrong*, it was held that if it was made clear to the plaintiff that violence against him would occur in future, assault was committed. [1969] 2 NSWLR 451.

[82] *Mulvullha v. Steenkamp* 1917 CPD 571; *Perera v. Perera* 48 NLR 575.

[83] Majeed (n 78) p. 526.

[84] See DK Srivastava and AD Tennekone, *The Law of Tort in Hong Kong* (4th ed) pp. 92, 93.

[85] *F v. West Berkshire Health Authority* 1990 2 AC 1.

[86] *W v. Meah* [1986] All ER 935.

[87] University Grants Commission, Federation of University Teachers' Association, and CARE International Sri Lanka (2015) 'Preventing Sexual and Gender-Based Violence (SGBV) Strategies for Universities', https://www.ugc.ac.lk/downloads/publications/SGVB.pdf.

[88] *Krishnan Nalinda Priyadarshan v. Kandana* SC Appeal No 67/2012. See also Priya Soyza 2001 2 SLR 293; *Priyangini Navaratne and others v. Chandrassena* (1998) Sri LR 170.

As mentioned above, a students union leader crashed a heavy computer monitor on the victim's head.[89] In another case seniors threw a tractor tyre while a fresher was descending down the stairs. He fell to the ground and suffered severe brain damage.[90] In both these cases, the plaintiff could have had a cause of action in battery.

- False Imprisonment

False imprisonment means putting a total restraint on a person's freedom of movement without any reasonable means of escape.[91] Imprisonment here has not been used in the same sense as imprisonment in a prison under the control of the police. Our focus is on delictual remedies, i.e., damages. Atkin LJ said[92] that "it appears to me that a person could be imprisoned without knowing it ... while he is asleep or while he is in a state of drunkenness or while he is unconscious or while he is lunatic".[93] Thus, the tort of false imprisonment is committed even if the plaintiff was unware of his detention.[94] However in such cases the, the plaintiff will get no more than nominal damages.[95] It is a defence that the defendant did not take any part in the imprisonment of the plaintiff and that he simply gave certain information to an officer of law who in his own discretion arrested the plaintiff.

Hazing scenarios can be taken into account to explain when a successful action in false imprisonment would succeed. These include locking a fresher in a classroom or hostel room; kidnapping and bringing the fresher to an unknown place from where the fresher could not escape. False imprisonment of a fresher as part hazing, which is a forbidden activity would attract greater punishment. The victim could also receive aggravated and punitive damages. Where the defendant acted maliciously towards the victim, this should also be taken into account in assessing damages.[96]

It is a defence that the plaintiff was detained at a certain place because the plaintiff had consented to it;[97] but it is no defence that defendant made an inevitable mistake[98]

---

[89] Gunatilleke (n 15).

[90] Himaya Perera and Asiri Ekanayake, 'Tradition vs Trauma: Hazing in Universities Worsen', *The Sunday Times* (online, 3 May 2020) https://www.pressreader.com/sri-lanka/sunday-times-sri-lanka/20200503/282664689550934.

[91] See *Prohibition Act (n 16)* (secs 4–6). It is a criminal offence to restrict a persons liberty and freedom of movement.

[92] *Meering v. Grahame-White Aviation Co Ltd* (1920) 122 LT 44, approved obiter by the House of Lords in *Murray v. Minister of Defence* [1988] 1 WLR 692.

[93] *Meering v. Graham-White* (1920) 122, L.T. 44; Majeed (n 78), p. 531.

[94] Majeed (n 78), p. 531; *Meering v. Grahame-White Aviation Co Ltd* (1920) 122 LT 44. Ed, (2020) p. 88.

[95] Rajapakshe (n 79), p. 245. See also *Prohibition Act (n 16)* s 11 & 13); *Gunawardena v. Perara* 1983 (1) SLR 305.

[96] Majeed (n 78) p. 532.

[97] See *Herd v. Weardale Steel, Coke & Cole Co Ltd* (1915) AC 67, per Solomon J, p. 268; *Mohamado Abdulla v. Lushington* (1909) 13 NLR 38.

[98] See *Davidson v. Johannesberg Turf Club* (1904) T.H. 260.

and that the wrongful act was committed in good faith and without negligence. Thus to succeed, the plaintiff is merely required to establish that he was falsely imprisoned.[99]

- Defamation

Defamation is the publication of a defamatory statement concerning the plaintiff without any lawful justification or excuse which injures the plaintiff's reputation among the right thinking members of society. It is also defamation to make others shun or avoid the plaintiff.[100] Defamation is publication of any matter with the intention (*animus injuriandi*) of injuring the plaintiff's reputation and to bring plaintiff into hatred, contempt or ridicule or lower the plaintiff's esteem. The defendant must intend to have serious consequences of the statement.[101]

Thus, the false imputation that the plaintiff has committed a crime, or was involved in cheating and blackmailing others to extort money is a defamatory statement. In the context of hazing, there are several false imputations against the plaintiff that could lead to a claim in defamation. These include allegations of unchastity to a girl, accusing her of participating in orgies, or incest.[102] Forcing male students to wander around naked in streets or in the presence of huge crowd[103] could also lead to a cause of action in defamation. "Where, in an action for defamation the words used by the defendant are prima facie actionable it is not necessary to give proof of special damage. Plaintiff may recover a verdict for damages without giving evidence of actual pecuniary loss".[104] The Roman-Dutch law and English law of defamation appear to be practically identical, except that English law distinguishes between spoken and written defamation, i.e., slander and libel.[105]

(i) *Publication*

The defendant's defamatory statement must be published to a third party. Communication to the plaintiff or their spouse is not treated as being a communication to a third party.[106]

Publication will be presumed where the defamatory statement is contained in a newspaper or a book. Spoken words, speeches and statements are supposed to be heard by the persons within the earshot. *Fernando v Fernando*[107] made it explicit

---

[99] Ibid.

[100] Majeed (n 78) p. 602.

[101] Ibid, p. 610; Voet Commentary [47:10.20] on the Pandects.

[102] Tina Kelly, 'When the Cool Get Hazed', *The New York Times* (online, 26 September 2009) http://www.nytimes.com/2009/09/27/weekinreview/27kelly.html?_r=3&ref=education.

[103] Joe Faretra, 'University Students Performed Naked Hazing Dance Ritual in Front of Women', *Dailystar.co.uk* (online, 19 July 2022) https://www.dailystar.co.uk/news/world-news/university-students-performed-naked-hazing-27516522.

[104] *Wickramanayake v. The Times of Ceylon Ltd* 29 NLR 547.

[105] Majeed (n 78) p. 601.

[106] Ibid, p. 604.

[107] 26 N.L.R 84. Ibid, p. 603.

that the plaintiff must show that the words were intended to allege defamatory connotation.

For example, where a defendant called the plaintiff, son of a whore. If this statement was intended to allege the plaintiff's base birth, it would be treated as defamatory.[108] On the other hand, where these words were just mere vulgar abuse and there is no possibility of any defamatory connotation, the plaintiff would not succeed.[109]

(ii) *The defamatory statement must refer to the plaintiff*

The defamatory statement must refer to the plaintiff either by their name or by their position or designation or by some acronym or nickname. The test is objective; if a reasonable person would have thought that the defendant's defamatory statement referred to the plaintiff, the plaintiff's identification will be treated as proved.

(iii) *Damages and maliciously published defamatory statement*

As far as damages for defamation is concerned, they are in line with damages for personal injuries. Apart from compensatory damages, aggravated and punitive damages can also be awarded in an appropriate case.[110] The plaintiff's 'plaint' or complaint might include the words, 'the defendant's statement was made maliciously' to inflate the plaintiff's damages.[111]

4.5.2 University's Liability in Negligence

The concept of duty of care was unknown in the Roman-Dutch law. It was imported from English law.[112]

- Duty of care

The test laid down by *Caparo v Dickman* is currently applied to determine whether a duty of care exists in a certain situation to make the defendant liable. Lord Bridge, adopting a three-fold test for duty, said:

> What emerges is that, in addition to the foreseeability of damage, necessary ingredients in any situation giving rise to a duty of care are that there should exist between the party owing

[108] Ibid, p. 603.

[109] Ibid, p. 603. *Thorley v. Kerry* (1812) 4 Taunt, 355, p. 365. See also *Philip v. Barthelot* (1863–68) Ram. 189; Lalith W Athulathmudali (1964) 'The Law of Defamation in Ceylon: A Study in the Inter-Action of English and Roman-Dutch Law', 13(4) *The International and Comparative Law Quarterly* 1368.

[110] Iulia Filip, 'Cox Accused of Defamation in Hazing Story', *Courthouse News* (online, 14 June 2012) https://www.courthousenews.com/cox-accused-of-defamation-in-hazing-story/.

[111] Majeed (n 78) p. 604.

[112] Rajapakshe (n 79) p. 150.

> the duty and the party to whom it is owed a relationship characterised by the law as one of "proximity" or "neighbourhood" and that the situation should be one in which the court considers it fair, just and reasonable that the law should impose a duty of a given scope upon the one party for the benefit of the other.[113]

Thus, to be successful in negligence, the plaintiff must establish (i) reasonable foreseeability of harm, (ii) proximity of relationship with the defendant, and (iii) fairness, justice and reasonableness for the imposition of liability on the defendant. Besides these tests, another overriding requirement to impose liability is policy considerations, meaning the plaintiff will only succeed where policy considerations would support the imposition of liability on the university.[114]

(i) *Foreseeability*

"The concept of reasonable foreseeability is derived from the standard of a reasonable person. That standard has been adopted to eliminate personal idiosyncrasies and peculiarities of the defendant and make the law objective".[115] The defendant needs to take only reasonable precautions; the defendant need not take every precaution imaginable. The defendant would be liable if a reasonable person in the defendant's position would have foressen the risk of injury to the plaintiff.[116]

When a tradesman renovating the plaintiff's house leaves it unlocked and a theft of jewellery occurs from the property, the court held that a reasonable person in the position of the tradesman should have foreseen the possibility of theft and guarded against it.[117] Likewise, where the owner of a bus company operates their buses along a dangerous route on which stone throwing and petrol bombing of buses were common, it would be deemed foreseeable that passengers travelling in such buses are in danger of injury.[118] The violence that comes with hazing at Sri Lankan universities is well-known.

As discussed in the sociological background, 57% of university students face hazing (psychological hazing—51%; physical hazing—34%, sexual hazing—17%).[119] Students commit suicide and leave their higher education.[120] According to the Ministry of Education, 2000 students drop out of university every year because of hazing.[121] The university has a duty to use every weapon in its armoury to protect naïve freshers.

---

[113] 2 AC 60 [1990] All ER 568 (HL).

[114] See D K Srivastava, Aashish Srivastava, and Neerav Srivastava (2018) '"A Hazy Shade of Liability": Duty of Care of Universities to Prevent Hazing', 25(1) *Torts Law Journal* 25.

[115] D.K. Srivastava and A.D. Tenekone *The Law of Tort in Hong Kong* (LexisNexis, Fourth Edition, 2020) p. 265.

[116] Rajapakshe (n 79) p. 155.

[117] See also *Stansbie v. Troman* [1948] 2 KB 48(CA) [1948] 1 All ER 599.

[118] *General Accident Insurance Co of South Africa v. Xhego* 1992 (1) SA 580 (A).

[119] Gunatilaka et al. (n 3).

[120] Perera and Ekanayake (n 29).

[121] Senanayake (n 9).

According to a committee appointed by the UGC-SL under the chairmanship of Justice Dr. Saleem Marsoof (the Marsoof Committee) the primary responsibility for curbing hazing lies with the university.[122] Where the university fails in its duty, it would be liable to a fresher injured as a result of hazing on the university premises.

(ii) *Proximity*

Apart from reasonable foreseeability, there must also be a sufficient degree of proximity between the defendant and the plaintiff to make the former liable. There is no liability in an indeterminate amount for an indeterminate time to an indeterminate class.[123] Here the question is whether there is any proximity between the university and its students to make the former liable for failure to prevent injury to a fresher. According to the UGC-SL Guidelines, a university in Sri Lanka must take measures to control hazing. These include: (i) forming an anti-hazing committee and requiring it to prepare a handout detailing hazing acts, punishments for the wrongdoer; (ii) disseminating information relating to hazing through posters and brochures in prominent places, (iii) educating all university staff, including security staff, on all aspects of hazing, and (iv) conducting an orientation program on hazing for new students and their parents. These requirements show a sufficient degree of proximity between students and the university.[124]

(iii) *Fairness, Justice and Reasonableness*

University is a second home for most students. "The modern university provides a setting in which every aspect of student life is, to some degree, university guided".[125] Students subjected to cruel and barbaric hazing cannot focus on their studies. They need a salutary study environment to thrive. The university's duty does not end with providing good teachers and learning facilities. A student's success largely depends on the university providing a safe and secure environment. According to the National Education Policy Framework (2020–2030), the sub-culture of inhumane hazing has eroded the overall conditions of learning environment and quality of student life in Sri Lankan universities. Thus, it is fair, just and reasonable to impose a duty on the university to protect its students.

(iv) *Policy Considerations*

Fairness justice and reasonableness and policy considerations are all related. Where the plaintiff argues for the imposition of liability, the defendant may put forward the plea of policy considerations to negate liability.[126] Policy considerations were taken into account to refuse to impose liability on the police because of the concern that it

---

[122] Marsoof et al. (n 25).

[123] *Ultramares Coroporation v. Touche* (1931) 174 NE 441.

[124] DK Srivastava and AD Tennekone (n 115) p. 214.

[125] *Furek v. University of Delaware* 594 A.2d 506 (Del.1991) (Supreme Court of Delaware) p. 516.

[126] Legal Studies (SL), 'Law of Obligations' (28 May 2017) https://sjmsassociates.wordpress.com/.

could "lead [the police] to the exercise of a function being carried in a detrimentally defensive frame of mind".[127] Policy considerations are also used to deny the plaintiff's claim on the ground that it could have ripple effect and lead to floodgates of claims.[128] What policy considerations should prevail is not easy to determine. Considerations which were relevant a generation ago may not be relevent today because of new developments, changes in the demands of society and attitude of people. In the U.S. prior to the decisions in *Mullins v Pine Manor College*[129] and *Furek v University of Delaware*,[130] university going students were taken as responsible adults, capable of organising their own affairs. It was thought that "the modern American college is not an insurer of the safety of its students".[131] Now there are several policy considerations in favour of imposing liability on universities. In *Regents of University of California v Superior Court*[132] the court said that policy favoured the imposition of a duty on the university to protect its students.

In Sri Lanka, hazing has become increasingly vicious in the last five decades. Society and the people would like to see an end to it. Hazing mostly occurs on university campuses. As noted earlier, Marsoof Committee said that the primary responsibility for curbing hazing at universities is exclusively with them.[133] Furthermore, UGC-SL stated that academic institutions must themselves develop policies and procedures for the elimination of hazing. The National Education Policy Framework (2020–2030), observed that a major cause "of the erosion of overall conditions of learning environment and quality of student life in Sri Lankan Universities is the... inhumane hazing".[134] In November 2022, the Higher Education State Minister told the media that unless drastic measures are adopted, extreme form of hazing would continue.[135]

The UGC- SL Guidelines require universities to take measures to prevent hazing and punish those found guilty of hazing. The Guidelines also require universities to appoint an Anti- Hazing Committee consisting of VC, DVC, Deans and one Council member and several other staff and the University Medical Officer. In *Priyangini Navarane and Others v Chandrassena*[136] the Supreme Court observed that as far

---

[127] *Hill v. Chief Constable of Yorkshire* (1989) AC 53.

[128] *Ultramares Coroporation v. Touche* (1931) 174 NE 441.

[129] *Mullins v. Pine Manor College* 389 Mass. 47, 449 N.E.2d 331 (1983) (Supreme Judicial Court of Massachusetts). [1973] 1 QB 27.

[130] *Furek v. University of Delaware* (n 125).

[131] *Bradshaw v. Rawlings*, 612 F 2d 135 (3d Cir 1979).

[132] *Regents of University of California v. Superior Court of Los Angeles County* 4 Cal 5th 607 413 P 3d 656 2018.

[133] Marsoof et al. (n 25).

[134] National Education Commission (Sri Lanka), National Education Policy Framework (2020–2030) (June 2022), para 1.5.4.

[135] Perera (n 2).

[136] (1998) 1 Sri LR 170.

as hazing was concerned, "public interest demands deterrent, rather than lenient punishment for admitted and proven misconduct…".[137] Pending cases under the Anti-Hazing Act are given special importance. Section 15 of the Act provides that "Every Court shall give priority to the trial of any person charged with any offence under this Act…".[138]

(v) *Incremental Approach*

Sri Lanka has been much influenced by English law to determine the issues of liability of a university in negligence. It is a novel question. The courts are not only required to analyse foreseeability, proximity, fairness, justice and reasonableness and policy considerations but also the application of the incremental approach. In *Caparo*,[139] Lord Bridge endorsed the incremental approach to resolve the existence of a new duty of care. The essence of incrementalism is that when confronted by a novel situation, the court must decide the case on the basis of analogy from earlier cases. Lord Bridge was much influenced by Brennan J's decision in *Sutherland Shire Council v Heyman*.[140] As mentioned earlier, the primary responsibility for curbing hazing at universities is exclusively with them and they are required to take the necessary measures to prevent it.[141] That hazing is a dangerous activity is public knowledge and that failure by a university to take the required steps to control hazing that causes injury to a student is breach of its duty towards the injured student. As far as criminal law is concerned, the Sri Lankan Supreme Court is of the view that in hazing cases deterrent punishment should awarded.[142] The UGC-SL Guidelines, the Supreme court's view and Justice Marsoof's comments make it clear that universities in Sri Lanka are already under a duty to prevent hazing. "As a matter of pragmatism holding institutions accountable is probably the only way to prevent future harm to students".[143]

- Breach of duty of care

"Roman-Dutch law, like English law, requires, the existence of a duty to take care owed by the defendant to the plaintiff".[144] "The existence of a duty of care is a legal question, its breach is a question of fact".[145] U.S. cases are instructive on the question

---

137 (1998) 1 Sri LR 170.

138 *Prohibition Act (n 16)* s 15.

139 2AC 605 at 617–618, [1990] All ER 568 (HL).

140 (1985) AJR I, p. 43–44. Cited with approval in *Murphy v. Brentwood in District Council* (1990) 2 ALL ER 908.

141 Marsoof et al. (n 25).

142 *Priyangini v. Navrani and others v. Chandrassena* (1998) 1 Sri LR 170.

143 Neerav Srivastava, Aashish Srivastava and DK Srivastava (2019) 'A Million Winslows: Private Liability of Universities for Ragging in India', 19(2) *Oxford University Commonwealth Law Journal* 227, p. 245.

144 Majeed (n 78), p. 80. See also *Perlman v. Zoutendyk* 1934 CPD 158.

145 Ibid, p. 80. See also *Nock v. Ministry of Internal Affairs* 1939 SR 268.

of breach by a university of its duty to prevent hazing. In *Furek*,[146] the university had assumed a duty to prevent hazing. However, hazing still continued unabated.[147] Where students are living in private residential colleges and the university has no control over the day to day activities of private colleges, there is no question of any university liability. In Sri Lanka hazing of freshers is common. Over the years various laws and regulations have been passed imposing a duty on universities to take precautions to protect its students. Jutice Marsoof's report mentions about strengthening security and discipline in all universities and establishing greater co-ordination between police and universities.[148] The UGC-SL Guidelines require universities to appoint an Anti-hazing Committee; brief the security staff on anti-hazing measure taken; inform the media about the measures taken to curb hazing; create public awareness about hazing; inform the local police of the places and periods of time when hazing is most likely to occur; and to arrange posters to be displayed in prominent places on all measures taken relating to hazing. These provisions vividly manifest that because of hazing the task of universities and higher educational institutions has become onerous. Since universities have exclusive duty to prevent hazing, they are required to take a number of security measures, e.g., they must maintain round the clock vigil and, among others, be in touch with the police constantly.

The Higher Education State Minister in his interview to the media in November 2022 said that: "I met all the state university marshals and asked them whether they had received any training to handle hazing and to counsel students. They said 'no'".[149] Given that universities have a duty under the UGC-SL Guidelines that "all security staff should be detailed on the preventive measures" to tackle hazing, failure to do so by the university is a breach of that duty.

- Causation

Even if the plaintiff suffered any injury or loss, the plaintiff must also prove on the balance of probabilities that the damage was in fact caused by the defendant. This is called factual causation. The courts generally apply the but for test, i.e., but for the defendant's conduct the plaintiff would not have suffered any damage.[150] The following three cases (not related to hazing) illustrate that it is easy to establish duty of care and breach but proving causation is not easy.

---

[146] *Furek v. University of Delaware* (n 125).

[147] *Mullins v. Pine Manor College* (n 129).

[148] Marsoof et al. (n 25). See Points 3 and 4.

[149] Yoshitha Perera (n 2).

[150] Rajapakshe (n 79) p. 235.

In *Priyani Soyza v Arsecuaratne*[151] the question was whether the death of a four year old child, Suhani was caused by the defendant doctor. Dheeraratne J said:

> the mere proof of the fact that the defendant was negligent in not ordering a CT scan on Suhani (which led to the non-diagnosis of BSG), does not make the plaintiff entitled to damages. The plaintiff must further prove that such non-diagnosis caused or materially contributed to the deterioration in the condition of Suhani and her death.[152]

In *Barnett v Chelsea Hospital*[153] the plaintiff's husband visited the defendant hospital as he was vomiting. The doctor advised him to go home and consult his own doctor. As the plaintiff's husband was suffering from arsenic poisoning, he died. It was clear that the doctor breached his duty but the breach was not the cause of husband's death. Even if the deceased was admitted into the hospital, he would have died before any treatment was given by the doctor. In *R v Blaue*[154] the defendant asked a woman to have sex with her which she refused. The defendant then stabbed her four times. To save her life both surgery and a blood transfusion were needed. Being a Jehovah's Witness, she refused any treatment and died. The Crown accepted that refusal to have blood transfusion, not stabbing, was the cause of her death.

Likewise, where a fresher during hazing suffers a heart attack, his success in the action for damages would depend on what caused the heart attack. If a thorough medical examination reveals that the heart attack was caused due to several previous medical conditions, not hazing, the fresher cannot succeed in his claim.

- Remoteness of Damage

The fact that the plaintiff's injury was caused by the defendant is not by itself sufficient to make the defendant liable.[155] "Damage which is too remote is not recoverable even if there is a factual link between…the duty and the loss".[156] "[T] here 'must be some limit beyond which consequences of the act are too remote to be attributable to the wrongdoer".[157] Liability will only be extended to natural, probable and reasonable consequences of the defendant's act or omission. The onus of establishing this is on the plaintiff.[158] Thus, where a fresher suffers some injury during hazing which was negligently treated by a doctor, the fesher cannot make any claim for injuries caused by the doctor's negligence.

---

151 2001 (2) Sri L.R. 249.

152 2001 (2) Sri L.R. 249, p. 293.

153 [1969] 1 QB 428. See also *Bolitho (Deceased) v. City and Hackney Health Authority* [1996] 4 All ER 771.

154 1975 61 Cr App R 271.

155 Rajapakshe (n 79) p. 235.

156 Ibid.

157 Majeed (n 78) p. 400. See also *Overseas Tankship (UK) Ltd v. Morts Dock and Engineering Co Ltd* [1961] AC 388.

158 McKerron (n 76) p. 52.

(vi) *Defences*

- Contributory Negligence

"Contributory negligence is an act or inaction on the part of an injured party that combines with the negligence of another in causing the injury".[159] It should be noted that in Sri Lanka the common law has been replaced by the introduction of *Contributory Negligence and Wrongdoers Act* 1968. Sec. 3(1) (a) of the Act states that:

> Where any person suffers damage which is caused partly by his own fault and partly by the fault of any other person, a claim in respect of that damage shall not be defeated by reason only of the fault of the claimant, but the damages recoverable in respect thereof shall be reduced by the court to such extent as the court may deem just and equitable having regard to the degree in which the claimant was at fault in relation to the damage.
>
> (b) Damage shall, for the purpose of paragraph (a) of this subsection, be regarded as having been caused by a person's fault, notwithstanding the fact that any other person had an opportunity of avoiding the consequences thereof and negligently failed to do so.

Further under section 3 (2) the court must find and record the total damages which would have been recoverable if the claimant had not been at fault.

Thus, in Sri Lanka, where any hazee suffers damage partly due to his own fault and partly due to the fault of the hazer, a claim in respect of that damage shall not be completely defeated by reason of the fault of the hazee, but the damages recoverable in respect thereof shall be reduced by the court to such an extent as the court may deem just and equitable having regard to the degree in which the hazee was at fault.

Where the hazer relies on the defence of contributory negligence, the onus is on the hazer to prove the hazee's negligence, which contributed to the latter's injury. This is also the current legal position prevailing in the U.K., Australia, and India. Contributory negligence is not an absolute defence but a partial one.[160]

In *W.H. Bus Company Ltd v Samaranayake*,[161] it was held that the issue of the plaintiff's contributory negligence is decided by applying "the test of reasonableness". In *Perera v Charles* the plaintiff was travelling in a bus with his arm resting on the window. There was a collision between his bus and another bus. The plaintiff sued his bus company for the injury and damages. The Supreme Court held that the cause of the accident and injury to the plaintiff was because of the negligence of the bus company and the plaintiff has not in anyway contributed to the collision by protruding his arm outside the bus. No reduction therefore was allowed in damages awarded to the plaintiff.

---

159 Rajapakshe (n 79) p. 201.

160 See Legal Studies (SL) (n 126).

161 (1952) S. C. 427.

- Volenti Non-fit Injuria

The maxim *volenti non-fit injuria* (voluntary assumption of risk) under the Roman-Dutch law means that no person can complain of any act to which they have voluntarily consented.[162] The plaintiff's consent could be express or implied. There are various everyday examples of volenti, e.g., consent by a cricket player not to complain for any injury or physical harm caused during a match. But the injury suffered must have been in the normal course of the game. As regards to hazing, where a fresher agrees to have sex with a senior student, the fresher cannot complain of sexual assault. But consent to having sex does not mean consent to physically abuse the fresher. Consent also cannot be given to an illegal act.[163] To successfully plead the defence of *volenti non-fit injuria,* the hazer must satisfy the following requirements[164]:

1. The hazee was aware of the specific danger;
2. The hazee fully understood the nature and extent of the danger; and
3. The hazee must have agreed to take the risk without any force or fraud on the part of hazer.[165]

Waring & Gillow Ltd v Sherborne,[166] Innes J said that "it must be clearly shown that the risk was known, that it was voluntarily undertaken…knowledge does not invariably imply appreciation [of risk] and both together are not equivalent to consent". In *Furek,* the Supreme Court of Delaware held that U.S. universities owed a duty to protect their students from hazing. As to the defences of contributory negligence and *volenti non-fit injuria*, the Court said that

> while Furek voluntarily participated in the hazing, he was not chargeable with the knowledge that he would be exposed to the risk that someone would pour a caustic substance over his head as part of a fraternity ritual….one does not assume a risk unless he appreciates its danger but takes no step to avoid it….In gauging the conduct of the plaintiff, the standard to be applied is a subjective one.[167]

The above summation of these two defences by the court explains their applicability to hazing cases not only in the U.S. but also in Sri Lanka.

[162] Rajapakshe (n 79) p. 210.

[163] Ibid, p. 212. This defence cannot be set up as a defence in criminal proceedings, for the reason that no person can licence another to commit a crime.

[164] Rajapakshe (n 79) p. 212.

[165] See Legal Studies (SL) (n 126).

[166] *Waring and Gillow Ltd v. Sherborne* 1904 TS 344.

[167] *Furek v. University of Delaware* (n 125).

- Vicarious liability

Vicarious liability is defined as "[t]he liability of one person for the delictual acts of another, such liability arising from the relationship between the person who commits the delict and the person who is held liable, but existing independently of any relationship between the injured party and the person who is held liable"[168] This is a form of no-fault liability, also described as strict liability.[169] Vicarious liability is concerned with compensating those who have suffered delictual harm. In *Ellis v Paranavitane*, T.S. Fernando J said that there was no difference between the Roman-Dutch law and English law on the question of vicarious liability.[170] The modern-Roman Dutch law, adopts the English law doctrine of vicarious liability.[171] "Whoever, appoints a person to any function is answerable for the wrongs and neglects which his agent may commit in the exercise of the functions to which he is appointed. In effect it is identical with the English rule that a master is responsible for the torts of a servant committed in the course of his employment".[172]

Where a senior student who is guilty of hazing and at the same time is an employee (e.g., research assistant, tutor, and student union leader) of the university, then it is a clear case of vicarious liability. The word employee is liberally interpreted. In *Perera v Marikar Bawa Ltd*,[173] the plaintiff was the head-cutter of the defendant's company. He was provided a cubicle to do his work but employed his own workmen and tools. The company passed on tailoring orders to him and on execution he was paid commission. The company collected payment from the customers and kept the account. The court held that the plaintiff's work was an integral part and parcel of the company. Therefore, he was a workman and an employee.

The university would be vicariously liable where a student union leader (who gets paid by the university for running day to day matters relating to student affairs) is involved in hazing activities. It does not matter whether the student leader is executing orders of the employer or he has a discretion how to carry out his duties.[174] It is also immaterial that the student union leader's action was negligent or intentional.[175]

---

168 Rajapakshe (n 79) p. 175; TB Barlow, *The South African Law of Vicarious Liability in Delict and a comparison of other legal principles.* (1939) p. 1.

169 Ibid, p. 176.

170 Ibid, p. 177.

171 See Legal Studies (SL) (n 126).

172 *Mkize v. Martens SALR* (1914) App. Div. 382 at 390; Majeed (n 78) p. 177. Srivastava et al. (n 143) p. 251

173 [1989]1 SLR 347.

174 See *DeSilva, T.H.I v. Trust Co.* 55 NLR 241; Rajapakshe (n 79) p. 183.

175 See Srivastava et al. (n 143). p. 251–254; *Brueckner v. Norwich University* 730 A2d 1086 1999; *Emoakeh v. Southern University* 654, So.2d 474 (LaCt app1995). See also *Lister v. Lesley Hall* [2002] 1 AC 215 where a boarding school warden sexually abused boys residing in the boarding school. Lord Steyn said that the warden torts were so "closely connected with his employment and the boarding school should be vicariously liable. After all the sexual abuse of the boys was inextricably interwoven with carrying out by the warden of his duties".

4.6 Conclusion

Three major legislation, (Anti-Hazing Act 1998, Anti-toture Act 1994, Universities Act 1978) and the UGC Circular No. 919 dated 15.01.2010 and UGC Circular No.946 dated 10.02.2022 have failed to stem the tide of hazing in Sri Lanka. Hazing continues unabated as before. The UGC Circular 919 dated 15.01.2010 stated that it has been drafted because the anti-hazing legislation had failed. Ironically even UGC-SL circulars have also failed. There are more concerns amongst freshers now than ever before. The Higher Education State Minister in November 2022 said that out of 3500 complaints made to the anti-hazing helpline and the police only a few complaints have been investigated. This does not augur well for hazees or tackling hazing.[176] The Minister said that:

> state university authorities give some 'other mental / physical health reasons' for all deaths of [hazees]. Most of the time this is done in order to avoid a black mark [on the educational institution]. The best way of avoiding all troubles is denying the truth.[177]

In the circumstances the Minister recommended strict punishment for hazers and blacklisting them from all state and private universities as well as foreign universities.[178]

The Marsoof Committee has recommended in its report dated 31 August 2020[179] a number regulatory measures that must be adopted to reduce hazing in Sri Lankan universities. They seem positive and practical. We are listing the important ones below.

1. The primary responsibility for curbing hazing at universities is exclusively with them.
2. The UGC-SL and academic institutions must themselves develop policies and procedures for the elimination of hazing.
3. Security and discipline should be strengthened in all universities and the heads of such educational institutions should create incentives for due compliance of anti-hazing laws and disincentives for failure to comply.
4. Greater coordination between police and academic institutions should be established.
5. It is necessary to develop wide public awareness of the disruptive or adverse consequences of hazing and the UGC and educational institutions must develop such awareness and set in place anti-hazing measures.
6. Educational institutions to control hazing must be proactive rather than reactive. They should put in place programmes that enhance awareness of human values and potentials, human rights, personality development and other similar programmes that help redress the underlying causes of hazing.

---

[176] Perera (n 2).

[177] 'End of Road for Ragging', Daily News (online, 26 September 2022) https://archives1.dailynews.lk/2022/09/26/features/287881/end-road-ragging.

[178] Ibid.

[179] Marsoof et al. (n 25).

7. Educational institutions should review the management of hostels and canteens. Quite a lot of hazing occurs in those places.
8. Periodic training programmes for all educational institutions' staff on hazing must be organised by them regularly.[180]

The practice of hazing is so deep rooted in Sri Lankan universities that it cannot be eliminated by making a few laws, circulars, guidelines and reports. While these can help, the main problems are with the ingrained culture of hazing and lackadaisical attitude, especially of those who are tasked to prevent hazing. The real problem is with the enforcement and implementation of legal sanctions.

[180] Ibid, p. 2.

Chapter 5
Hazing in Australia

Hazing is the abuse of new or prospective group members.[1] It is sometimes confused with bullying. Bullying is exclusionary.[2] Hazing purports to be inclusive. It is the price of admission for new students; an initiation ceremony. Hazees purportedly 'submit' to hazing, and that complicates the legal analysis. This chapter first discusses the current state of hazing in Australia. There have been cruel incidents that has resulted in lasting harm and trauma for the hazee. Unlike the US and India, Australia has not developed hazing-specific regulations. It is both under-examined and under-regulated. Like the US and India, the authors adhere to the view that Australian universities bear responsibility for and are best positioned to prevent hazing. In 2018, Mr Simon Birmingham, the federal education minister at the time, stated that it is for universities to make sure the culture is changed.[3] The shadow education minister at the time, Ms Tanya Plibersek stated that universities need to step up and shoulder some of the responsibility for college culture.[4]

Second, it considers the legal position. Unlike the US and India, Australia has not developed hazing-specific regulations. Therefore, any claim must be brought under the general law. The claims can be divided into ones that can be brought against (a) the hazer or (b) the university. Regarding the hazer, proceedings can be brought in both tort and crime for assault and sexual assault. Civil proceedings can be brought for mental harm and discrimination. An issue that has caused problems in hazing situations is whether the hazee consented to the initiation because they want to join the community. Consent should be carefully circumscribed.

---

[1] A legal definition is discussed below.

[2] Jennifer Lamb, Debra J Pepler, Wendy Craig (2009) 'Approach to bullying and victimization', 55(4) *Canadian Family Physician* 356.

[3] Matthew Doran, "Bullying Has No Place in Australia', PM Tells School Principals, Amid Tough Talk on University Hazing', *ABC News* (online, 1 March 2018) https://www.abc.net.au/triplej/programs/hack/labor-tells-residential-colleges-to-clean-up-their-act/9494780.

[4] Shalailah Medhora, 'Labor Issues Warning to Colleges Over Assaults: Clean Up Your Act or Else', *ABC News* (online, 1 March 2018) https://www.abc.net.au/triplej/programs/hack/labor-tells-residential-colleges-to-clean-up-their-act/9494780.

A. Srivastava et al., *Hazing (Ragging) at Universities: A Legal Perspective*,
https://doi.org/10.1007/978-981-99-5215-1_5

As for universities, although there is no direct local authority, it seems that a university can be sued in negligence for a failure to exercise reasonable care to prevent hazing. Australian law has made a contribution in this area by clarifying a university's responsibility when handling a victim complaint. If the complaint is poorly handled and the victim is further traumatised, the university might be liable for the secondary wounding. The same substantive claim can probably also be made under the consumer guarantees in the *Australian Consumer Law*. There is also the possibility of an implied term in the university-student contract that the university should take reasonable care to prevent hazing.

Third, specialist hazing laws in the US and India do not seem to have dented the practice. Therefore, the chapter asks:

- why does hazing occur?
- what are the cultural and behavioural levers of hazing?
- rather than just being proscriptive, can the law also foster cultural change?

A key contributor to hazing persisting is that universities are not taking ownership of its prevention. As for hazers, it seems that they seek to dominate and test the commitment of new students. Hazees are willing to submit to humiliating acts so that they gain acceptance in the community. As young adults, acceptance in the student community is hugely important. Alcohol emboldens hazers and makes hazees vulnerable. Finally, hazees know they may pay a heavy price if they report the hazing. They could be ostracised, and the authority to whom they report may have conflicting interests.

Fourth, hazing laws for Australia are proposed. These consist of (a) traditional proscriptive and prescriptive regulations from other jurisdictions that could be usefully imported and (b) non-traditional laws designed to foster cultural change. The behavioural levers that foster change regarding an ingrained harmful practice seem to be creating a sense of duty, communication and education as to the harm caused to third parties, the certainty of repercussions, persuading individuals that the desired behaviour is good for the individual concerned, and creating practical constraints. Proposed laws should seek to engage these levers. On that basis, it is recommended that:

(a) The legislation should be explicit that universities are primarily responsible for student safety and preventing hazing. Universities should have anti-hazing taskforces headed by the vice-chancellor and compulsory education for staff and students on student safety. An independent body should give every university an annual student safety score out of 10.

(b) Hazing needs to be defined to plug legal gaps. Humiliation, harassment, and activities that endanger students, such as forced consumption of alcohol, should be included in the definition of hazing. For consent, a reverse onus provision should be introduced, such that it is for the hazer to show that the hazee genuinely consented to the activity.

(c) The student body and leadership should be engaged in hazing prevention. Students should be appointed as anti-hazing leaders and as a support network for victims.
(d) Orientation week is when most hazing occurs. It is when new students are most vulnerable. They are keen to join the community and do not have friends among existing students who can help them. Alternate teambuilding O-week activities should be organised that reduce the distance between freshers and the existing cohort. If required, O-week should be postponed.
(e) Alcohol has been an enabler of hazing, and practical measures should be implemented to reduce its availability at campuses and colleges during O-week.
(f) Reporting is an extremely challenging issue. The legislation should mandate that there be independent channels to whom reports can be made. The university must have a victim support team that includes student leaders.

The tenor of the chapter is that universities and residential colleges should take ownership of preventing hazing. That tenor is reflected in the arguments made.

5.1 Current State

5.1.1 Prevalence and Culture

Hazing has not been subject to quite the same scrutiny in Australia as in the US and India. To be sure, Australia does not have a pervasive fraternity culture that exists in the US, and hazing deaths are rare.[5] That does not mean hazing is not a real problem in Australia. Nor that Australian hazing is any less barbaric or cruel. Hazing occurs at Australian private schools,[6] the military,[7] and universities.

The Australian Human Rights Commission's report on sexual assault at universities contends that hazing is so entrenched at residential colleges that the *culture* 'cannot reform itself'.[8] Likewise, a paper on hazing in the Australian military is headed 'A Culture of Denial?'[9] The word' Culture' repeats in the title of a study

[5] One instance that might have been a hazing death was regarding Stuart Kelly. See Naaman Zhou, 'Inquiry Demanded as Hazing Culture in Top University Colleges Revealed', *The Guardian* (online, 26 Feb 2018) https://www.theguardian.com/australia-news/2018/feb/26/family-of-stuart-kelly-demand-inquiry-as-hazing-culture-revealed. See Chaps. 2 and 3, respectivley, for the US and India positions.

[6] Ben Fordham, 'Made to Bark Like Dogs: 'Gutles' Students Expelled from Waverley College', *2GB* (online, 8 December 2022) https://www.2gb.com/made-to-bark-like-dogs-gutless-students-expelled-from-waverley-college/.

[7] Richard Evans (2013) 'Hazing in the ADF: a Culture of Denial?', 10 *Australian Army Journal* 113.

[8] Australian Human Rights Commission (2017) 'Change the Course: National Report on Sexual Assault and Sexual Harassment at Australian Universities', https://humanrights.gov.au/our-work/sex-discrimination/publications/change-course-national-report-sexual-assault-and-sexual.

[9] Evans (n 7).

commissioned by the University of Sydney to look into its residential colleges. It is entitled 'Cultural Renewal at the University of Sydney Residential Colleges' ('the Colleges Report').[10] The privately commissioned Red Zone Report, which accused the Colleges Report of being a gloss, states that:

> there is a clear link between the coercion of hazing rituals, and the high rate of sexual assault and harassment at colleges. Through these rituals, college students are initiated into a culture in which personal boundaries and consent are routinely disregarded.[11]

Hazing rituals at Australian universities include sexual assault or harassment, forced drinking, the 'dead possum'—bashing and kicking intoxicated students, and students masturbating into shampoo bottles belonging to female students. The 'walk-about' is a practice where freshers—on their hands and knees—are auctioned to second-year students to perform tasks such as stealing.[12] It is alleged that the 'bone room' is a tradition at a residential college where fresher women are invited by a senior to a party. Attendees are wined and dined before being led to the Rogers Room, which has been described as 'a room as full of mattresses'. As one former student observed, 'If you're an 18, 19-year-old girl and this institution of men deigns to recognise you and invite you to this secret event that you [don't] know anything about [...] saying no [...] is impossible[13] Another student stated that 'unless you drink, unless you participate' in the hazing activities everybody knows 'you're probably going to have a shit time at college'.

Alcohol has been the predicate to many hazing activities and requires specific treatment. It enables hazers and makes hazees vulnerable. Universities provide 'a unique social context' for excessive drinking.[14] This is because students, having turned 18, have only recently been able to drink legally, there is declining parental control, the structures and routines of high school are absent, and there is peer pressure to drink.[15] A student recently suffered brain damage due to alcohol hazing.[16]

---

[10] See Elizabeth Broderick (2017) 'Cultural Renewal at the University of Sydney Residential Colleges', https://www.sanctasophiacollege.edu.au/wp-content/uploads/2017/11/Cultural-Renewal-Overarching-Report-2017.pdf.

[11] Nina Funnell, Anna Hush and Sharna Bremner (2018) 'The Red Zone Report: An Investigation into Sexual Violence and Hazing in Australian University Residential Colleges', *End Rape on Campus (EROC) Australia*, https://apo.org.au/node/134766, p. 84.

[12] Madeline Ward, Lara Sonnenschein & Nina Dillon, 'Racism, Sexism, Hazing: New Allegations Surface Over Behaviour at St Andrew's College', *Honi Soit* (online, 17 May 2020) http://honisoit.com/2020/05/racism-sexism-hazing-new-allegations-surface-over-behaviour-at-st-andrews-college/.

[13] Natalie Buckett and Victoria Zerbst, 'The Bone Room' Honi Suit (24 February 2016) https://social.shorthand.com/honi_soit/jydosyK7zf/the-bone-room.html.

[14] Ann Roche and Kerrianne Watt (2000) 'Drink smart: a Qualitative Evaluation of an Alcohol Intervention for University Students', 10(3) *Health Promotion Journal of Australia* 245.

[15] Broderick (n 10).

[16] Shireen Khalil, 'Student now blind with Brain Damage After Hazing', *News.com.au* (online, 9 June 2022). https://www.news.com.au/lifestyle/real-life/news-life/student-now-blind-with-brain-damage-after-hazing/news-story/e437de3039ac39619103fd5fe9d619f0.

The Colleges Report noted that 'a particularly large number of submissions identifying alcohol as a factor contributing to College-based sexual assault and sexual harassment'.[17] As adults, it is a student's decision whether to drink.[18] Forced drinking involves coercion rather than being an exercise of pure autonomy. But we should be aware of the dangers.

In the US, about 2000 alcohol-related deaths occur each year among American college students; and it is a factor in about half a million student injuries each year.[19] For the 'Mott walk' ritual at Charles Stuart University, students are fed alcohol for hours before being abandoned several kilometres from the university. In one incident, after being left drunk and naked at midnight in a rural area without phones, the students were attacked by a third party.[20] A 2017 report by the Australian Human Rights Commission reached the 'unavoidable' conclusions that sexual assault are too prevalent at universities and universities are not doing enough to prevent it.[21] But matters do not seem to have improved. A 2021 survey of 43,819 students regarding sexual assault at universities found that[22]:

- 16% of students had experienced sexual harassment, and 4.5% had experienced sexual assault in the past 12 months.
- As for the location, 43% of sexual harassment occurred in the general campus area. For sexual assault, 25% occurred at student accommodation and 25% at a university club or society.
- As for reporting sexual assault or harassment to universities, the figures are low. This raises concerns about whether hazing has been adequately documented. 3% of sexual harassment victims, and 5% of sexual assault victims complain. Most complaints were not referred to the police, and the overall experience of university's responses was mixed, although most complainants were dissatisfied.[23]

The 2023 Senate Report on Current Proposed Sexual Consent Laws in Australia singled out universities and put in stark terms: According to two creditable surveys [...] sexual violence on campus is as prevalent in tertiary education settings as it is in the community, if not more so [...] Some stakeholders expressed a view that the university sector pays 'lip service' to the persistent issue of sexual violence on

---

[17] Broderick (n 10).

[18] Ann Roche and Kerrianne Watt (1990) 'Drinking and University Students: From Celebration to Inebriation', 18 *Drug and Alcohol* 389.

[19] David J Skorton, 'A Pledge to End Fraternity Hazing', New York Times (online, 23 August 2011) https://www.nytimes.com/2011/08/24/opinion/a-pledge-to-end-fraternity-hazing.html.

[20] Adelaide Lang, 'Naked and Drunk University Students Attacked During Hazing Ritual', *The West Australian* (online, 26 June 2022) https://thewest.com.au/news/naked-and-drunk-university-students-attacked-during-hazing-ritual-c-7304342.

[21] Australian Human Rights Commission, *Change The Course: National Report on Sexual Assault and Sexual Harassment at Australian Universities* (1 August 2017).

[22] Wendy Heywood, Paul Myers, Anastasia Powell, Gillian Meikle & Diana Nguyen (2022) 'National Student Safety Survey: Report on the Prevalence of Sexual Harassment and Sexual Assault among University Students in 2021', *The Social Research Centre,* https://www.nsss.edu.au/.

[23] Ward et al. (n 12).

campus. The committee acknowledges that this is partially a corollary of entrenched cultural and societal attitudes and beliefs [...] the committee heard that the university sector's commitment has, at best, waned and, at worst, stalled. Preventative measures and support services are inconsistently delivered at Australian universities. Some universities appear to be approaching consent education and reducing sexual violence within their community proactively and with genuine commitment. Others appear to find the issue too confronting or difficult; their responses might be generously described as inadequate but are, in some cases, outright damaging and deeply troubling. The committee finds such approaches by certain Australian universities utterly unacceptable'.[24]Australian universities are primarily autonomous and not subject to a central authority, as is the case in India.[25] Further, residential colleges are independent of the university. Universities have claimed there is little they can do to prevent hazing at colleges,[26] where it is especially prevalent. A former Head of College at ANU stated:

> there are definitely pressures brought to bear on our newly arrived residents to conform to a lifestyle that embraces amongst others, drinking beyond moderation, being casually flippant about matters a reasonable person might regard as weighty and important - for example referring to Fellows Oval as "Rape Oval", or joking about terminologies hat have troubling sexual assault overtones. A good example of this is the term "rockspidering" which refers to a practice I haven't seen evidence exists but is supposed to involve one resident knocking on another resident's door late at night and if he/she opens the doors, this being interpreted as consent to sexual relations.
>
> [...] there is a dominant culture here that celebrates behaviours and attitudes that ethical, moral and upright people find abhorrent and these behaviours, which are little more than hedonistic, pursued in the name of "fun" by a sizeable and influential minority, some might say majority, within the College community.[27]

The impact of hazing on victims can be severe. There is physical injury, immediate trauma, and potentially long-term psychological issues.[28] In India, the Raghavan Committee Report states that two-thirds of victims of hazing had lasting emotional problems, adversely impacting their self-esteem and confidence.[29]

---

[24] Legal and Constitutional Affairs References Committee, 'Current Proposed Sexual Consent Laws in Australia' Senate, https://parlinfo.aph.gov.au/parlInfo/download/committees/reportsen/RB000074/toc_pdf/CurrentandproposedsexualconsentlawsinAustralia.pdf.

[25] Universities Australia is a committee with no binding authority over Universities. It issues guidelines and good practice advice. See 'About Universities Australia' Universities Australia (Accessed 16 November 2023) https://universitiesaustralia.edu.au/about/.

[26] See Naaman Zhou, 'University of Sydney Says It Is Powerless to Stop Violent Hazing of Students', *The Guardian* (online, 27 February 2018) http://www.theguardian.com/australia-news/2018/feb/27/sydney-university-says-it-is-powerless-to-stop-violent-hazing-of-students.

[27] *SMA v. John XXIII College* (No 2) [2020] ACTSC 211, [17].

[28] RK Raghavan et al. (2007) 'The Menace of Ragging in Educational Institutions and Measures to Curb It', http://dos.iitd.ac.in/anti-ragging/menace.pdf.

[29] Timothy C Marchell, Laura Beth Santacrose, Anne C Laurita & Elizabeth J Allan (2022) 'A Public Health Approach to Preventing Hazing on a University Campus', 10 *Journal of American College Health*, https://doi.org/10.1080/07448481.2021.2024210.

5.1.2 Why Does Hazing Occur?

As to why hazing occurs:

> When viewed as a socio-ecological phenomenon, hazing is the result of the interaction of multiple factors that operate at the levels of the individual, group, institution, community, and society. These factors include psychological processes that may motivate hazing, foster tolerance of the behavior, and contribute to its perpetuation.[30]

The three parties to hazing are the hazers, the hazee, and the institution. As for hazers, the motivations are complex and do not reduce to one reason.[31] A common[32] theory is 'dominance': hazers seek to establish or reaffirm a dominant position concerning hazees. The commitment theory is that severe gang initiations act to 'weed out the weak and uncommitted', such as those seeking to join a fraternity in the US, because newcomers are an unknown quantity.[33] It, too, is well represented in scholarship.[34] For example, military hazing purports to weed out the weak to protect the group's safety. More recently, Aldo has proposed 'automatic accrual theory', which is that hazing functions, in part, to prevent the near-term exploitation of group-controlled benefits by new members.[35]

As to why hazees subject themselves to dangerous humiliation, there are multiple factors including

- the need of emerging adults to separate from family and forge their own identities;
- obedience to authority, specifically older students; and
- 'solidarity', i.e. the desire to be accepted in a group.[36]

---

30 'Ibid'.

31 (n 32).

32 On it being common Aldo Cimino (2011) 'The Evolution of Hazing: Motivational Mechanisms and the Abuse of Newcomers', 11 *Journal of Cognition and Culture* 241 traces this 'Durkheim (1912) notes that group members haze newcomers to "make them understand how superior [they feel]" (p. 318). Bryshun (1997) writes that athletic hazing allows veterans to have their dominant position "consolidated" (p. 100). Whiting (1958) argues that hazing in male adolescent initiations is used to suppress "open and violent revolt" (p. 361). Honeycutt (2005) describes veterans of a discussion group hazing to "maintain their power" (Analysis section, final paragraph). Robidoux (2001) describes athletic hazers "celebrating their power over rookies" (p. 104). Keating et al. (2005) suggest that vertically-organized groups use severe initiations to "establish social control" (p. 107). Waldron and Kowalski (2009) write that athletic hazing rituals "help maintain…the power structure of the team" (p. 292). Nuwer (2000) actually defines hazing as an imposition of dominance, stating that hazing involves "any activity that requires new members to show subservience to old members" (p. 20), and so on (e.g., Webster, 1908; Stone, 1946; Johnson, 2001; Allan and DeAngelis, 2004; Tooby et al., 2006)'.

33 JD Vigil (1996) 'Street baptism: Chicano gang initiation', 55 *Human Organization* 149, p. 151.

34 Cimino (n 32).

35 Ibid.

36 Aldo Cimino (2022) 'Does Hazing Actually Increase Group Solidarity? Re-examining a Classic Theory with a Modern Fraternity', 43 *Evolution and Human Behavior* 408.

Group solidarity theory holds that individuals who undergo hazing justify their high levels of effort because it increases their acceptance within the group.[37] They are showing their willingness to accept and conform to College norms, gain social acceptance, and demonstrate their commitment even if it comes with pain.[38] For all these factors, there is an 'us and them' element. It has been argued that hazing tries to create a dependence and, like the Stockholm Syndrome, increases hazees' liking of hazers.[39]

For both hazers and hazees, alcohol facilitates the practice. Hazers are emboldened and less restrained. Hazees become more vulnerable. Freshers are also inclined to drink because they are in a new environment, and drinking helps them relax.[40]

A real difficulty is student unwillingness to report hazing activities. When students report hazing, they risk their own alienation from the student body and disbelieving authorities with conflicted loyalties.

Finally, when it comes to institutions and the broader community, hazing takes place when there is a tradition of it and a permissive culture.[41] An empirical study[42] by Allen et al. ('Allen Study') found that:

> commitment emerged as a predominant theme. Commitment refers to dedication of resources and support structures that foster a campus climate conducive to hazing prevention. Our data indicate that campus leaders, working closely with staff, demonstrated commitment by upholding expectations and accountability for group environments to be free from humiliation and abuse (i.e., non-hazing), and thereby more inclusive and safe for student learning and development. A resounding theme in our data is that without such commitment, hazing prevention efforts may lack credibility and traction to transform campus hazing culture … hazing policies are more impactful if senior leaders make them visible […][43]

There has been a tendency to see hazing as a problem between students, rather than something for the institution to solve.[44] Other factors that are relevant to hazing prevention are capacity, properly assessing the state of hazing at the university, planning, evaluations, commitment, educating senior leaders, and cultural competence. Cultural competence refers to 'understanding sociopolitical and other identity-based characteristics of students, student groups, and of the institutions'.[45]

We will return to the causes of hazing when considering proposed laws in Australia.

---

[37] Ibid.

[38] Jennifer J. Waldron (2015) 'Predictors of Mild Hazing, Severe Hazing and Positive Initiation Rituals in Sport', 10 *International Journal of Sports Science and Coaching* 1089.

[39] Cimino (n 32).

[40] Broderick (n 10) [3.1].

[41] Elizabeth J. Allan, Jessica M Payne & David Kerschner (2018) 'Transforming the Culture of Hazing: A Research-Based Hazing Prevention Framework', 55 *Journal of Student Affairs* 412, https://doi.org/10.1080/19496591.2018.1474759.

[42] Ibid.

[43] Ibid.

[44] Ibid.

[45] Ibid.

5.2 Primary Perpetrators: Crimes and Tort

Subject to some thorny issues, a hazer can be sued in both criminal law and in torts for an individual incident.

5.2.1 Sexual Assault

The main criminal categories are sexual assault and offences against the person. Statutory sexual offences are at Pt 1, Div 1 of the *Crimes Act 1958* (Vic). Under s 38, rape is committed when a person (A) intentionally sexually penetrates another person (B); B does not consent; and A does not reasonably believe that B consented. In Victoria, rape has recently been amended to include an affirmative consent model. For sexual assault offences, the position now is that 'A's belief that B consents to an act *is not reasonable* if, within a reasonable time before or at the time the act takes place, A does not *say or do anything to find out* whether B consents to the act'. A hazer has to positively confirm that the hazee consents.

In addition, a non-exhaustive list of circumstances in which B does not consent has been added as a new s 36AA. A number of these circumstances are relevant to hazing, including

- the person does not say or do anything to indicate consent;
- there is force, harm, or the threat of either;
- coercion or intimidation;
- unlawful detention;
- the person is overborne by the abuse of a relationship of authority or trust;
- the person is asleep or unconscious;
- the person is so affected by alcohol or another drug as to be incapable of consenting to the act; and
- a withdrawal of consent.

The new regime is a significant and welcome change. Under it, perpetrators of the 'bone room' practice would be vulnerable to prosecution. So too would the perpetrator in the *SMA* case discussed below.

Other criminal offences that may be relevant to hazing include administering an intoxicating substance for a sexual purpose,[46] which may catch certain perpetrators of the Rogers Room practice, and abduction or detention for a sexual purpose.[47]

---

[46] *Crimes Act 1958 (Vic)* s 48.

[47] *Crimes Act 1958 (Vic)* s 47.

5.2.2 Offences Against the Person

Relevant offences against the person under the *Crimes Act 1958 (Vic)* include assault or threats of assault; causing serious injury intentionally, recklessly, or negligently; murder; endangering the person; and threatening serious injury. It is possible that the Mott walk practice, in extreme circumstances, could amount to endangering the person. In criminal law, an assault is the direct or indirect application of force by a person to the body '(a) without lawful excuse; and (b) with intent to inflict or being reckless as to the infliction of bodily injury, pain, discomfort, damage, insult or deprivation of liberty'.[48] The 'dead possum' practice above is an assault. False imprisonment is a common law offence in Victoria. It is the intentional deprivation of another person's liberty by way of physical force, threats, or coercion in circumstances where the other person is not consenting and has no reasonable means of escape, and no lawful excuse for the conduct exists. In the novel *A Fine Balance,*[49] Mistry describes an incident where new students are locked in a freezer. It is conduct that would be actionable as false imprisonment.

It should be added that prosecution for a 'hazing' offence seems to be very rare. That is, it does not seem there are consequences for hazing. This is relevant to the discussion of cultural change below.

5.2.3 Intentional Torts

The victim can pursue a parallel claim in tort for intentional torts. Intentional torts include battery, assault, false imprisonment, defamation, and the intentional infliction of nervous shock. In tort, a battery is a direct and intentional act that has the effect of causing contact with the body of another without the latter's consent.[50] It is possible that masturbating into a shampoo bottle amounts to an assault. Trinidade and Cane point out that 'An act that set in motion an unbroken series of continuing consequences, the last of which ultimately caused contact with the plaintiff, was still regarded as sufficiently direct for the purposes of trespass'.[51] It also likely to be regarded as an intentional act.[52] An assault is a threat by the defendant that places the plaintiff in reasonable apprehension of being assaulted.[53] Touching or hitting a new student, or threatening to do so, can be actionable. In tort, false imprisonment is

[48] *Crimes Act 1958 (Vic)* s 31(1)(ba)(2).

[49] Rohinton Mistry, *A Fine Balance* (Faber, 2007).

[50] Frances Trinidade et al. *The Law of Torts in Australia* (OUP, 4th ed, 2011), [2.2.1]. In Australia, unlike the UK, it is possible to sue for negligent trespass to person provided it was caused negligently. This chapter is concerned with intentional hazing.

[51] Ibid, [2.2.1.1].

[52] In the US, the doctrine of substantial certainty applies but the point seems undecided by local authority. Trinidade et al. (n 49), [2.2.1.2].

[53] Trinidade et al. (n 49), [2.2.2].

a wrongful total restraint on the liberty of the plaintiff that is directly brought about by the defendant.

Defamation is the publication of material that causes serious harm[54] to the plaintiff. The serious harm threshold is a recent introduction. It makes it harder to claim in defamation, and the courts still have to work through what serious harm requires. The defences to defamation include justification[55] (truth) and honest opinion.[56] Loose talk on social media can be defamatory but may not be regarded as serious harm. The online environment creates new dimensions in that a defamatory statement can spread rapidly through multiple forwards, and trying to prevent its spread can have the opposite effect:

> two women at Yale Law School were subject to anonymous sexual defamatory statements on AutoAdmit.com, a law school admission online board. The owner of the site was unsympathetic. When they brought proceedings, it had the opposite effect, known as the "Streisand effect", of "exploding" the issue.[57]

Claims for intentional infliction of 'nervous shock',[58] where there is no physical injury, are uncommon—but may apply in a hazing situation. Nervous shock is a misnomer and is essentially a recognised psychiatric illness.[59] There has been uncertainty as to the elements of the tort. In the most recent pronouncement by an appellate court, the UK Supreme Court held that there were three elements to the tort:

(a) Conduct. Words or conduct directed towards the claimant for which there is no justification or reasonable excuse.
(b) Mental. Intention to cause physical harm or at least mental or emotional distress.
(c) Consequence. Recognised psychiatric illness.

Regarding (c) consequences, if the conduct results in mental distress, such as humiliation or embarrassment, it is *not* actionable. To be actionable, the consequence must be a recognised psychiatric injury. An alternative, discussed below, is where a recognised psychiatric injury was *negligently* caused. In any event, activities like the dead possum, the shampoo bottles, the walkabout, the bone room, and the Mott walk could all potentially lead to psychiatric harm and a claim. For the Mott walk, leaving naked students in the wilderness cannot be justified. It could cause mental or emotional distress, and may very well lead to a recognised psychiatric illness.

---

[54] Under s 10A of the *Defamation Act 2005* (Vic), it is an element of the cause of action that there be 'serious harm' to the plaintiff or the likelihood thereof.

[55] *Defamation Act 2005* (Vic) s 25.

[56] *Defamation Act 2005* (Vic) s 31.

[57] Neerav Srivastava (2020) 'The Iron Curtain: Controlling Unreasonable Defamation Immunity Clauses', 50 *Hong Kong Law Journal* 685.

[58] *Wilkinson v. Downton* [1897] 2 QB 57.

[59] *Mount Isa Mines v. Pusey* (1970) 125 CLR 383, 394 and *Hinz v. Berry* [1970] 2 QB 40, p. 42.

5.2.4 Consent

The defence of consent is an issue in both criminal and tortious proceedings regarding intentional conduct. While consent is a lawful excuse, the law has ‘carefully circumscribed’ the situations when it can be given.[60] A consent can be withdrawn.[61] If the victim can show duress, then it vitiates consent.[62] Should the hazee be a minor, that may be a factor in assessing whether it is genuine. At common law, in general, a person cannot consent to the application or threat of actual or grievous bodily harm.[63] In *Pallante v Stadiums Pty Ltd (No 1)*, it was held that such consent is nugatory because ‘it injures society if a person is allowed to consent to the infliction on himself of such a degree of serious physical harm’.[64] While there is a conceptual difficulty with this principle in that it may infringe on a person’s autonomy, for the purposes of hazing where the consent is not genuine but likely brought about by pressure, it is a check against arguments that consent was given. As per s 36AA of the *Crimes Act 1958* (Vic), the veracity of a purported consent under the influence of alcohol or drugs will probably be scrutinised by the courts.

Finally, there is a distinction between consenting to the risk of harm and consenting to intentional harm.[65] In *Neal v The Queen*,[66] it was held that a person could give informed consent to the risk of contracting HIV or any other sexually transmitted diseases, provided there was no intention on the part of the accused to infect the other person. In sporting activities, the consent is with respect to the risk of harm occurring while the rules are being obeyed. The consent is based on the premise that the sport is not inherently dangerous to life or limb, and the participants’ predominant motive is not the infliction of grievous bodily harm, although actual bodily harm is an incident of the sport.[67] For example, a victim in sport does not consent to an intentional battery that is not the byproduct of playing within the rules.[68] A victim does not consent to be, say, punched when the football is on the other side of the pitch.

If we apply these principles to an assault during hazing, consent should be a limited defence. The hazer has little scope to argue that the hazee consented to any more than the *risk* of incidental and unintentional harm occurring during inherently non-harmful hazing. As a factual matter, that was probably the extent of their consent, and even that is questionable.

---

[60] Kenneth J. Arenson (2014) ‘Consent as a Common Law Defence to Non-Sexual Assaults: The Effect of *Neal v. The Queen*’, 33(2) *University of Tasmania Law Review* 300.

[61] *R v. L* (1992) 103 ALJ 588.

[62] *Alridge v. Booth* (1988) 80 ALR 1.

[63] *Pallante v. Stadiums Pty Ltd (No 1)* [1976] VR 331, p. 340.

[64] Ibid.

[65] E.g. volenti non fit injuria.

[66] (1982) 149 CLR 305.

[67] *Feleccia v. Lackawanna College*, 156 A 3d 1200 (Pa, 2017); DK Srivastava, Aashish Srivastava & Neerav Srivastava (2018) ‘A Hazy Shade of Liability: Duty of Care of Universities to Prevent Hazing’, 25 *Tort Law Journal* 25.

[68] *McNamara v. Duncan* (1971) 26 ALR 584.

5.2.5 Discrimination

Reports speak to the discriminatory nature that hazing can descend into.[69] There is a patchwork of legislation regarding discrimination in Australia. There is federal legislation on age,[70] disability,[71] race,[72] and sex[73] that apply in the education sector. In Victoria, there is also the *Equal Opportunity Act 2010 (Vic)*. While there are differences in the respective legislation, discrimination generally involves being treated less favourably. Under s 28F of the *Sex Discrimination Act 1984 (Cth)*, it is unlawful for an adult student to sexually harass[74] another student. Section 28A defines harassment as an unwelcome sexual advance, request for sexual favours, or conduct of a sexual nature in circumstances in which a reasonable person would have anticipated the possibility that the person harassed would be offended, humiliated, or intimidated. Further, the *Racial and Religious Tolerance Act 2001 (Vic)* protects against vilification, such as hate speech, which is defined at ss 7 and 8 as 'conduct that incites hatred against, serious contempt for, or revulsion or severe ridicule of, that other person or class of persons'. Masturbating into shampoo bottles is a form of sexual harassment. So too might be the bone room incident might be and elements of the Mott walk.

5.2.6 Mental Harm

Even where there was no intentional infliction of mental harm, potential liability can arise due to negligence. Section 72 of the *Wrongs Act 1957* (Vic) provides[75] that:

> A person (the defendant) does not owe a duty to another person (the plaintiff) to take care not to cause the plaintiff pure mental harm unless the defendant foresaw or ought to have foreseen that a person of normal fortitude might, in the circumstances of the case, suffer a recognised psychiatric illness if reasonable care were not taken.

Under s 74(1)(a), a person is not entitled to recover damages unless it was foreseeable that a person of normal fortitude might suffer a recognised psychiatric illness. Alternatively, under s 74(1)(b), if the defendant knew, or ought to have known, that the person was a person of less than normal fortitude and, therefore, it was foreseeable that they might suffer a recognised psychiatric illness. Recognised psychiatric

---

[69] Madeline Ward, 'Racism, sexism, hazing: New allegations surface over behaviour at St Andrew's College' *Honi Suit* (17 May 2020) http://honisoit.com/2020/05/racism-sexism-hazing-new-allegations-surface-over-behaviour-at-st-andrews-college/.

[70] *Age Discrimination Act 2004* (Cth).

[71] *Disability Discrimination Act 1992* (Cth).

[72] *Racial Discrimination Act 1975* (Cth).

[73] *Sex Discrimination Act 1984* (Cth).

[74] Or to harass on the grounds of sex. Section 28AA of the *Sex Discrimination Act 1984* (Cth).

[75] The common law remains unaffected under s 71 of the *Wrongs Act 1957* (Vic) but s 72 is now the conventional basis for arguing a duty arises.

injury is not defined in the *Wrongs Act 1957* (Vic). The *DSM-5 (Diagnostic and Statistical Manual of Mental Disorders)* is a handbook used by health professionals to help identify and diagnose mental illness. Some of the main groups of mental disorders that it lists are[76]:

- mood disorders (such as depression or bipolar disorder)
- anxiety disorders
- personality disorders
- psychotic disorders (such as schizophrenia)
- eating disorders
- trauma-related disorders (such as post-traumatic stress disorder)
- substance abuse disorders.

Statistics in other countries reinforce that a significant proportion of victims of hazing suffer long-term mental health consequences.[77] It is foreseeable that severe hazing rituals, such as harassment and humiliation, could potentially lead to a recognised psychiatric illness such that the hazer is liable. A potential issue is whether the hazer, as a young adult, 'ought to have foreseen' this. Education on the harms of hazing, discussed below, will put the issue beyond reasonable doubt.

A distinction between the intentional infliction of 'nervous shock' and negligence is that, for the former, it must be the consequence of the conduct, while for the latter, it ought to be foreseeable. The authors would argue that psychiatric injury ought to be foreseeable for the dead possum, the bone room, and the Mott walk. The Mott walk is humiliating and endangers the hazees. It is foreseeable that it could lead to mental illness.

5.3 Liability of Universities and Negligence

Assault or sexual assault might be a purely individual criminal act or one that is as discussed above, facilitated by a hazing culture. A university is not vicariously liable for the hazing under Australian law, which still operates within the confines of an employment relationship.[78] As a matter of policy, a legal regime that limits liability to the direct perpetrator i.e. the hazer, when there is an underlying permissive culture is 'treating the symptoms rather than the cause'. The legal position should align with the general proposition that universities need to foster an anti-hazing culture and have a responsibility to take reasonable steps to prevent hazing. Hence, when considering

[76] 'Mental Illness' Health Direct (Accessed 16 November 2023) https://www.healthdirect.gov.au/mental-illness.

[77] Raghavan et al. (n 28).

[78] Neerav Srivastava, Aashish Srivastava & DK Srivastava (2019) 'A Million Winslows: Private Liability of Universities for Ragging in India', 19 *Oxford University Commonwealth Law Journal* 227.

potential liability under current laws, it is vital to understand when the university might also be liable.

5.3.1 *Duty of Care*

It is submitted that Australian universities owe a duty to take reasonable care to prevent hazing. In Australia, this point has not been decided, and for novel categories of negligence, the common law develops incrementally and by analogy with established categories. There is support for such a duty arising. Decisions like *Furek* and *Regent* in the US support that conclusion.[79] The NSW Court of Appeal has held that a 'University is bound by a general duty of care towards its students to protect them from a risk of injury of which it is aware or ought to be aware'.[80] That dicta was applied in *SMA v John XXIII College (No 2) ('SMA')*.[81] However, Elkaim J did not go so far as to hold that a tertiary institute owes its students a duty to take reasonable care to prevent hazing. Nevertheless, we seem to be moving in that direction.

In *SMA*, the plaintiff was a high-achieving law student. She voluntarily attended a drinking hazing ritual called the 'Pub Golf Event'. By 830 pm, the students were incredibly drunk, and 'there was vomit in hallways, stairwells, and rooms, along with garbage and broken glass bottles'.[82] The students were directed to leave the college. They went to a pub. At some stage, the plaintiff was tied, back-to-back, to another first-year student, and their hands were taped to a bottle of alcohol. The plaintiff was so drunk that she had no recollection of having non-consensual sex with another student in an alleyway next to the pub. When the plaintiff found out what had happened, she suffered significant psychological injury. She left her law degree and took up another degree in which she obtained moderate marks. But for the injury, she probably would have completed her law degree and achieved better marks. It should also be pointed out that under the new Victorian laws, the hazer could have been convicted of rape.

It was held that the college *was not* liable to the student for failing to prevent the alcohol ritual from going ahead as that would interfere with the plaintiff's autonomy, specifically her decision to drink. The college was held *liable* for directing the students to leave:

> By this time the students were very much intoxicated. The College was therefore directing the students, over whom it had assumed a pastoral role, to leave the relative safety of the John's premises and venture out to other venues, and inevitably and eventually to Mooseheads. When the direction was made, therefore, the plaintiff and the other students were not exercising a conflicting autonomous decision, rather they, and in particular the female students, were

[79] See Chaps. 2 and 3 for further discussion of these decisions.

[80] *Waters v. Winter and The University of New England* [1998] NSWCA 248.

[81] [2020] ACTSC 211.

[82] *SMA v. John XXIII College (No 2)* [2020] ACTSC 211, [255].

> vulnerable and entitled to the pastoral care of the defendant ... that as a matter of policy the care for students by a residential college would enhance the existence of the duty of care.[83]

Apart from drinking being a voluntary and autonomous act, the other difficulty with imposing a duty of care to prevent hazing is that the common law does not generally impose a positive duty to act as opposed to liability for acting negligently. A positive duty to act is only imposed where there are special circumstances. The learned judge works through these difficult issues, but there are counterarguments. If we apply the salient features,[84] they support there being a duty of care. It is foreseeable that there will be hazing activities, which can lead to physical and physiological harms. After all, the Pub Golf Event was a known practice.[85] It is foreseeable that freshers are vulnerable to sexual exploitation. It would have been possible for the college to have put in place measures to ensure there was no hazing, abuse, or exploitation of freshers. It can educate, control existing students, have control over the physical environment, and can put in place checks.[86] Schools and employers owe a duty of care to prevent bullying. In Kaplan v State of Victoria (No 8), the school was held liable in negligence for failing to take reasonable and more systemic steps to discourage and modify antisemitic student bullying and harassment behaviour; and to discourage swastika graffiti. Regarding the workplace, it has been held that:

> the prevention of bullying or harassment in the workplace is 'unquestionably one of the modern responsibilities of an employer'. Moreover, it was no answer to the plaintiff's claim to say that training or instruction given by the defendant would not likely have eliminated any bullying to which he was subjected.[87]

Both are analogical to the position of a university that can exert control over students.

The authors have sought to demonstrate how freshers are vulnerable. As for a positive duty arising to take reasonable care to prevent hazing, there is an assumption of responsibility. A residential college purports to provide pastoral care, i.e. looking after the welfare of students and safety from the outset. Further, any event at the college had to be approved, and a risk assessment carried out.[88] There is no indeterminacy of liability. While choosing to drink is generally an expression of one's autonomy, hazing is about initiation and wanting to join a community. A plaintiff is under pressure to drink. It is questionable whether they genuinely choose to binge drink, or drink without the support of pastoral protection. Hence while not settled yet by local authority, it is submitted that an Australian court would adopt *Furek* if that was the issue before it. That is, legally, universities will be liable for failing to take reasonable care to prevent hazing. That is in keeping with how we see modern universities.

---

[83] Ibid.

[84] As per *Caltex Refineries (Qld) Pty Limited v. Stavar* (2009) 75 NSWLR 649.

[85] *SMA v. John XXIII College (No 2)* [2020] ACTSC 211, [77].

[86] Srivastava et al. (n 78).

[87] *Stevens v. DP World Melbourne* [2022] VSCA 285.

[88] *SMA v. John XXIII College (No 2)* [2020] ACTSC 211, [168].

5.3.2 *Breach and Causation*

If universities and residential colleges owe a duty to take reasonable care to prevent hazing, the next question is whether there has been a breach? What is required is a contextual and balanced assessment of the reasonable response to a foreseeable risk.[89] A university or residential college can satisfy this requirement by ensuring there is education, security, proactive student support, and real-time management during heightened times. In *SMA*, it seems that the college's practices were poor. The learned judge found that:

> there would always be Senior Residents on duty at night and they could call a Community Coordinator for extra support. He said that the primary role of the Senior Residents was pastoral care […] overall supervision was carried out by the presence of persons around the College, rather than by direct instruction. […] Senior Residents receive training through the ANU, at a retreat at the beginning of the year and also at the College. Mr Brent Sanders was invited to speak to the Senior Residents, as well as students, about consent and sexual assault […] not only did the College condone events like Pub Golf, but it fostered the consumption of alcohol as a normal part of college life. It did this through events which it did sanction, like Out the Back Day, and its general approach to the excessive drinking that was prevalent at John's […] Rather than an intention to change the drinking habits of the College, I had the impression that John's almost held its reputation as a haven for the excessive consumption of alcohol as an accomplishment rather than a mark of shame.[90]

In addition, the following questions might be asked, all of which can be answered in the affirmative. Would freshers be pressured to 'join' in activities they might not genuinely consent to? Would the student body have benefitted from anti-hazing education? Would it be prudent on the night for there to be at least some oversight to ensure students did not succumb to unconsented acts? Would it be prudent for the college to directly keep an eye on the safety of students? Should there have been a duty, therefore, a breach would have been established. As for causation, but for the lack of reasonable care by the college, student harm would not have occurred.

The college's approach to student safety in *SMA* was inadequate. The management was disengaged, and rather than addressing the dangers posed by excessive drinking, it seems to have been encouraged. It is an instance where the college has contributed to an entrenched culture. What is unclear is to what extent the college's unsatisfactory approach is representative of Australian institutions. It is one reason why institutes should be given a student safety score.[91]

5.3.3 *Liability for Secondary Wounding*

A contribution made by Elkaim J to the anti-hazing fabric was holding the college liable for 'secondary wounding'. Secondary wounding is a dismissive, disbelieving,

---

[89] *Roads and Traffic Authority of NSW v. Dederer* (2007) 234 CLR 330.

[90] *SMA v. John XXIII College* (No 2) [2020] ACTSC 211, [168]–[206].

[91] See below.

hostile, or non-protective response[92] to a disclosure of sexual abuse. Negative responses may traumatise the victim further.[93] Unfortunately, negative responses by institutions do not appear uncommon around the world.[94] As above, students are reluctant to report an incident and wary about how the institute will deal with it.

In *SMA*, when the plaintiff reported the matter to the college, she met the head of the college, who was initially sympathetic. At a subsequent meeting, comments were made that were gratuitous, insulting, and entirely unnecessary, including questioning whether the incident happened and how she got drunk. His Honour concluded that the stance taken was designed to protect the college's reputation. The only reasonable explanation was an intent to undermine the plaintiff's confidence so that she would not continue with her complaint. Administrators' first loyalty is to the institution, and they might be conflicted rather than independent arbitrators of a hazing dispute.

The college was held liable for not taking reasonable care when dealing with a complaint of sexual abuse. It was plainly foreseeable that a person making such a complaint is vulnerable and susceptible to psychological harm should the complaint be improperly dealt with, and that was what occurred here. Given the reluctance to report, and the potential adverse consequences of a hostile response, this is a significant development.

5.3.4 Consumer Guarantee of Due Care and Skill

An alternative to the claim in negligence would be the non-excludable consumer guarantee of due care and skill at s 60 of the *Australian Consumer Law* ('ACL').[95] Section 60 has been described as akin to negligence.[96] One benefit of s 60 is that it *might* be unencumbered by the intricacies of the common law's distinction between omissions and acts. The plaintiff is a consumer under s 3 of the *ACL*. The same analysis regarding negligence applies in support of the submission that there was a contravention of s 60. That is, under s 60, there is an obligation to take reasonable care to prevent hazing.

The challenge for the claimant is that the service must have been supplied by the university 'in trade or commerce' for a s 60 claim. It is submitted that this requirement

---

92 Debbie Allnock & Pam Miller (2013) 'No One Noticed, No One Heard', https://learning.nspcc.org.uk/research-resources/2013/no-one-noticed-no-one-heard. *ONNOHASDCA*.

93 Tamara Blakemore, James Leslie Herbert, Fiona Arney & Samantha Parkinson (2017) 'The Impacts of Institutional Child Sexual Abuse: A rapid Review of the Evidence', *Child Abuse & Neglect*, https://doi.org/10.1016/j.chiabu.2017.08.006 Abstract, p. 79.

94 E.g. India. See Srivastava et al. (n 78).

95 The full name is the *Competition and Consumer Act 2010* (Cth) sch 2 The Australian Consumer Law.

96 Philip Clarke & Sharon Erbacher, *Australian Consumer Law: Commentary and Materials* (Lawbook, 6th ed, 2018) [13–10]; *Russell V Miller, Miller's Australian Competition and Consumer Law Annotated* (Lawbook, 40th ed, 2018) [*ACL* 60.20].

can be met. It would be hard for the three[97] private universities in Australia to argue that they are not engaged in trade or commerce. The better view is that public universities are also involved 'in trade or commerce'. Prof Corones points out that universities 'now compete for students on the basis of price (tuition fees and other costs of attendance) and service (courses offered, teaching quality, the standard of facilities, and research opportunities).[98] He concludes that 'there can be no doubt' that the services are supplied in trade or commerce. Another point is that universities provide a variety of services beyond the educational and academic ones. For example, they provide accommodation for a fee.

5.3.5 Implied Term

Another alternative is that the university-student contract includes an implied term that the university take reasonable steps to prevent hazing. Under the *BP Refinery* principles,[99] for a term to be implied it must be (1) reasonable and equitable; (2) necessary to give business efficacy to the contract so that no term will be implied if the contract is effective without it; (3) so obvious that 'it goes without saying'; (4) capable of clear expression; and (5) not contradict any express term of the contract.[100] For (2), we have previously argued that:

> A number of leading cases on implication of a term involved safety. When it comes to selling goods and services to consumers, implied terms as to safety are commonplace. The landlord-tenant safety cases concern geographical space over which the landlord has control [...] The employment cases concern activities over which the employer has control [...].
>
> Universities have reasonable control over both the physical space and student activities on their campus. Universities generally maintain law and order on campus and provide security. Like tenants, students spend a great deal of time on campus. Like employees, they are dependent on the university to police activities and safety on campus. [...] A more specific question is whether this safety obligation extends to the prevention of [hazing]. There are strong reasons why it does. In Mullins, a student was raped in a dormitory. It was held that adequate security was an indispensable part of the bundle of services that students pay colleges for [...].[101]

---

[97] Bond University, University of Notre Dame Australia, and Australia's Torrens University.

[98] Stephen Corones (2012) 'Consumer Guarantees And The Supply Of Educational Services By Higher Education Providers', 35 *University of New South Wales Law Journal* 1.

[99] *BP Refinery (Westernport) Pty Ltd v. Shire of Hastings* [1977] UKPC 13.

[100] In Australia, the implication would not be prevented by an entire agreement clause.

[101] Srivastava et al. (n 78).

5.4 Hazing-Specific Proscriptive Laws in Other Jurisdictions

5.4.1 US

Thus, many acts of hazing will be covered by the general law in Australia. However, there are lacunas. Hazing-specific laws from other countries may therefore be relevant to what should be done in Australia. In the US, 44 states have hazing-specific laws.[102] For example, the *Massachusetts General Code* criminalises hazing. Institutions are required to distribute anti-hazing laws to students. Further, a person—which appears to include university authorities—who knows of a hazing incident is obliged to report it to the criminal authorities unless it puts them in peril or danger.[103]

The *Code* criminalises hazing, which it defines as:

> any conduct or method of initiation into any student organization, whether on public or private property, which wilfully or recklessly endangers the physical or mental health of any student or other person. Such conduct shall include whipping, beating, branding, forced calisthenics, exposure to the weather, forced consumption of any food, liquor, beverage, drug or other substance, or any other brutal treatment or forced physical activity which is likely to adversely affect the physical health or safety of any such student or other person, or which subjects such student or other person to extreme mental stress, including extended deprivation of sleep or rest or extended isolation.

As for this hazing-specific crime, these provisions address some of the gaps. They criminalise initiation activities that

(a) endanger the mental health of a student,
(b) involve forced consumption of alcohol, drugs, and food as recognised forms of hazing,
(c) involve forced physical activity, and
(d) subject a student to extreme mental stress, including deprivation of sleep.

It *may* be difficult to fit (a)–(d) into an existing Australian cause of action such as assault. Further, the definition captures certain Australian hazing practices.

5.4.2 India

When it comes to passing anti-hazing laws, India has been a pioneer. The Supreme Court was exasperated by the inaction of universities, and constituted the Raghavan Committee to look into hazing and how to curb it.[104] In time, the Raghavan

[102] This is discussed in the US chapter.

[103] *Massachusetts General Code* s 18.

[104] Raghavan et al. (n 28).

Committee's recommendations led to the national University Grants Commission (UGC) passing anti-hazing laws. They:

> contain a general requirement that a university take all necessary steps to eliminate ragging. The Regulations are detailed and prescriptive. Universities are obliged to conduct anti-ragging vetting and orientation, constitute anti-ragging committees that include senior students, illuminate, tighten security and keep a close watch, especially in areas known to be vulnerable to ragging, and maintain a round-the-clock vigil at hostels.[105]

These Regulations have failed due to institutional apathy persisting,[106] and there have been calls in parliament for recalcitrant universities to be derecognised.[107] Nevertheless, insights from the UGC Regulations, such as university accountability to a centralised body and engaging student leaders, may inform proposals in Australia.

Many of these US and Indian laws would address lacunas in Australian laws and should be adopted. *However*, anti-hazing laws do not appear to have dented the practice in the US and India.[108] Of themselves, they are not a panacea. This is because hazing is an entrenched culture. Merely proscribing or prescribing conduct is not enough to regulate the practice.

5.5 Entrenched Culture of Hazing

If we are serious about hazing prevention, the reality of it being an entrenched culture should be confronted. It is significant that the Colleges Report is headed 'Cultural Renewal' and that *Honi Soit*, the student weekly publication, alleges that hazing continues unabated: 'Sexism, white nationalist sentiment, hazing and public defecation plague St Andrew's College'.[109] The college has expressed the opposite view.[110] For this chapter, it will be *assumed* that there is truth to Honi Suit's allegations. The question then becomes what is required to change an ingrained culture, and can the law help foster cultural change?

---

105 Srivastava et al. (n 78).

106 Ibid.

107 Baijayant Jay Panda (Twitter, 6 January 2018) www.twitter.com/PandaJay/status/949848639320420352, following the death of student Sreyas Kesharwani. See 'Ragging in Vizag College Claims Life of Odisha Boy!' *Odisha Sun Times* (online, 6 January 2018) www.odishasuntimes.com/ragging-in-vizag-college-claims-life-of-odisha-boy.

108 See Chaps. 2 and 3.

109 Ward et al. (n 12).

110 St Andrew's College (2018) 'Cultural Renewal at the University of Sydney Colleges Progress Report on Implementation of Recommendations—End of Year One', https://www.standrewscollege.edu.au/wp-content/uploads/Broderick-End-of-Year-One.pdf.

5.5.1 *Hazing Prevention*

The field of hazing prevention is still at a nascent stage.[111] One of the first universities to develop a successful anti-hazing programme is Cornell University. In 2011, a Cornell student died while participating in a hazing episode that included mock kidnapping, ritualized humiliation, and coerced drinking.[112] Following the incident, the eminent university president pledged to end hazing in a New York Times editorial.[113] The program introduced has led to a significant decline in hazing.[114] It includes a task force, education, training, and communication; comprehensive anti-hazing information being available; non-hazing team-building activities; and alcohol abuse prevention strategies. The Cornell University experience is instructive. It shows that hazing practices can be reduced *when there is institutional engagement*.[115]

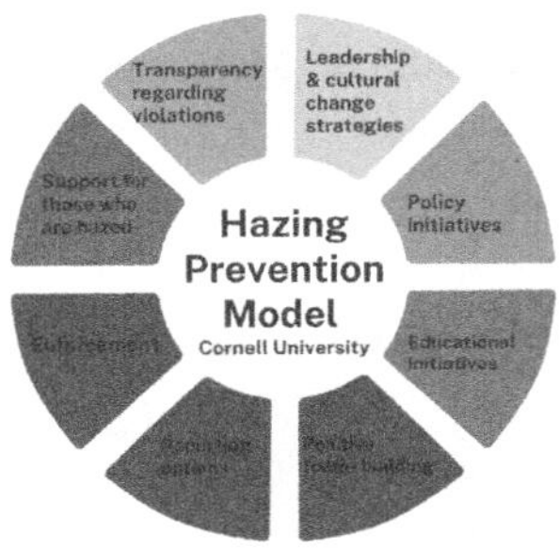

The Indian UGC Regulations have a similar approach to Cornell but have failed. This is probably because, to put it in terms of the Allens Study,[116] there was a lack of commitment, planning, sustainability, and cultural competence.

5.5.2 *Cultural Change*

The contrast between Cornell's success and the failure of the UGC Regulations leads to a question. The laws discussed so far follow a traditional pattern. They provide the code. They proscribe and sometimes prescribe conduct. In doing so, they reflect[117]

---

[111] Marchell et al. (n 29).

[112] Skorton (n 19).

[113] Ibid.

[114] Marchell et al. (n 29).

[115] Cornell University, 'Hazing Prevention Model', *Hazing at Cornell*, https://hazing.cornell.edu/prevention/hazing-prevention-model.

[116] Allan et al. (n 41).

[117] As they should.

societal norms. A breach of those laws leads to sanctions. However, while the US and India have adequate hazing laws, they have not dented the practice. It seems that effective hazing prevention depends not only on laws that prohibit it. It also requires a change in culture, institutional leadership, and practical measures. The question: what if regulations sought to foster that change?

In their recent book, *The Behavioural Code* Van Rooij and Fine describe law draftsmen as 'behavioural novices'.[118] They add that other disciplines, such as economics, have been transformed by behavioural economics. So far, the law remains largely untouched. They begin with a story about seatbelts in America:

> In 1984, New York became the first state to require drivers to use seatbelts. Soon all states—except [...] New Hampshire—followed suit, and seatbelt usage across the country shot up from 10 percent to 50 percent—a 400 percent increase. Simply introducing the law mandating seatbelt usage hugely impacted people's driving safety habits. But half of Americans still weren't buckling up. In response, states began organizing enforcement campaigns with catchy slogans like 'Click it or Ticket.' Seatbelt slackers were warned that they could face fines [that] were low, mostly well below a hundred dollars [...]. Concurrently, authorities broadcast public service announcements showing unbuckled, lifelike crash-test dummies to warn about the potential gruesome effects of not wearing seatbelts. And car manufacturers installed those seatbelt warning alarms, reminding (or really just irritating) us into buckling up. With all of these combined, today about 90 percent of American drivers and car passengers wear a seatbelt. And most strap in automatically.[119]

Van Rooij and Fine characterise this as a successful marriage between the legal and behavioural code. They point out that a number of behavioural mechanisms were at play.[120] First, *people were educated* about the new rule. New laws are not always supported by public education. Second, a *sense of duty* towards laws was created. Third, there was the fear of *personal repercussions*. Studies have found that, when it comes to deterrence, the certainty of sanctions is more important than their scale.[121] Fourth, beyond deterrence, there was *persuasion*. Public messaging campaigns conveyed that buckling up was also a matter of *self-interest*. Fifth, the annoying warning beeps created a *practical obstacle*. In time using a seatbelt became habitual and automatic—the norm. Finally, Van Rooij and Fine add that offering a carrot, instead of using a stick, has met with success. Instead of punishing, rewarding good behaviour has been more effective in effecting cultural change. US schools, for instance, use a 'positive behaviour incentive system'.[122]

An instance where Australia is a world leader in bringing about cultural reform is reducing smoking.[123] In 1985, 35% of Australians were regular smokers. Now it

---

[118] Benjamin Van Rooij and Adam Fine, *The Behavioural Code* (Beacon, 2021) p. 10.

[119] Ibid, p. 7.

[120] Ibid, p. 7–8.

[121] Ibid, p. 68–69.

[122] Ibid, Chap. 3.

[123] Michelle Scollo, Megan Bayly & Melanie Wakefield (2015) 'Plain packaging: A Logical Progression for Tobacco Control in One of the World's 'Darkest Markets', 24 (Suppl 2) *Tobacco Control* ii3.

is 10.7%[124] or a reduction of 70%. Australia adopted a comprehensive[125] strategy that involved reducing both the supply of cigarettes and the demand for them. Again behavioural levers were used. First there was persuasion. The public were educated on how smoking can harm them. Required information on cigarette packs[126] now include graphic pictures, and there have been mass marketing campaigns. The promotion of tobacco has been restricted.[127] Second, practical constraints have been deployed. There are restrictions on smoking in public places. Raised taxes have made smoking in Australia the most expensive in the world and three times the price in the US.[128] Finally, anti-smoking sentiment has been fostered and has become the norm.

In both these examples, there are behavioural levers that foster change:

(a) a sense of duty
(b) communication and education, including direct communication
(c) repercussions
(d) persuasion that not only will there be repercussions, but the desired behaviour is good for the individual
(e) practical constraints.

There are crucial differences between the seatbelt and smoking examples and the hazing paradigm. For the former, the authorities have driven the change. With hazing, universities have been accused of being recalcitrant. They are part of the problem. The other difference is that, for a hazer, the danger of physical self-harm is not present; the action itself does not harm them.

5.6 Proposed Laws for Australia

On the basis of the above, we now consider whether legislation can mandate a comprehensive anti-hazing strategy in addition to proscriptive laws. There will be proscriptive laws that cover lacunas in the general law with respect to hazing. Further, what if the legislation was conscious that hazing represents an entrenched culture and tries to tackle the behavioural levers that cause it? It will be recalled that the psychological and cultural factors that lead to hazing are:

---

124 Elizabeth Greenhalgh, Michelle Scollo & Margaret Winstanley, Tobacco in Australia (Cancer Council Australia, 2019) Chap. 1.3. 'Prevalence of Smoking - Adults', https://www.tobaccoinaustralia.org.au/chapter-1-prevalence/1-3-prevalence-of-smoking-adults.

125 Scollo et al. (n 123).

126 Greenhalgh et al. (n 124) Chap. 12A.1 'History of Health Warnings in Australia', https://www.tobaccoinaustralia.org.au/chapter-12-tobacco-products/attachment-12-1-health-warnings/12a-1-history-health-warnings.

127 Scollo et al. (n 123).

128 'Price Ranking by Country of Cigarettes 20 Packs (Marlboro) (Market)', *Numbeo*, https://www.numbeo.com/cost-of-living/country_price_rankings?itemId=17.

- universities not committing to hazing prevention and taking a relaxed approach;
- dominance, commitment, and automatic accrual theory that is not free riding; obedience and solidarity
- alcohol; and
- the cost of reporting.

Central to these proposals is the theme that universities should take responsibility for eliminating hazing. We are trying to get potential hazers *and universities* to change their behaviour. It is not being suggested that students should not drink or engage in sex. They are adults. The concern is when an individual is coerced as part of an initiation ceremony.

5.6.1 Universities Committing to Hazing Prevention

Legislation could be introduced in the Australian states. It could begin by stating that its purpose is to ensure student safety and eliminate hazing and that universities are primarily responsible for ensuring this. The legislation should be proscriptive, prescriptive, and engage with behavioural levers. As per the Allen Study,[129] universities should be committing to student safety. Universities should be under general obligations to take reasonable steps to ensure student safety, prevent hazing, and to inculcate an anti-hazing culture. For the avoidance of doubt, there should be an actionable duty of care to take reasonable care for the safety of students, including the prevention of hazing.

Specific obligations of universities would include constituting a student safety/anti-hazing task force headed by the vice-chancellor. In accordance with the Allen Study, senior leaders should commit to hazing prevention measures that address commitment, education, planning, evaluation, and cultural competence. The task force would have to issue an annual public report on hazing. Residential colleges would be subject to the same obligations. Anti-hazing education of key staff, which includes senior management, should be compulsory. The Colleges Report states 'College staff have a critical leadership role in shaping College culture and creating and sustaining a values-based community'.[130]

The education should be 'plain' so that there is no misunderstanding as to the possible dangers.[131]

---

[129] Allan et al. (n 41).

[130] See Broderick (n 10).

[131] An evolution of health warnings up until 2012. See Scollo (n 123).

There should be no ambiguity as to a university's responsibility. There have been developments that may not have been understood by staff. For potential sexual offences the university should clarify the new affirmative consent laws discussed above. That the university might be liable for secondary wounding under *SMA* should be made clear to staff. Two areas that universities should specifically tackle are O-week and alcohol.

Universities need to be accountable to an independent third party. Ideally, this should be a central organisation such as Universities Australia. Alternatively, it can be to a state authority. They should be required to submit an annual report on student safety to the organisation and make it publicly available. Universities and residential colleges should be given an annual student safety score out of 5 by a central authority, with a general schedule explaining the range of scores from 1–5. The list of scores should be published annually. The comparison will provide clarity regarding the state of hazing in Australia. Saying that hazing is a problem at University A is less meaningful then saying University A is less safe than University B. That score may influence student decisions as to which university or college they choose. There is a carrot in that a high score may attract students. It may be relevant to funding. Should the student safety score fall below a minimum threshold, there might be further repercussions.

These proposals have elements of both prescription and behavioural science. Regarding the latter, a sense of duty would be fostered at universities, there would be education, and repercussions as presumably universities would like a good student safety score. Transparency will facilitate accountability and ownership on the part of universities.

5.6.2 Define Hazing

A common definition of hazing should be adopted. It can be similar to the one in Massachusetts. In particular, it should include activities that endanger the mental health of a student, involve forced consumption of alcohol, and forced physical activity, including deprivation of sleep. Initiation activities that discriminate, humiliate, harass, or vilify a student should be included in the definition. Unlike the patchwork of discrimination laws, all remedies should be available under this model. The practices of 'walkabout' and the 'Mott walk' would be caught by this definition.

As discussed, consent has proved problematic in the context of hazing. If someone attends an event, they have at least consented to being there. At one residential college, students were asked to sign consent waivers. As one of the authors of the Red Zone observes:

> Getting students to sign consent waivers so that institutional responsibility is abnegated is the very opposite of cultural reform and accountability [...] Students should be provided with a safe living environment, not asked to sign waivers accepting that they understand the environment is unsafe.[132]

Recognising the reality that the hazee does not really consent, the legislation should include a reverse onus provision. People do not normally consent to physical or psychological harm, being humiliated, or to a situation where there is a risk of these harms. A reverse onus provision will put the onus on the hazer to show that the hazee genuinely consented, i.e. not under duress or undue influence, to the *specific* activities. As for the consent waivers, as discussed, students are consumers under the *ACL*. That means that s 60 on due care and skill applies, is non-excludable, and includes obligations to prevent hazing. Further, a consent waiver is likely to be void as an unfair term under the *ACL*.[133]

There are three possible consequences for a hazer. They might be liable in private law to the victim, criminal prosecution by the state, or subject to disciplinary proceedings by the university. It is submitted that all three should be available as options under the legislation, although it should be tailored to reflect gravity.

Hazers are students too, with a potential career ahead of them, and perhaps acted in accordance with an entrenched culture. That is not to excuse their behaviour but is relevant to a criminal prosecution and disciplinary proceedings or the consequences thereof.

5.6.3 Student Body and Leadership

Crucial to fostering an anti-hazing culture is student body engagement and education. Community values should be built and made explicit.[134] All students should be required to complete compulsory anti-hazing education. Like the smoking campaign, the information should be graphic and include real-life examples. The education should make clear that there is zero tolerance[135] and the potential consequences[136]

---

[132] Ward et al. (n 12).

[133] Sections 23–27 of the *ACL*.

[134] Broderick (n 10), [5.3.2].

[135] Ibid, [5.3.2].

[136] Ibid, [5.2.1].

to both the hazer and hazee. This includes the affirmative consent model and coercive drinking. The potential long-term impact of sexual assault or hazing on the victim should be made clear.

Student leaders, including a fresher, should be engaged as support and safety agents. As the Colleges Report noted:

> Best practice recognises that student leadership is integral, not supplementary, to educational institutions. When enabled and supported, student leadership is associated with increased positive outcomes including in the areas of cultural change and renewal. Developed specifically for university student leadership, the 'social change model' has been identified as one of the most broadly applicable, successful, and well-known leadership development models for higher education.[137]

Student safety agents should work with the university task force. The university, residential colleges, and student leaders should feel a sense of duty to prevent hazing. Student agents should informally encourage an understanding of how dangerous hazing is and what help can be sought. Having student agents should facilitate a sense of duty and improve communication. They should be specifically tasked during O-week:

> at Rhodes University in South Africa [in] response to problematic hazing during their orientation week, new guidelines were set which recommended that orientation week student leaders be given annual training dedicated to 'initiation' and its potential problems, and that the education make students 'aware of their power and the potential for unwitting peer pressure to be applied'. As a result, orientation week leaders removed hazing behaviours and new students experienced an overwhelmingly positive and inclusive orientation week.[138]

5.6.4 O-Week and Team Building

O-week is when most hazing activities occur. At this point, hazers are at their most powerful and hazees at their most vulnerable position. Hazers are driven by dominance and automatic accrual theory. Hazees are new and subject to feelings of solidarity and obedience. It is when heavy drinking begins, and that may set the pattern for the year.[139] One student stated that 'O Week was intense, insane and I think a lot of it was because of the drinking. I didn't expect it'.[140] O-week should have specific regulations. There should be greater supervision and security by staff during O-week or consideration given to postponing it until there are greater community bonds. As the students get to know each other, the likelihood of serious hazing reduces.[141] Soon

---

137 Ibid, [2.2.4].

138 Ibid.

139 Benjamin Riordan, Damien Scarf & Tamlin Conner (2015), 'Is Orientation Week a Gateway to Persistent Alcohol Use in University Students? A Preliminary Investigation', 76(2) *Journal of Studies on Alcohol and Drugs* 204.

140 Broderick (n 10), [2.2.4].

141 Vigil (n 33).

after O-week, freshers are no longer strangers, and it is harder to pick on them. These are practical measures to reduce hazing.[142]

Team building is a carrot and can be rewarded.[143] Like Cornell, alternate[144] safe O-week activities should be organised that reduce the distance between freshers and the existing cohort and address automatic accrual theory. New students can be paired with existing ones. Prizes can be awarded. Again, legislation can stipulate this. There is no longer a need to wait till O-week for students to meet. Prior to O-week social media should facilitate freshers getting to know the existing students and each other. This will help break down barriers. Rather than being seen as outsiders joining the group, freshers should be seen as part of the community to which existing students belong.[145] In short, foster team building rather than entry through initiation.

5.6.5 Alcohol

As discussed, alcohol is a key enabler of hazing. The Colleges Report points out that drinking at residential colleges is characterised by binge drinking and drinking too quickly. The *National Alcohol Strategy 2019–2026* identifies young adults as a group that experience disproportionate levels of harm.[146] As mitigation, it suggests there needs to be education on alcohol-related harms; reduced availability and promotion of alcohol, and limitations on affordable pricing in 'hotspots'. Education and practical constraints are also identified by Van Rooij and Fine. The legislation should require education on alcohol. Drinking too much may have personal repercussions and endanger self-interest. Freshers should understand how vulnerable they become to hazing and sexual assault when intoxicated. Existing students should understand that they may do things that they regret later and that coercing a new student to drink is hazing, albeit hard to prove. By building bonds between new and existing students as soon as possible, the pressure on freshers to drink is reduced.[147]

The availability of alcohol on campus should be controlled during O-week, both with respect to volume, places where it can be consumed on campus, and pricing. Given the tendency to binge and to drink too quickly during O-week, the types of alcohol made available and using smaller glasses can be considered.

Finally, it is critical that institutions be active when it comes to alcohol management. They, too, need to be educated.

---

[142] Rooij and Fine (n 118) p. 7–8.

[143] Ibid.

[144] Broderick (n 10) [5.2.1].

[145] Ibid, [2.2.4].

[146] Department Of Health And Aged Care, 'National Alcohol Strategy: 2019–2028', https://www.health.gov.au/sites/default/files/documents/2019/12/national-alcohol-strategy-2019-2028.pdf.

[147] Broderick (n 10) [3.1].

5.6.6 Reporting

As discussed, the cost of reporting an incident is potentially high to a student. First, the university might be conflicted and, at least historically, untrained when it comes to dealing with a disclosure of hazing or a sexual offence. Second, the student further risks being ostracised by the student community. Not surprisingly, the vast majority of incidents go unreported. The Colleges Report found only 3% of students that reported experiencing sexual harassment and only 9% of students that reported experiencing actual or attempted sexual assault made a formal report.[148] That does not seem to have changed in the five years since its publication.[149] A study commissioned by Universities Australia reported in 2022 that

- *sexual harassment*: 1 in 6 students have experienced harassment; and 1 in 30 victims report it.
- *sexual assault*: 1 in 20 students have experienced assault; and 1 in 20 victims report it.[150]

This is a grim reality. The Chair of Universities Australia, Professor John Dewar described the findings as 'distressing, disappointing and confronting' and said the situation was 'unacceptable'.[151] Van Rooij and Fine have pointed out that the certainty of sanctions is more important than their severity.[152] A lack of reporting may therefore undermine an anti-hazing regime.

Regarding whom to report to, there should be multiple options. Legislation should specify that it includes an option of reporting to those who are independent of the university, such as Universities Australia, a student representative, and the option of reporting to a female representative.[153] The legislation should also specify that those involved in handling a report should be trained.

There is the risk of secondary wounding and potential liability for causing this. Students should understand that reporting will happen in a safe and confidential environment. It is not suggested that Australia adopt the duty-to-report-to-authorities model at this stage. It may lead to survivors being even further isolated. As for being ostracised, the legislation can require institutions to have a trained support network for survivors that includes existing students. Reluctance to report sexual offences is a general problem. As Rooij and Fine observe, these things can take time and involve incremental steps.

---

[148] Ibid, [55].

[149] Alison Henry, 'Sexual Assault and Harassment on Campus: Universities Need Regulation', *UNSW Newsroom* (online, 28 March 2022) https://newsroom.unsw.edu.au/news/general/sexual-assault-and-harassment-campus-universities-need-regulation.

[150] Heywood et al. (n 22).

[151] John Dewar, 'Response to the 2021 National Student Safety Survey', *Universities Australia* (online, 23 March 2022) https://universitiesaustralia.edu.au/media-item/response-to-the-2021-national-student-safety-survey/.

[152] Rooij Fine (n 118), p. 68–69.

[153] https://www.universitiesaustralia.edu.au/.

5.6.7 Personal Repercussions

Finally, as discussed, it seems that the certainty of sanctions is more important than their severity. That philosophy can be adopted by the legislation.

5.7 Conclusion

In summary, hazing prevention requires a university to commit to student safety. Legislation can make this explicit. The proposed reforms are (a) proscriptive—identifying conduct for which there should be a legal remedy in line with traditional law reform; and (b) using legislation to encourage cultural reform. It may be that (b) is also relevant to other jurisdictions.

Legislation that is informed by behavioural science may have a better chance of changing the culture and reducing hazing. Cornell's success through ownership and engagement stands in contrast to the failure to prevent hazing by recalcitrant universities. Some of the changes proposed may seem onerous. But they are consonant with the broader societal change that we are seeing. Students are entering the next stage of their life. They attend university to build a future. A serious incident of hazing is a life-changing event.

Chapter 6
Conclusion

We believe hazing can be prevented and lives can be saved.
—Parents of a fresher who died in a hazing incident
('REACH-Info_updatedAug2022.Pdf' https://stophazing.org/wp-content/uploads/2022/08/REACH-Info_updatedAug2022.pdf)

Hazing is despicable. Young students joining universities have died, committed suicide and suffered physical and emotional harm. We have focused on four countries, U.S., India, Sri Lanka and Australia. In all these countries, hazing is typical of university life. Hazing is practised on university campuses, at clubs, organisations (fraternities and sororities), and student residences and hostels. Students joining a university are subjected to humiliation and degradation.

Ironically, in all the countries there remain proponents of hazing who believe that it builds social cohesion and helps students to become a rounded person.[1] Such arguments are specious and based on false premises. Empirical research suggests that severity of initiation ceremony in the university, residences, hostels, fraternities, sororities, sporting clubs, and other organisations, leads to less not more affiliation into the community.[2] Negative emotions such as humiliation have no positive consequences.[3] A study of hazing, especially focused on university athletes in the U.K. proves that hazing does not build social cohesion.[4] As Van Raalte, Cornelius, Linder,

[1] See Lisbeth Mann, Allard R. Feddes, Bertjab Doosje & Agneta H. Fisher (2016) 'Withdraw or Affiliate? The Role of Humiliation in Initiation Rituals', 30(1) *Cognition and Emotion* 80; Harsh Agarwal, *Psychology Behind Ragging*, Paper presented at the seminar "Legal Awareness Programme on Anti-Ragging" in the session 'Understanding Psychology Behind Ragging' chaired by the acting Chief Justice of Delhi High Court, organised by the Delhi Legal Services Authority (DLSA), in the Vallabhbhai Patel Chest Institute (VPCI) Auditorium (New Delhi, India, March 20, 2010) http://www.humiliationstudies.org/documents/AgarwalPsychologyBehindRagging.pdf.

[2] Mann et al. (n 1). Hein F. Lodewijkx & Joseph E. M. M. Syroit (1997) '*Severity of Initiation Revisited: Does severity of Initiation Increase Attractiveness in Real Groups*?', 27 *European Journal of Social Psychology* 275.

[3] Mann et al., (n 1), p. 97.

[4] M. E. Lafferty, C. Wakefield & H. Brown, (2016) '"We Do it for the Team" – Students-athletes' Initiation Practices and Their Impact on Group Cohesion', *International Journal of Sport & Exercise Psychology*.

A. Srivastava et al., *Hazing (Ragging) at Universities: A Legal Perspective*,
https://doi.org/10.1007/978-981-99-5215-1_6

and Brewer (2007) noted that society and history believe hazing can build team cohesion, while research shows cohesion decreases with hazing behaviours.[5] Quite apart from hazing not serving its purported function, it is dangerous and can cause long-term mental health issues for hazees. To repeat, universities are contributing to the psychological and cultural factors by not committing to hazing prevention.

Seeking remedies for hazing requires a complaint. Not surprisingly, victims of hazing are reluctant to report their suffering and victimisation to the authorities. Several reasons are attributed for their reluctance i.e., shame, embarrassment, fear of retaliation, lack of faith in the institutional response, and possible alienation.[6] Some students do not even realise that they have been hazed. Universities weigh reporting a matter to external authorities as it could damage their reputation and lead to loss of students. For all these reasons cases reported in the media are only the tip of the iceberg.

This leads to a series of observations and recommendations. First, when it comes to the legal accountability of a hazer, for the most part the framework is already in place under the general law. Save for a few lacunas, a hazer is likely to be liable under criminal and/or civil law.

As for universities, in the U.S., India and Sri Lanka, efforts have been made to regulate hazing through specific anti-hazing laws, rules, regulations, and facilitating reporting mechanisms. These regulations impose prescriptive and proscriptive obligations on universities. Australia has not passed any specific anti-hazing laws and regulations yet. It should do so.

The common law has made good progress. When it comes to suing universities for negligence, US courts are no longer bound by the *in loco parentis* and the bystander doctrine. U.S. universities are now liable for their negligence causing harm to students as well intentional and negligent wrongs of their employees. This approach sets a good precedent for India, Sri Lanka and Australia, and it is fair to assume that the US position would be adopted in those respective jurisdictions. In Australia, it has been clarified that a university can be liable for secondary wounding;[7] that is a dismissive, disbelieving, hostile, or non-protective response[8] to a disclosure of sexual abuse.

---

[5] Judy L. Van Raalte, Allen. E. Cornelius, Darwyn E. Lydner & Britton W. Brewer (2007) 'The Relationship Between Hazing and Team Cohesion', 30(4) *Journal of Sport Behavior*, 491.

[6] Nadine Hoover (1999) 'National Survey: Initiation Rites and athletics for NCAA Sports Teams', https://www.alfred.edu/about/news/studies/_docs/hazing.pdf; Elizabeth J Allan & Mary Madden (2008) 'Hazing in View: College Students at Risk: Initial Findings from the National Study of Student Hazing', *Stop Hazing*, https://stophazing.org/wp-content/uploads/2020/12/hazing_in_view_study.pdf; Shelly Campo Gretchen Poulos and John W Sipple (2005) 'Prevalence and Profiling: Hazing among College Students and Points of Intervention', 29(2) *American Journal of Health Behavior* 137; Jennifer J Waldron (2008) 'I Have to Do What to Be a Teammate?', 79(5) *Journal of Physical Education, Recreation & Dance* 4; Victoria Banyard (2007) 'Sexual Violence Prevention through Bystander Education: An Experimental Evaluation', 35(4) *Journal of Community Psychology*, https://onlinelibrary.wiley.com/doi/abs/10.1002/jcop.20.

[7] *SMA v. John XXIII College* (No 2) [2020] ACTSC 211, [168]–[206].

[8] Debbie Allnock & Pam Miller (2013) No One Noticed, No One Heard: a Study of Disclosures of Childhood Abuse', https://learning.nspcc.org.uk/research-resources/2013/no-one-noticed-no-one-heard.

There are legal aspects that require refinement:

(a) The legislation should state at the outset that the primary responsibility for student safety rests with universities.
(b) The definition of hazing. Both, the US and India have specific state statutes but do not have a federal or central law on hazing. As noted, each state has its own law and they are not identical. Sometimes there are major differences between the law of two states. This leads to confusion. Federal or central legislation would help create national consistency in the area.[9] In the U.S. there is an excellent suggestion made in a Senate bill of 15th March 2021. The Report and Educate About Campus Hazing (REACH) Act seeks to have an inclusive definition of hazing.
(c) An affirmative consent model should be introduced for hazing and sexual offences in those jurisdictions where it does not exist. In the absence of a positive consent from the victim for the specific conduct in question, the hazer is potentially liable in criminal and civil law.
(d) While a duty for universities to take reasonable care to prevent hazing has been recognised, as noted before, by US courts, and would likely be followed by other jurisdictions, codifying a duty of care would put the matter beyond doubt. The statutory duty should be to take reasonable care for the safety of students, and that extends to taking reasonable steps to prevent hazing.
(e) Likewise, a duty for universities to take reasonable care to not cause secondary wounding should be codified.
(f) Psychiatric injury needs to be integrated into anti-hazing legislation. The regulation should make clear, for instance, that a hazer is potentially liable for resultant psychiatric injury.
(g) Australia should introduce hazing-specific laws.

Second, the central argument made in the book is that it is for universities to take responsibility for preventing hazing. Universities are in the best position to protect students from hazing. And any cultural change starts at the top. As we have seen, adequate measures without university ownership are hollow. Cornell has run a successful campaign against hazing because university management has led the campaign. University engagement is the foundation for hazing prevention. Research and case law support the idea that university must play a vital role to prevent hazing and student injuries.

Third, specific regulations have been identified in certain jurisdictions that other jurisdictions would benefit from introducing. They include:

---

[9] Note that a bill [REACH (Report and Educate About Campus Hazing) Act] has been introduced on 15th March 2021 before the Senate. REACH Act seeks to: have an inclusive definition of hazing; amend 485(f)(7) of the Higher Education Act of 1965 to require universities to disclose hazing incidents; and amend Section 485(f)(8)(B)(i) of the Higher Education Act of 1965 requiring universities to have an educational program on hazing that includes information on hazing awareness, hazing prevention, and policies on hazing. See Congress. Gov, S.744 - Report and Educate About Campus Hazing Act at https://www.congress.gov/bill/117th-congress/senate-bill/744/text?r=8&s=5.

- A mechanism where universities are accountable to a central authority as to their anti-hazing practices.
- Institutions being awarded student safety scores out of 10 by a central organisation.
- Senior management at institutions committing to hazing prevention.
- Plain education of staff and student about the harms of hazing.
- Student safety.
- A safety/anti-hazing task force headed by the vice-chancellor.
- Annual public reports on student safety.
- Student body engagement. Student leaders should be engaged to foster a change in culture. Victim support networks in the student body must be built.
- Alternate team-building activities during O-week and/or deferment of O-week. The barrier between existing and new students should be broken down as soon as possible.
- Regulating the availability of alcohol during O-week.
- Multiple reporting options for victims, including to an independent body.

The Supreme Court of India recommended that schools must include hazing as part of the human rights subject to sensitise students early about the evils of hazing. This should also be considered in other countries.

A country's future depends on its students. Hazing is an evil perpetrated against a victim and an entrenched culture at universities. The effects of hazing linger, affects families, and corrodes society as a whole.

Appendix A
India

Undertaking by the Student and Their Parent/Guardian

Undertaking by the Student

(1) I, (full name student with admission/registration/enrolment number) s/o d/o Mr./Mrs./Ms.______________________, having been admitted to (name of the institution),____
____, have received a copy of the UGC Regulations on Curbing the Menace of Ragging in Higher Educational Institutions, 2009, (hereinafter called the "Regulations"), carefully read and fully understood the provisions contained in the said Regulations.
(2) I have, in particular, perused clause 3 of the Regulations and am aware as to what constitutes ragging.
(3) I have also, in particular, perused clause 7 and clause 9.1 of the Regulations and am fully aware of the penal and administrative action that is liable to be taken against me in case I am found guilty of or abetting ragging, actively or passively, or being part of a conspiracy to promote ragging.
(4) I hereby solemnly aver and undertake that
    (a) I will not indulge in any behaviour or act that may be constituted as ragging under clause 3 of the Regulations.
    (b) I will not participate in or abet or propagate through any act of commission or omission that may be constituted as ragging under clause 3 of the Regulations.
(5) I hereby affirm that, if found guilty of ragging, I am liable for punishment according to clause 9.1 of the Regulations, without prejudice to any other criminal action that may be taken against me under any penal law or any law for the time being in force.
(6) I hereby declare that I have not been expelled or debarred from admission in any institution in the country on account of being found guilty of, abetting or

A. Srivastava et al., *Hazing (Ragging) at Universities: A Legal Perspective*,
https://doi.org/10.1007/978-981-99-5215-1

being part of a conspiracy to promote, ragging; and further affirm that, in case the declaration is found to be untrue, I am aware that my admission is liable to be cancelled.

Declared this_______ day of______month of____ year.

Signature of deponent

Verification

Verified that the contents of this undertaking are true to the best of my knowledge and no part of the undertaking is false and nothing has been concealed or misstated therein.

Verified at (place)________on this the (day)_______of, (month),________(year)__ ________.

Signature of deponent

Name:

Undertaking by Parent/Guardian

(1) I, Mr/Mrs/Ms. __________________(full name of parent/guardian) father/ mother/guardian of,______________________________(full name of the student with admission/registration/enrolment number)______________, having been admitted to_________________(name of the institution)________________ ____, have received a copy of the UGC Regulations on Curbing the Menace of Ragging in Higher Educational Institutions, 2009, (hereinafter called the "Regulations"), carefully read and fully understood the provisions contained in the said Regulations.
(2) I have, in particular, perused clause 3 of the Regulations and am aware as to what constitutes ragging.
(3) I have also, in particular, perused clause 7 and clause 9.1 of the Regulations and am fully aware of the penal and administrative action that is liable to be taken against my ward in case he/she is found guilty of or abetting ragging, actively or passively, or being part of a conspiracy to promote ragging.
(4) I hereby solemnly aver and undertake that
    (a) My ward will not indulge in any behaviour or act that may be constituted as ragging under clause 3 of the Regulations.
    (b) My ward will not participate in or abet or propagate through any act of commission or omission that may be constituted as ragging under clause 3 of the Regulations.

(5) I hereby affirm that, if found guilty of ragging, my ward is liable for punishment according to clause 9.1 of the Regulations, without prejudice to any other criminal action that may be taken against my ward under any penal law or any law for the time being in force.

(6) I hereby declare that my ward has not been expelled or debarred from admission in any institution in the country on account of being found guilty of, abetting or being part of a conspiracy to promote, ragging; and further affirm that, in case the declaration is found to be untrue, the admission of my ward is liable to be cancelled.

Declared this_______ day of______month of____ year.

Signature of deponent

Name:

Address

Telephone/Mobile No:

Verification

Verified that the contents of this undertaking are true to the best of my knowledge and no part of the undertaking is false and nothing has been concealed or misstated therein.

Verified at (place)________on this the (day)_______of, (month),________(year)__ ________.

Signature of deponent

Name:

Appendix B
Sri Lanka

Declaration to be Signed by the Student and Countersigned by the Parent/Guardian

Declaration by the Candidate or Student

1. I ....have carefully read and fully understood the law prohibiting ragging referred in the Prohibition of Ragging and Other Forms of Violence in Educational Institutions Act, No 20 of 1998 and the Commission Circular No: .... of 15th January, 2010.
2. I hereby undertake that;

   2.1 I will not indulge in any behaviour or act that may come under the definition of ragging
   2.2 I will not participate in or abet or propagate ragging in any form
   2.3 I will not hurt anyone physically or psychologically or cause any other harm

3. I hereby agree that if found guilty of any form of ragging, I may be punished as per the law enforced and by-laws of the University.

Signed this on the..day of the month of...in the year ....

....

Signature of the Student

Name:.....................................

Admission No: ....

Address: ....

A. Srivastava et al., *Hazing (Ragging) at Universities: A Legal Perspective*,
https://doi.org/10.1007/978-981-99-5215-1

Undertaking by the Parent/Guardian

1. I ....have carefully read and fully understood the law prohibiting ragging referred in the Prohibition of Ragging and Other Forms of Violence in Educational Institutions Act, No 20 of 1998 and the Commission Circular No: .... of 15th January, 2010.
2. I assure you that my son/daughter/ward will not indulge in any form of ragging.
3. I hereby agree that if he or she is found guilty of any form of ragging he or she may be punished as per the law enforce and by-laws of the University.

....

Signature of the Parent or Guardian

Name: ....

Admission No: ....

Address: ....

The manufacturer's authorised representative in the EU is Springer Nature Customer Service Centre GmbH, Europaplatz 3, 69115 Heidelberg, Germany. If you have any concerns regarding our products, please contact ProductSafety@springernature.com

Printed and bound by CPI Group (UK) Ltd, Croydon, CR0 4YY
05/10/2026
02228151-0005